D0944702

MODERN SEXUALITY

MODERN SEXUALITY

The Truth About Sex and Relationships

Michael Aaron

ROWMAN & LITTLEFIELD
Lanham • Boulder • New York • London

Published by Rowman & Littlefield
A wholly owned subsidiary of The Rowman & Littlefield Publishing Group, Inc.
4501 Forbes Boulevard, Suite 200, Lanham, Maryland 20706
www.rowman.com

Unit A, Whitacre Mews, 26-34 Stannary Street, London SE11 4AB

British Library Cataloguing in Publication Information Available

Library of Congress Cataloging-in-Publication Data

Names: Aaron, Michael, 1976– author.
Title: Modern sexuality : the truth about sex and relationships / Michael Aaron.
Description: Lanham : Rowman & Littlefield, [2016] | Includes bibliographical references and index.
Identifiers: LCCN 2016014797 | ISBN 9781442253216 (cloth : alk. paper)
Subjects: LCSH: Sex. | Sex (Psychology) | Sexual attraction. | Man–woman relationships.
Classification: LCC HQ16 .A27 2016 | DDC 306.7—dc23 LC record available at https:// lccn.loc.gov/2016014797

∞ ™ The paper used in this publication meets the minimum requirements of American National Standard for Information Sciences Permanence of Paper for Printed Library Materials, ANSI/NISO Z39.48-1992.

Printed in the United States of America

CONTENTS

Introduction   I

I: SETTING THE STAGE: THE BATTLE BETWEEN SEX AND SOCIETY

1 Through the Keyhole: Debunking the Biggest Sexual Myths   9

2 The Birds and the Bees: The Case for Sexual Diversity   23

3 Be Like Mike: Society's Incessant Demand for Social Conformity   43

4 Law and Order: I Fought the Law and the Law Won   57

5 Fear and Loathing: How to Create the Perfect Consumer   71

II: LIVES RECLAIMED: EMBRACING SEXUAL FREEDOM

6 Ch-Ch-Changes, Turn and Face the Strange: How the Process of Change Occurs   95

7 The Authentic Self: Resolving Internal Shame   109

8 Get Your Sexy On: Exploring New Horizons   129

9 Spreading Your Wings: Peak Sexual Experiences   149

10 Keeping the Flame Red-Hot: The Importance of Communication, Trust, and Transparency   161

Postscript   181

Notes   185

Acknowledgments   203

Bibliography   205

Index   213

About the Author   217

INTRODUCTION

This book is about sex. And society. And the uneasy friction between the two. And it's about my role as a sex therapist, witnessing this struggle each and every day as it plays out on my therapy couch.

Don't get me wrong: sex is everywhere. It's in popular music lyrics and in beer commercials featuring bikini-clad girls on the beach. So nicely packaged, yet so far removed from reality. With so much sex all around, you'd think we'd know it all when it comes to sex. But most of what we think we know about sex is completely wrong. And millions of people in the world are suffering because of these mistaken assumptions and the myths about sexuality that have developed around them.

Myths are not random stories that people tell each other. They serve an important social purpose: to keep society unified and cohesive. As individuals, we strive for freedom of expression, but as a group we're forced to stifle it. Human sexuality today stands at the crossroads between biological diversity and social conformity, and a battle between the two rages in the media, in social institutions, and in our daily lives.

Celebrities who have sex outside their relationships often get publicly shamed and go to sex addiction rehab facilities, while sexual imagery is used to sell products and attract viewers to the latest cable show. People who are into kinky sex are labeled as perverts and lose child custody battles, yet *Fifty Shades of Grey* sells seventy million copies and the movie version tops the box office. Porn performers are marginalized as social outcasts, yet some of them appear in Hollywood movies and get book deals. Sex addiction, same-sex marriage, human sex trafficking, feminism, sex-positive feminism, porn addiction, swingers, monogamy, polyamory, intimacy, kink, attachment, BDSM, soul mates, friends with benefits. So much noise, so little clarity. What the heck is going on? With so much contradictory information, how is anyone supposed to make sense of what is OK when it comes to sex?

This book tries to accomplish a few things. First, it strives to explain why we are so removed from our own sexualities. Why sex is so shrouded in misinformation and untruths. And why sex is used as a weapon—to market to us, to turn us into loyal consumers, and to keep us feeling unsatisfied and incomplete. Toward this, I aim to provide cutting-edge scientific, accurate information about what we actually do know about sex. What is normal and healthy? What is sickness? What is right in relationships? And what is wrong?

I am going to answer all these questions and then some by using groundbreaking brain-imaging studies and cutting-edge psychological insights to provide a complete, scientific perspective on what we currently know in the field of sexology. I will go into depth on a wide range of topics, including "nonnormative" sexualities encompassing orientation, nontraditional relationships, specific fantasies and kinks, and sex work and prostitution. I will leave no stone unturned in uncovering every aspect of sexual behavior. By doing this, I hope to achieve my second goal, which is to help individuals rid themselves of any unnecessary guilt or shame about their own sexualities that inhibit them from living a life full of personal authenticity and life satisfaction.

I then explain group formation and why social groups depend on conformity for survival. The book then explores the battle between biology and society as it rages on through the media, current events, public policy, and the lives of millions of individuals caught up in the drama. Even though the book addresses individuals with a wide range of unique sexualities, it highlights the very similar and common struggles most people have when coming to terms with their authentic identities in the face of severe social pressures and stigmas. These lives are illustrated through specific examples based on actual cases taken from my established sex therapy practice in order to shine a bright light on the sexual struggles of typical Americans. Although the cases presented are composites of numerous clients and do not represent any one individual specifically, they do provide a clear window into the challenges of my work.

My hope is that the stories I present of people marginalized by society's need to suppress sexuality will inspire readers as examples of courage, resilience, and search for identity, offering insights to their own problems and inhibitions. I will then provide concrete instructions on how you, the reader, can overcome the sexual difficulties you may experience as a result of social stigma.

Here's a typical example from my practice: Cody and Amy are newlyweds whose nine-month marriage seems headed for divorce. They haven't had sex for the past month, and only recently Amy discovered troubling porn on Cody's computer that depicted sexual activities with men and transsexuals and included seemingly violent depictions of people, men and women, tied up and whipped. What kind of sex pervert did she marry? Was he gay? A sex addict? Maybe a potential sex offender? Did he also want to hurt her? Should she be afraid of him? All these questions raced through her mind. Whatever was wrong with him, he needed psychological treatment or the marriage was over.

I see these situations in my therapy office every single day. I see people struggling with and trying to make sense of their sexualities. All that intense stuff that Cody was watching online . . . those were all consensual acts that can be classified under the umbrella of BDSM—which stands for bondage, discipline, sadism, and masochism—which, as *Modern Sexuality* will reveal, is benign, nonpathological, and, surprisingly, a much more prevalent activity than most people realize. There is nothing wrong with Cody or any of the other dozens of individuals, both men and women, who have come through my office. They are simply caught up in the eternal struggle between our own human biological needs for sexual diversity and society's needs for social conformity.

This book is how I help individuals navigate this struggle and how the reader can use the specific techniques and exercises that I provide my clients to break free from the stranglehold of sexual myths and social taboos to achieve their own sexual authenticity. It represents the culmination of my entire life's work to this point, personally and professionally.

Some readers may be wondering what personal significance, if any, this subject holds for me as the author. As I was writing this book, I kept going back and forth regarding how much of my own personal life I wanted to share with readers. In the end, a close friend and colleague encouraged me to share my own story, convincing me that my own narrative would strengthen the arguments made in the book as well as provide even more inspiration for readers who may be looking for answers about their own sexuality. That was enough to sway my decision to provide some transparency about my own life.

I first volunteered for social service organizations before going back to school. My first experience in the field was as a harm reduction specialist for a clinic in midtown Manhattan that specialized in working with transgender people, intravenous drug users, and street prostitutes—basically anyone at risk of acquiring HIV and other STDs. Often the individuals fit into all three categories. Indeed, because they are so discriminated against in our society, trans people often find themselves outcast from their families and unemployable and so turn to drugs in despair and to prostitution as the only means to support themselves.

I would walk around the streets of Hell's Kitchen, looking for the spots where these folks could often be found. I carried with me medical supplies, condoms, and clean needles, along with a special package for disposing of the dirty needles given back to me in exchange for the clean ones. I would have some official-looking ID with me just in case a cop stopped me so that I wouldn't be hauled off to jail.

As I worked with marginalized people, I realized that while their problems were severe, they weren't unique. Just as my transgender clients felt alienated by society's response to their sexuality, so too did thousands of other people who were not homeless or drug addicted but went through their daily lives with a more quiet, yet hopeless desperation. I wanted to reach a much broader group of people who were suffering needlessly, not just a small subset of our society.

I studied all the important sexologists of the past, from Alfred Kinsey to Masters and Johnson and Shere Hite. I became particularly fascinated with the theorists Robert Stoller and John Money, who focused their research on the origins of "paraphilic," or deviant, sexual behavior. But while I found these ideas intriguing, I came to realize that most of what had been written about nonnormative sexual behavior came from a perspective of pathology. Indeed, the entire field of sexology throughout history mostly viewed sexual behavior through a very narrow range of what was "normal" and what was pathological. I recognized that there was a shortage of material approaching nonnormative sexual behavior from a lens that was not pathological.

Fortunately, the past five years have seen a surge of new research demonstrating that individuals who practice a wide variety of nonnormative sexual behaviors are normal and healthy. This has begun to change the discourse within the academic community, but much of this information has not yet filtered through to the public.

In the past few years, we have seen the legalization of same-sex marriages, the runaway best-seller success of *Fifty Shades of Grey*, a book centered on BDSM, and dozens of reality TV programs focusing on alternative relationships such as swinging and polyamory. However, the public is still mostly in the dark. Most of the information that reaches the public has been sensationalized and distorted simply to make a profit, not to educate, and so millions of people are still confused and frustrated, unable to make sense of the tension between their own desires and what is socially acceptable.

As a therapist, I work with people who are cut off from their full sexual and personal potential due to internalized shame and social stigma. Indeed, I work with all kinds of people with all kinds of sexual problems, including sexual minorities, adult survivors of childhood sexual abuse, and individuals with sexual anxieties and dysfunctions, gender and orientation confusion, and sexual compulsivity issues.

Even to this very day, mental health professionals are not trained in sexuality and continue to pathologize nonnormative sexual expression. According to my clients, finding a therapist who truly understands the wide range of sexual behavior is like finding a needle in a haystack. I have come to realize that I fill a huge gap by providing accurate sex education and therapy where often it's sorely lacking. *Modern Sexuality* is the product of this realization. It is my attempt to bring help from one to many—from one client at a time to the millions of people who might benefit from my knowledge.

Modern Sexuality is the by-product of countless therapy sessions where I witnessed normal people struggling immensely with their sexuality and unnecessarily suffering, all due to mixed-up and nonsensical sexual messages they learned as kids and continued to believe as adults. On a daily basis, I see how so much of what my clients have learned about sexuality is totally wrong and is needlessly destroying their lives.

Modern Sexuality is my attempt to undo this damage for the millions of individuals who are not my clients but could still use my help.

Modern Sexuality consists of two parts. Part I, "Setting the Stage: The Battle between Sex and Society," sets the stage for understanding the specific struggles that individuals experience while trying to balance their innate sexual diversity with society's need to enforce conformity. It then takes a thorough look at how the clash between biological and sexual diversity and social conformity plays out in the issues of the day, such as media representations of sexuality, the sex addiction industry, same-sex marriage, monogamy, prostitution, and pornography. Specific examples from my sex therapy practice illustrate the daily struggle that individuals experience in balancing their sexual desires with social pressures.

Part II, "Lives Reclaimed: Embracing Sexual Freedom," provides specific steps to help readers explore and reclaim their sexual identities and break free from unnecessary social stigma. It presents readers with the necessary tools while again providing specific examples from my sex therapy practice, to start the initial journey of self-discovery and sexual growth. It then explores how readers can integrate their new authentic sexual identities into the rest of their lives.

Ready to get started? So let's begin . . .

I

Setting the Stage: The Battle between Sex and Society

I

THROUGH THE KEYHOLE

Debunking the Biggest Sexual Myths

EXTERIOR SCENE: A man passionately holds a young woman close to his chest.

Man: Where have you been my whole life?

Woman: Searching. Searching for you.

Man: Now that we've finally found each other, I will never let anything come between us again.

Woman: You complete me. Without you, my world was dark and empty. But now that I'm with you, the world seems full of possibilities.

Man: You are all that I've ever wanted, ever needed. And with you, only you, I will share the rest of eternity.

FADE TO BLACK

This is the typical Hollywood fairytale ending we are so accustomed to. Boy meets girl, courts her, falls in love, loses her due to some stupidity or ineptness, and then wins her back. And they live happily ever after. This is typical in the movies, but is it typical in real life? Not really.

For many millions of people who don't fit into this cookie-cutter model, making their way through the world presents an obstacle course filled with self-doubt, insecurity, and shame. Sure, millions get married in heterosexual couplings, stay faithfully monogamous, and maintain harmonious "intimate" communion for the rest of their lives, but this view of normality misses out on the even larger number of people who are not rigidly hetero, maintain their relationship(s) through a large assortment of nonmonogamous behavior, and define intimacy radically different from the classically romantic notions of yesteryear.

This is all because now we as a society have more freedom than ever to live the way we want. Some very specific social reasons explain why that is now the case, and I'll describe them in chapter 3. The myths that once held sway over human behavior are still there, but cracks are forming on the surface. These myths do not exist by accident, however, but serve a very specific social purpose.

AESOP'S FABLES: THE SECRET PURPOSE OF MYTHS

So why do we need myths? Famed mythologist Joseph Campbell identified four main functions of myths. According to Campbell:

1. The first function of mythology [is] to evoke in the individual a sense of grateful, affirmative awe before the monstrous mystery that is existence.
2. The second function of mythology is to present an image of the cosmos, an image of the universe round about, that will maintain and elicit this experience of awe. [or] . . . to present an image of the cosmos that will maintain your sense of mystical awe and explain everything that you come into contact with in the universe around you.
3. The third function of a mythological order is to validate and maintain a certain sociological system: a shared set of rights and wrongs, proprieties or improprieties, on which your particular social unit depends for its existence.
4. The fourth function of myth is psychological. That myth must carry the individual through the stages of his life, from birth through maturity through senility to death. The mythology must

do so in accords with the social order of his group, the cosmos as understood by his group, and the monstrous mystery.[1]

The first two functions deal more with a sense of awe and connection with the universe, the fourth function with stages of life. It is function number three, however, that bears the most importance for our discussion here. Let's look at it again. According to Campbell, myths "validate and maintain a certain sociological system: a shared set of rights and wrongs, proprieties or improprieties, on which your particular social unit depends for its existence."[2]

In other words, myths are necessary not only for social cohesion but really for the very existence of the social unit. Myths protect the social order. Through myths, we include everything that fits into the social fabric and exclude anything that poses a threat.

In this chapter, I look at the top five sexual myths that run through our social fabric. As you'll see, they feed into one another and often overlap.

MYTH NUMBER ONE: SEXUALITY IS MOSTLY LEARNED AND SO CAN BE CHANGED

Whether it's orientation, fetishistic preferences, or specific sexual behaviors, much of the stigma about sexual behavior has to do with the myth that people pick up their sexual interests through their social environment, usually in childhood. As a result, that allows a lot of opportunity for picking up "deviance" along the way.

Recent research, however, shows that most of human sexuality, from sexual orientation to specific behaviors, is innate. Don't get me wrong— other research suggests that sexuality isn't fixed or rigid, but rather fluid. It can change over time, but not due to some sort of conscious intervention, such as willpower or behavioral modification. This fluidity is most likely due to a process called *epigenetics*, but I'll take a look at the bulk of this research in chapter 2. Often, coming into one's own sexuality is a process of uncovering. Not changing.

Suffice it to say, much of sexual behavior, such as orientation, appears to be mostly determined by prenatal influences. Even those behaviors that would seem to have been created by some external environmental influence, such as childhood trauma of some sort, appear to affect only those who are already genetically predisposed to it.

For example, the scant evidence we have, starting from the studies of psychiatrist Richard von Krafft-Ebing (more on him below), shows that men are much more likely to have fetishistic arousal patterns than women.[3] (Here I am differentiating between fetishes and BDSM, which as we shall see in chapter 2 appears to encompass women almost as much or just as much as men.) When qualitative studies are conducted, about half of respondents state that they have been aware of their desires as far back as they can remember, while about another half typically can recall a specific moment in time when they developed their interest. Sometimes these moments have been traumatic. Sexologist John Money, for example, cited numerous examples of individuals who developed their sexual interests due to some specific traumatic event.[4] For example, in his seminal book *Love Maps*, Money details the childhood origins of a man with acrotomophilia (attraction to amputees) and another who was aroused by autoerotic asphyxiation. Ogi Ogas and Sai Gaddam, the authors of *A Billion Wicked Thoughts* provide the example of a young man who developed a sexual arousal toward being crawled on by insects.[5]

As a sex therapist, I have also encountered individuals in my practice who can recall a specific (sometimes traumatic) event (typically in childhood) that was the catalyst for an entire series of sexual proclivities. Indeed, recent research on rats showed that they could be conditioned to connect sexual arousal to wearing a special rat-outfitted jacket.[6] Virgin rats who wore the jacket the first nine times they had sex generally had less success achieving orgasm the tenth time if they did not wear the jacket. Still, 60 percent of the rats had no problems at all despite the researchers' best efforts to manipulate their sexuality.

That said, even with clear examples of environmental influences, we are still left with the question of why it is men and not women who are much more likely to develop fetishistic influences. If environment is the sole cause, why don't women with similar traumas also form similar kinks? (Note: for purposes of clarity, I'm using the word "fetish" to describe a sexual interest in a nonliving, inanimate object. For simplicity, I'm also including body parts under this term, although the correct word for an interest in a foot or elbow would be "partialism.")

The answer to this question may be found in the research of Cambridge psychologist Simon Baron-Cohen, cousin of *Borat* creator Sacha Baron-Cohen. Much of his research revolves around autism and, specifically, sex differences in the human brain. He found, for example, that higher levels of fetal testosterone accounted for the prevalence of autism in males.[7] In one specific research study, and the one most relevant to this discussion, he took female and male babies that were all of one day old and showed both groups of babies a human face and an object, such as a toy. The girls were much more likely to focus on the expressions of the human face, while the boys were significantly more likely to fix their gaze on the inanimate object.

So according to these research results, boys are wired from the very time of birth to be much more object oriented than girls. A comprehensive study showing these tendencies was conducted by Dr. Richard Lippa at UCLA, in which he analyzed the kinds of occupations that individuals chose and found that men generally are more attracted to objected-oriented fields (dealing with machinery, tools, gadgets) and that this trend applies across the board regardless of country or culture.[8] I will go more into the absolutely fascinating and essential role that testosterone plays in sexual development in chapter 2.

The point of this is that boys already enter their environment with a predisposition toward objects. Is it any surprise, then, that they are far more likely to gather impressions from their environment that play into their natural tendencies and that then become imprinted for life? For example, let's take a boy who had a neighbor girl seductively rub her foot in his face while playing in the backyard and then developed a foot fetish. If he wasn't already wired to home in on objects, would the foot ever make such an indelible impression on him? Probably not. And here we have the interaction of nature and the environment. In this scenario, the environment clearly was a catalyst, but the fetish could never take hold if the boy didn't have a vulnerability for a visual stimulation toward objects, in this case, the foot. We have a term for this interaction, where the environment triggers underlying genetic tendencies—epigenetics. I'll get more into epigenetics later on, but for now, let's just take a look at the possibility that even in the most obvious cases of environmental meddling, genetics still play a big, pretty big, heck, let's say really, Really, *Really* B-I-G part.

MYTH NUMBER TWO: NONNORMATIVE SEXUAL BEHAVIOR IS PATHOLOGICAL

This is a big one that perpetuates itself all over and especially within therapeutic circles—the idea that any nonnormative sexual behavior, from the whole range of kinky fetishes to polyamory to swinging, is somehow pathological. Recent research completely disproves this and even shows that these groups may actually tend to be more mentally healthy, mostly because they are enjoying rather than suppressing their diverse sexualities. I'll get into all the research in chapter 2, but for now, let's take a look at how this idea has taken hold.

German psychiatrist Richard von Krafft-Ebing in his magnus opus *Psychopathia Sexualis* was the first medical practitioner to attempt to chronicle and label the wide spectrum of sexual behavior. He presented 238 case studies ranging from homosexuality to bestiality to exhibitionism.[9] His writings coincided with a resurgence of interest in sexuality in the late 1800s, at the time that prudish Victorianism was the order of the day in England and the rest of Europe. I'll talk more about why this time was so fruitful in the annals of sexology in chapter 3, but for now, I am going to focus only on how Krafft-Ebing's work influenced psychiatry's view of nonnormative sexualities for the next 120 years. For those sex nerds out there, Krafft-Ebing was the one who coined the terms "sadism" (from the Marquis de Sade) and "masochism" (from the writer Leopold von Sacher-Masoch).

The one thing about Krafft-Ebing, to his credit, is that unlike his contemporaries such as Sigmund Freud, he believed that much of the sexual peculiarities he witnessed were due to biological reasons.

Prior to Krafft-Ebing, no one really saw the need to catalogue anything about sexual differences. Indeed, the term "homosexuality" did not even exist back then. In fact, no word to describe homosexuality even existed at all. Sociologist Michel Foucault wrote that a discourse around sexuality was created only after the decline of religion in the industrialized world and the subsequent need for some way of controlling sexual behavior arose in its absence.[10] This control took on the form of listing, labeling, and cataloguing every single variation of sexual behavior imaginable. And then pathologizing it.

Also, in the late 1800s, we witnessed the work of Sigmund Freud and the birth of psychoanalysis. Freud had many interesting theories about sexuality, but most of them again came up with some pathological conclusion. For example, for Freud, homosexuality was the result of some hitch in the anal phase of childhood, roughly age one and one-half to three years. Freud did acknowledge that children were inherently sexual, calling it "polymorphous perversity," but then also concluded that the inevitable result of that sexuality was to want to have sex with the opposite-gendered parent.[11] Indeed, the entire enterprise of psychoanalysis was formed from Freud's efforts to "cure" upper-class Viennese women of their hysteria with psychological means as opposed to the typical medical practice of the day, whereby the physician masturbated the aggrieved woman to orgasm (paroxysm). (Look up the history of the vibrator.)

As much as Freud went about the business of pathologizing most of everything, it was his followers who really cranked the illness making up a notch. In the 1920s, psychoanalyst Wilhelm Steckel coined the term "paraphilia" or literally "above or beyond love" to label nonnormative sexuality. This term came back up in the *Diagnostic and Statistical Manual III* (*DSM*, psychiatry's reference bible) in 1980 to define basically any kind of nonnormative sexual practice as a mental illness. Before that, the term of the day was "perversion" and literally libraries full of texts were written by psychoanalysts to explain the etiology of these perversions in pathological terms.

So depending on the author of choice, a perversion was a result of childhood trauma, a developmental arrest, a "transitional object" that would take the place of a real love object, an attachment glitch due to the fact that the individual was too impaired to actually attach securely to another human, or a symptom of a personality disorder, such as being schizoid. As I will show in chapter 2, research shows that none of this is true and that there is absolutely no correlation whatsoever between nonnormative sexual practices and pathology.

The same is true of forms of consensual nonmonogamy, such as swinging and polyamory. These are different cohorts, but still, no research study has shown any differences in mental health functioning between monogamous and consensually nonmonogamous individuals. A study by psychologist Elisabeth Sheff also found that children raised by parents in poly configurations grew up equally as healthy as the kids raised in monogamous environments.[12] Further, other studies have shown that poly folks have even greater levels of intimacy than their monoamorous counterparts.

One study, for example, found that open couples have better relationship quality—more trust and communication and less jealousy.[13] Another study found no relationship between attachment avoidance and type of relationship (poly or mono).[14] Actually, anxiously attached people were less satisfied in poly than mono relationships. In other words, for anxiously attached people, monogamy was a more ideal relationship structure, possibly due to not having to deal with as much relational jealousy. (By anxiously attached, I am referring to the body of research on attachment styles, in which individuals are either avoidantly, anxiously, or securely attached. Those who are avoidant or anxious often struggle to form stable romantic relationships.)

Much has already been written about sexual orientation in other tomes, and as a nation, we've experienced the recent breakthrough of the Supreme Court ruling on same-sex marriages. As a result, I will focus less on orientation in this book, although I will definitely touch on it. Suffice it to say, every study ever completed has shown absolutely no pathology or difference in mental health between gay and straight folks. Same goes for kinky or poly individuals and their "vanilla" counterparts.

MYTH NUMBER THREE: HEALTHY SEXUALITY INVOLVES INTIMACY

Go to your local bookshop and head to the "Relationship" aisle and you will be inundated with various books purporting to help you create, rebuild, enhance, find again, or deepen your intimacy. Turn on the TV and anytime any subject comes on about relationships and sex, inevitably it will all come back down to intimacy. *Intimacy*. That's what it seems to be all about. But what the heck is intimacy anyway?

Most of this material seems to be mainly centered on old, outdated ideas about monogamy and marriage, even the quality of married sex, such as the importance of eye gazing, sensual foreplay, and loving pillow talk. The truth is that intimacy takes on many forms. More on that in a moment.

The idea of intimacy centers on all kinds notions of what separates healthy versus unhealthy, or dirty, sexuality and really, in the big scheme of things, is a relatively new idea. The entire notion of intimacy rests on the foundation that healthy sexuality should be confined to a committed relationship or at least part of a defined courting process. This myth has broad ramifications, affecting the debate on sex addiction, pornography, and prostitution. The truth is that most "healthy" sexuality often has nothing to do with intimacy at all and often involves a healthy process of emotional and psychological exploration, which may or may not (but often does) feel intimate.

Again, intimacy is a fairly new idea in the annals of human history, so let's take a quick look at what it replaced and how it all came to be. Sociologist Anthony Giddens traces the notion of romantic love (and the basis of modern concepts of intimacy) to only as far back as the eighteenth century.[15] He sees this kind of love as culturally specific and mostly found in Western societies. According to him, this type of love focuses on the concept of finding "the One," that person who will be our soul mate, who will provide for all our emotional needs and make our life complete.

Don't get me wrong. Anyone who has ever read *Romeo and Juliet* or the chivalrous adventures of the knights of King Arthur knows that the concept of love has existed since the dawn of humanity. What I'm referring to is the heavy emphasis on love and romantic compatibility that is now placed on primary relationships. Before this, marriages had more of a utilitarian purpose. They were about preserving land ownership and class distinction as well as forming useful alliances. You married in order to survive and raise kids, and the more kids you had, the more likely some of them would survive and help out with the chores.

In many ways, the idea of finding the "One," of locating our true soul mate, and the heavy emphasis we as a society place on this new concept of intimacy is based on the notion that our romantic partner should somehow fulfill all our basic human needs, such as love, friendship, companionship, emotional support, and sexual satisfaction. That's a lot of pressure to put on just one person. And I think that it is no coincidence that this idea has taken hold at the same time as our society has become more fast paced, technology driven, and globalized, all aspects that have on one hand made us more connected but on the other more lonely and alienated.

According to two recent surveys, 40 percent of adults said they were lonely, compared with 20 percent in the 1980s.[16] That's a 100 percent increase. And social media, for all of its social features, doesn't seem to be helping. In fact, studies show that those who most commonly use Facebook are also more likely to feel lonely and insecure about their social lives.[17] Instead of meeting face to face, people (especially younger ones) are much more likely to communicate via social media or text messages. (Before I sound too bleak, technology does have its benefits, which I will address in further detail in chapter 3.)

We have tons more ways to communicate but less real interaction. Much more technology but less humanity. No wonder when or if we snag a mate, that person simply has to be everything to us, I mean literally everything, since so many lack a strong social net outside their primary relationship. Is this what we really mean by "intimacy"?

The more we privilege intimacy, the higher the divorce rate seems to be. Studies show that the divorce rate has skyrocketed since the 1970s, leveling off at about 50 percent in the past decade.[18] According to a study published in 2002, 70 percent of folks have stated that they have been cheated on at some point.[19] That's a vast majority. High divorce rates. Massive cheating. Is this what we have to show for all of our focus on intimacy? I would argue, and the research backs me up on this, that the problem isn't with the search or the desire for intimacy but rather with how we define it.

Recent research shows that intimacy is a highly subjective term that is experienced by people in a wide number of ways. The intimacy we commonly think of—sexuality fused with romance, fucking with love-making, physicality with tenderness, and commitment with monogamy is simply nothing but a myth. For many, things like rough sex and role play can be (and often are) experienced as deep intimacy as well. And, as studies show, many of them have better "intimacies" than their traditional counterparts. In fact, a recent study found that polyamorist couples have the highest rates of relationship satisfaction and lowest rates of STDs.[20] Which leads me to myth number four.

MYTH NUMBER FOUR: INTIMACY IS EASILY DEFINED AND MEANS THE SAME TO EVERYONE

Ask polyamorous and swinging couples, and they'll likely tell you that they find much greater intimacy in sharing their partners with others.

BDSM couples find intense intimacy through role play, experimenting with roles of dominance and submission, and connecting through powerful expressions of power exchange and pain. Funny how intimacy can mean so many things to so many different people.

Psychologist Donald Mosher, in his research of partnered sex, found that couples engage in three distinct categories of sex: (1) trance, (2) role play, and (3) partner engagement.[21]

According to Mosher, trance sex is purely physical—it's all about the tingling, the friction, and all the other sensations that go along with sex. It's not mental or emotional, just purely physical. No thoughts, no fantasies, and not necessarily any feel of connection. Still healthy. And stuff folks do all the time.

Role play refers to an exploration of the more psychological elements of sex. It doesn't necessarily mean dressing up in any kind of exotic costumes, but instead, it's a type of sex that focuses on exploring interpersonal dynamics. This stage is all about identity exploration. That identity can be an archetype, such as the hero or waif, or involve a creative exploration of one's dark side, what psychoanalyst Carl Jung called the "shadow."

And finally, partner engagement is the kind of sex that we think about when we think about happy Hollywood endings. You know, eye gazing, pillow talk, and all that other romantic stuff. Yeah, that's only just one type of sex, and not necessarily the most common either.

What Mosher discovered was that there is really no right kind of sex. In other words, people typically engage in one type of sex during one encounter and may then engage in a completely different type of sex the next time around. They often may even transition from one type to another within the same encounter.

So one night, two people can have slow sensual sex, just focusing on the sensations of penetration and physical touch, then the next morning get into some rough play involving power dynamics, hair pulling, butt slapping, and so on, and then finish things off in the afternoon with a soft, penetrative embrace filled with passionate kisses and tender "I love yous." Or better yet, they do this all during the same session.

So, for example, they may start out with the intention of just having a quickie but find themselves involved in some kink play, then slide into passionate "I love yous," then back into biting and hair pulling, then up into a rhythmic trance, then some more leaning in with eye gazing, followed by some orders and commands, leading up to a physical explosion where all sense of self is obliterated. Now that sounds like some fucking great sex. Yeah, and healthy too.

What Mosher actually found was that sexual difficulties arose when one or the other person could not transition between the three types of sex. In other words, they were either stuck in one of the stages and unable to experience pleasure any other way or able to experience pleasure in two stages but not in a third. So following this model, folks who require partner engagement to get into it are more likely to feel stuck in their sexual experience than folks who can enjoy it all. Following those conclusions, the folks who are ripping off each other's clothes, playing around with whips and chains, enjoying sex just for the physical stimulation, *and* engaging in pillow talk have far fewer issues than those exclusively locked in each other's embrace.

Now I'm not saying there's anything wrong or pathological with doing only one thing either. What I'm saying here rather is that healthy sexuality encompasses so much beyond traditional notions of intimacy and that actually, a fixation on traditional notions of intimacy leads to far "unhealthier" sex than just going with the flow and surrendering to whatever the moment lends itself to.

MYTH NUMBER FIVE: SEXUAL BEHAVIOR MUST HAVE A CLEARLY DEFINED PURPOSE

This myth is dualistic, separating sexual behavior into two extremes—intended for either procreation or pleasure. The truth is much different. Most sexual behavior serves a far broader range of functions, ranging from exploring personal identity (see above myth number four), experimenting with archetypical roles (also myth number four), working through past pains or trauma, seeking self-validation, looking for emotional peaks, connecting with others in a more transparent way, or as part of a transcendent spiritual practice. Sometimes sex involves several of these reasons, sometimes none at all. Most of all, sex is supposed to be fun, right? Or, if not, what's the point?

A 2007 study of 203 men and 241 women ages 17–52, published in the *Archives of Sexual Behavior*, found 237 reasons why people engage in sex.[22] The researchers then prepared this list, asked 1,549 psychology students to rate how often they engaged in sex for each of the reasons, and then ranked the most common themes in order. The most common reasons included the following: feeling desired by another; curiosity or seeking new experiences; marking a special occasion for celebration; mere opportunity; and "just happening due to seemingly uncontrollable circumstances." Other, less common reasons included: wanting to harm another person; getting resources (such as job, money, drugs, or gifts); enhancing social status; and as a means to a seemingly unrelated end (such as relieving a headache). I don't see procreation there.

Indeed, recent bio-evolutionary theories propose that sex serves the evolutionary purpose of providing connection to others more than it serves procreation.[23] And what is connection? Well, here again, we circularly go back to the earlier myth about intimacy. Connection means different things to different people, which is why we find 237 reasons in the study mentioned above.

As we'll see, it is this search for connection that makes sex feel so necessary, so important, yet at the same time has fostered the need for conformism and stigmatization of those types of sexualities that pose a threat to social cohesion. Let's read on.

2

THE BIRDS AND THE BEES

The Case for Sexual Diversity

WHAT'S THE MATTER WITH KINSEY? LESSONS RELEARNED FROM A HALF-CENTURY OF SEX RESEARCH

Alfred Kinsey's groundbreaking research in the 1940s and 1950s put a real wrench in America's attitudes and conceptions around sexuality. In his qualitative studies, he found that people do all kinds of things, way more than we ever suspected, and sure, heterosexual vanilla sex was a part of the picture, but there was a lot more to human sexuality than that.

His *Sexual Behavior in the Human Male*,[1] published in 1948, stunned the nation, but it was his *Sexual Behavior in the Human Female* that got him blacklisted and ended his career.[2] Folks just couldn't imagine that their wives, daughters, and girlfriends were horny, sexual creatures. Ever since then, we have had a dearth of research on anything sexual due mostly to a lack of funding. The free love of the sixties and seventies transformed into the conservativism of the eighties and the advent of AIDS, the evangelical movement, and sex addiction treatment.

The good news is that we are experiencing a renaissance of sex research in recent years, research that is starting to shed some significant light on our understanding of human sexuality. I'm going to be discussing a lot of that scientific research in this chapter, so bear with me. I'll try to make it as painless as possible. But science is really, really important because if we're going to make therapeutic or public policy decisions about sexuality, we have to have hard science behind us. Otherwise, it's only mythology and personal bias.

I think it's also important to go through all the science in order for me to substantiate why I work the way I do. In other words, I use science to support my clinical therapeutic decisions every single day. So if you are going to make sense of the subsequent chapters, where I go into detail on how I help my clients (and also how you can help yourself), I think it's really important that we have the science in front of us as a common language.

HOT (XXX) OFF THE PRESSES: WHAT THE LATEST PSYCHOLOGICAL RESEARCH TELLS US ABOUT SEX

Earlier, in chapter 1, I briefly introduced the myth that much of our sexuality is learned from the environment. Here, I'll go into greater detail on why that is not true. Let's start with the big elephant in the room—testosterone. I'll keep coming back to this little hormone because it's a doozy.

Testosterone has been shown to influence everything from gender identity to orientation and even to predisposition to fetishistic interests (see chapter 1). I'm sure most of you have heard the cliche "the brain is the biggest sex organ." Well, in honor of that most accurate phrase, let's start our survey of human sexuality by looking at the human brain.

Let's take a look at what current brain research shows. Recent advances in brain imaging, particularly PET scans, prove that brains of men are different from brains of women, brains of homosexual men are different from brains of heterosexual men, brains of homosexual women are different from brains of heterosexual women, and brains of transgender individuals are different from those of cisgender (same gender expression) individuals.

Brains of heterosexual women and homosexual men were found to be symmetrical, with more nerve connections in the left side of the amygdala, while the brains of homosexual women and heterosexual men showed asymmetry, with more nerve connections in the right side of the amygdala, according to researchers at Karolinska Institute in

Sweden.[3] Further, in 1991, neuroscientist Simon LaVey examined brain tissue samples from forty-one human autopsies and found a significant difference between heterosexual and homosexual men in a part of the brain called the anterior hypothalamus, a region known for managing emotions.[4]

In addition, there are other markers. Research has shown that homosexuals are more likely to have a lower birth order and more prevalence of left-handedness. When it comes to birth order, sex researcher Ray Blanchard coined the term "fraternal birth order effect" to designate his discovery that males are 33 percent more likely to be gay with each older brother (this is limited only to older brothers, not sisters, and also does not appear to affect lesbians).[5] Blanchard theorizes that this effect is due perhaps to an immunological response of the mother to her son's male hormones released in her system.

Another researcher, Dean Hamer, studied pairs of gay brothers in 1993 and identified a stretch of the X chromosome (the chromosome coming from the mother) called Xq28, which appears to possess genes that predispose a man to being gay.[6] This finding was controversial, as a few other studies confirmed these findings while others appeared to invalidate Hamer's conclusions. Most recently in 2014, the largest study to replicate the original research examined 409 gay brothers and found a link to the same region in the X chromosome.[7] The authors of the study concluded, "Our findings, taken in context with previous work, suggest that genetic variation in . . . these regions contributes to development of the important psychological trait of male sexual orientation."

Current research seems to indicate that roughly 2–3 percent of the male population is gay, with a 2014 National Statistics Report coming in at a lower number, 1.6 percent of the population identifying as gay or lesbian.[8] However, when identical twins of gay men and women were studied by researcher Michael Bailey in 1991, about 50 percent of the identical twins were also gay, a much higher rate, but not 100 percent as might be expected of identical twins that have exact replicas of each other's genetics.[9] Other studies have shown smaller concordance rates. A study of 4,901 Australian twins found rates of homosexuality of 20 percent for male identical twins and 24 percent for female identical twins,[10] and a 2002 study of 289 pairs of identical twins found concordance rates of 7.7 percent for males and 5.3 percent for females.[11]

Taking all this into account, we can see that the identical twin studies are all over the map; however, they clearly show higher concordance rates between identical twins than the rate of homosexuality in the general population, although not the 100 percent one would expect of identical twins. So what does this mean? Most likely, orientation is not purely genetic but epigenetic, meaning that something environmental affects inborn predispositions.

So in the twin studies, both siblings have the genetic disposition toward homosexuality, but in some it is triggered, and in others it is not. A groundbreaking new discovery announced in October 2015 appears to provide compelling proof. UCLA molecular biologist Tuck C. Ngun, studying forty-six pairs of identical twins, reported finding specific "epigenetic marks" in nine areas of the human genome. These marks predict homosexuality to within 70 percent accuracy rates.[12]

We don't know exactly how this process works, but recent research shows that the same epigenetic dynamic is at play with multiple sclerosis. In a 2010 study, researchers studied identical twins where one twin had multiple sclerosis and the other did not, and they found that both twins had the same genetic makeup—another point of evidence toward epigenetic factors.[13]

So the best evidence we have is that orientation is epigenetic—it is based on the complex interaction between genetic disposition and environmental triggers in the womb. This is why orientation is hardwired and has proved resistant to any efforts toward change.

In the 1950s, Czech psychologist Karl Freund started employing a device called the penile plethysmograph to screen out recruits who were trying to avoid military service in the Czech army by claiming to be homosexuals. The penile plethysmograph (PPG) is a little contraption that attaches to the penis and measures blood flow while a subject typically watches erotic visual material. Although there are techniques that may allow someone to fake results (more on that later), the PPG is still considered an accurate assessment tool and is often used in research even today.

One of Freund's assigned tasks using the PPG was not only to screen out the fakers but also to find the "real" homosexuals, the folks who were authentically aroused by erotic images of other men, and then convert them into heterosexuals using behavioral aversive techniques. These aversive techniques may include masturbating to gay material once the subject has already orgasmed and is no longer feeling aroused (and so the imagery supposedly becomes associated with discomfort and lack of interest) or in worst-case scenarios, shocking the subject with pain as soon as he becomes aroused by gay imagery. Lovely, isn't it? Thankfully, these painful techniques are no longer practiced due to ethical reasons, but unfortunately, a few aversive techniques are still sometimes employed in the "treatment" of fetishes.

Freund was one of the first to show, through his large-scale studies that extended throughout much of the 1950s, that conversion therapy was futile and that no matter what he tried, his subjects did not change their arousal patterns.[14] Even those who married women and had apparently "given up" homosexuality were still aroused by other men. Every other study to date has shown similar results. In other words, there is not one single controlled study that has demonstrated any concrete evidence that orientation can be changed.

The PPG has been used to study not only homosexuality but other possible orientations, such as bisexuality, and even asexuality. Yes, asexuality is a unique orientation. Which leads to an even greater theme that runs throughout this book—there are many types of orientations. And none of them should be pathologized.

Let's first start out with a look at bisexuality. A 2005 study by Northwestern University researchers reported that bisexuality is a myth. They recruited 101 men, 30 of whom identified as heterosexual, 33 as bisexual, and 38 as homosexual.[15] Using the PPG to study genital arousal, they concluded that three-quarters of those who identified as bisexual were much more aroused by homosexual imagery, while about one-quarter showed a more heterosexual pattern. Thus, they surmised, even though individuals may identify as bisexual, true bisexual arousal does not exist. This finding appeared to confirm other studies that found similar results.

For example, a 1979 study of thirty men found that bisexuals were indistinguishable from homosexuals on measures of genital arousal,[16] and a 1994 survey by the gay community magazine *The Advocate* found that prior to identifying as gay, 40 percent of survey respondents had initially identified as bi.[17]

OK, so the research seems to show that bisexuality is not a true orientation, right? Not so fast. The same researchers from Northwestern decided to revisit their 2005 study when they realized they had made methodological errors in their research. Specifically, and most seriously, they had totally stacked the deck in the way they had recruited their subjects. Instead of recruiting from a wide range of sources, they had merely placed advertisements in gay-oriented publications and then somehow expected to get an accurate sample of bisexual respondents. Talk about research bias; this takes the cake.

This time around, the researchers amended their protocol and recruited bisexual-identified subjects from online sites that specifically catered to bisexuals. In addition, they required that subjects had had at least two sexual experiences with people from each sex and a romantic relationship of at least three months with at least one person of each sex. Not surprisingly, the results were radically different.

In this study, bisexual men responded genitally to both male and female erotic content, while the gay and straight men did not.[18] Their subjective experiences of arousal also matched their genital response. These findings corroborated another study done that year, published in the prestigious *Archives of Sexual Behavior*, that found that self-identified bisexual men were genitally aroused by both men and women as well as bisexual material of a man interacting with a woman and another man, and they were much more likely to experience arousal to this material than either heterosexual or gay men.[19] So the science seems to indicate that when a study is done correctly without recruitment bias, bisexuality is as real as homosexuality and heterosexuality.

But I also mentioned asexuality. Is that an orientation too? Let's take a look at the evidence. First, and curiously enough, those who identify as asexual tend to have some common characteristics with homosexuals (in the aggregate), such as higher prevalence of left-handedness and lower birth order (born later than other siblings).[20] That may mean something, or it might not. But what does the PPG say? Do asexuals experience genital arousal like others do?

A recent study attempted to find this exact answer. Researchers from the University of British Columbia studied differences in genital (using vaginal photoplethysmography [VPG], not PPG) and subjective arousal between asexual woman and nonasexual women and found that asexuals did not actually differ at all in their genital arousal.[21] The only difference was in their subjective experience of arousal. In other words, asexual women were genitally aroused like the other subjects but did not report any increase in sexual desire. Further, they did not experience any change in their emotional state, so fear or aversion could not explain their lack of desire. To recap, asexuals appear to have some genetic markers similar to homosexuals, and their lack of desire cannot be attributed to lack of genital arousal, fear, aversion, trauma, or any other adverse life events. Based on the evidence, asexuality appears to be largely innate.

We've covered a bunch of ground so far. Homosexuality, bisexuality, asexuality. All orientations. All probably mostly, if not completely, genetic. None pathological. What about other forms of sexuality? Lots of stuff is in the media lately about things way out of the mainstream, like fetishes, BDSM, and polyamory. These can't possibly be orientations or in any way remotely connected with anything genetic, right? Well, let's take a look at the evidence.

ALTERNATIVE UNIVERSE

First, let's start with some definitions. Fetishes are sexual interests in inanimate objects. Partialisms are sexual interests in body parts. For the sake of simplicity, I will group these two items together under the umbrella of "fetishes" to designate sexual interests that are extremely focused on specific things. Like shoes, feet, rubber, elbows, stuff like that. Those are only mainstream varieties. There are literally hundreds of different types of fetishes with all kinds of arcane Latin names such as acrotomophilia (amputees), autonepiophilia (diapers), coulrophilia (clowns), and formicophilia (insects). Again, I am differentiating between fetishes and the broader topic of BDSM, which I will discuss in more detail in a moment.

Where do all these fetishes come from? Surely they must be based on some kind of negative experience or trauma? If you reflect back to chapter 1, you'll recall that no doubt some individuals can trace their unusual sex interest to some specific intense or life-changing event. No doubt about it. But I also posed this question in chapter 1: Why are the majority of fetishists male? That doesn't seem environmentally based to me. In fact, in his book *What You Can Change, and What You Can't*, psychologist Martin Seligman states that he believes basically almost all men are fetishists except that it is called a "fetish" only when it is frowned on.[22] In other words, an interest in breasts, buttocks, and genitals is okay, but a desire for anything less commonplace, well that's a fetish.

If you recall, recent research shows that due to the influence of testosterone, males are much more inclined to focus on objects, females on faces. If both males and females are as likely to have a negative experience with a bad clown or a creepy crawly insect or some other thing that could be linked in the heat of the moment to sexual arousal, why is it that almost universally, it is men who experience fetishes? A purely environmental, trauma-based explanation simply does not hold up. And scientific evidence confirms this.

A study of 262 members of a homosexual foot fetish club found that 50 percent of respondents could not identify a point of origin of their fetish.[23] The majority of the other 50 percent could point to either childhood play with peers or contact with the feet of an older male as point of first awareness. This group did not show any tendency toward pathology or high incidence of childhood trauma.

I think an important unanswered question here is whether the childhood incident caused the fetish or was merely the first time the individual became aware of it. This is an important distinction. But with the research facts in front of us—50 percent cannot determine any etiology, 50 percent can remember a starting point of awareness but not necessarily causality, and no evidence of statistically significant tendencies toward pathology or experiences of childhood trauma—it really makes you wonder what's really behind the fetish.

Other studies provide similar evidence. An unpublished study of forty-five foot fetishists by Dr. William Granzig of the American Academy of Clinical Sexologists found that 36 percent of respondents became aware of their fetish by age two or three (so literally, as long as they had been alive), and a total of 69 percent became aware before puberty.[24] A total of 70 percent could not identify any cause or etiology whatsoever. One respondent stated that he developed an interest in feet only after learning about the subject, an important point that will come up later in the subject of sexual addictions. Doesn't sound environmentally based, does it?

Another research project by Amy Lykins and Phillipa Nothman in Australia studied the interests of vorarephiles (those aroused by a fantasy of being eaten alive) as well as those with other fetishes besides vorarephilia. The preliminary findings indicate that the vast majority became aware of their interest(s) at an early age of from three to seven.[25] Even those who started to sexualize their interests at puberty were aware of a "fascination" with the subject at a much earlier age.

Let's open up the subject a bit more and enter the larger arena of BDSM. Often there is an overlap between the two groups, as fetishists often do engage in BDSM activities. Although BDSM is a separate category from fetishes, researcher Elisabeth Sheff found these groups to be so similar as to be indistinguishable for the purposes of her analysis. As most will know, BDSM stands for bondage and discipline, dominance and submission (and/or sadism and masochism). It is a big umbrella term, but most importantly, it designates a specific type of relationship based on "eroticized power," according to David Ortmann and Richard Sprott in their book *Sexual Outsiders*.[26] While fetishes are part of sex play for many, BDSM may often be experienced as part of an overall identity or type of relationship.

Several studies have examined the origins of the interests of BDSM participants and found similar results but with an interesting caveat. Let's start with the oldest one, done in 1977 by psychologist Andreas Spengler, of 245 male West German sadomasochists that found that 17 percent of respondents first became aware of their sexual interests before age twelve.[27] Similarly, in a 1987 study, sexologists Charles Moser and Eugene Levitt found that 16 percent of their respondents had first experience of their interests before age twelve.[28] The number jumps to 24 percent in sexologist Gloria Brame's online survey of 6,997 BDSM participants.[29] 17 percent, 16 percent, 24 percent—seem like relatively small numbers, right? Note that this research was all done before the year 2000 and the first two studies in the 1970s and 1980s, respectively. Why does this matter?

Well, in a more recent online survey of 1,800 individuals conducted by therapist Galen Fous, a whopping 70 percent of respondents stated that they were aware of their sexual proclivities before age twelve.[30] Now this particular study does not differentiate between kink and more "vanilla" sexual interests. Still, how do we explain these seemingly incongruent results?

I think some of the answers may lie with research on gender composition of BDSM participants. Early research indicated that BDSM was a purely male activity. The same Spengler study from above suggested that few or even no women were involved in BDSM unless pressured by a male partner. A leaflet from 1978 from a lesbian organization stated "S/M is a male perversion. There are no lesbians into S/M."[31] Moser and Levitt, in their same 1987 study, concluded that BDSM was largely the province of men since they found that males outnumber females four to one.[32]

Moving along to Brame in 2000, we find a gender ratio of nine men for every seven women of BDSM participants. An even more recent survey in 2008 in Australia of 1,500 respondents found a similar ten to seven ratio.[33] Further, the study found that younger women are significantly more likely to be kinky than older women. Fous's most recent online survey actually found a slightly higher demographic of women (51 percent). It is important to note that this online survey, along with a few others cited such as the Brame survey, are not peer reviewed, and so we cannot absolutely claim them to be scientific as they may contain methodological and sampling errors and such.

However, taking a step back and looking at the larger picture, we can start to see some trends. At the same time that more and more people started becoming aware of their BDSM interests at a young age, more and more women started identifying an interest in BDSM as well (remember, we are talking about BDSM, not fetishes, which are predominantly male). And both of these rise almost in lockstep, as if they are very closely correlated.

We have a few possibilities here. One is that folks are suddenly becoming innately more kinky in rapid numbers. The other is that folks who previously did not identify as kinky now do, and at earlier ages as well. How could this be possible?

One theory is that less stigma and shame are now attached to coming out kinky as well as more awareness of BDSM through the media. So those who were kinky all along are now able to be more honest in questionnaires as well as fearlessly explore their own sexualities rather than stifle them. In other words, if this is the case, then social stigma bears great responsibility in preventing individuals from accessing their innate natural tendencies.

A new study in the prestigious *Journal of Sexual Medicine* might shed some light on this issue. The researchers surveyed over 1,500 respondents about their sexual fantasies and determined that almost none of them are really that unusual.[34] Let's take a close look at the nuts and bolts of this survey. It breaks down the sexual fantasies into very specific details and separates participants by gender. The most interesting findings were that only two of the fantasies were found to be rare and that men and women were found to differ significantly in the amount and content of their fantasies. The two more rare fantasies were having sex with a child younger than twelve (pedophilia), at roughly 1.5 percent (0.8 percent women and 1.8 percent men), and having sex with animals (zoophilia) (3 percent women and 2.2 percent men). Remember, these numbers reflect the people who were willing to disclose these kinds of fantasies—self-reports like these are notorious for under-reporting.

More unusual but by no means rare fantasies included fantasies around urination (water sports) for both women (7 percent) and men (9 percent) and the following fantasies only for women: wearing clothes of the opposite gender (6.9 percent), forcing someone to have sex (10.8 percent), abusing a person who is drunk, asleep, or unconscious (10.8 percent), having sex with a prostitute (12.5 percent), and having sex with a woman who has very small breasts (10.8 percent). *None* of these were found to be unusual at all for men. In general, men had way more fantasies than women and indicated a higher desire to experience them in real life.

Some other examples include these:

- A total of 61.2 percent of men had fantasized about interracial sex; only 27.5 percent of women had such fantasies.
- A total of 57.0 percent of men had fantasized about having sex with someone much younger; only 18.1 percent of women had such fantasies.
- A total of 56.5 percent of women surveyed had fantasized about having sex with more than three people, both men and women; only 15.8 percent of men had such fantasies.
- Finally, 64.6 percent of women had fantasized about "being dominated sexually"; only 53.3 percent of men had such fantasies.

The authors of the study state, "Among women, it was found that sexual fantasies (SF) of being dominated, being spanked or whipped, being tied up, and being forced to have sex were reported by 30%–60%. . . . The fantasy of being dominated was significantly greater for women than for men, on average, whereas the fantasy of dominating was statistically stronger for men than for women, on average."

Of the fifty-five sexual fantasies studied, which included a wide gamut of scenarios, thirty-six were found to be common (more than 50 percent), including all themes of domination and submission, and five were typical (more than 84.1 percent of the sample). Perhaps most interesting of all is that despite men having only a slight edge in frequency of fantasies, they were far more likely to act on them than were the women.

So what do all these numbers mean? First, it appears that a wide range of sexual fantasies, including BDSM fantasies, are fairly common, and I daresay even mainstream. However, only a certain percentage of those who fantasize actually act out on them, and an even smaller percentage identify as "kinky."

My point isn't to overwhelm you with studies and reams of numbers and data but simply to point out an undeniable theme—most people experience a wide variety of harmless but "unusual" fantasies, to the point that almost none of them are atypical, but relatively few (in comparison) act on them. Clearly a gap exists between "fantasizers" and "doers." To some extent, I imagine that this gap has shortened over the years, as more women now identify as kinky, particularly younger women (see above), and more people regardless of gender identify as kinky at younger ages.

We can speculate that media attention and destigmatization have played roles. For example, the *DSM-5*, which came out June 2013, depathologized kink by differentiating between "paraphilias" (the clinical term for fetishistic and SM interests) and "paraphilic disorders."[35] The crucial differences are that paraphilic disorders are nonconsensual in nature and cause distress to the individual that is not societally created. So, for example, an exhibitionist who flashes unsuspecting and nonconsenting women would suffer from a paraphilic disorder and require treatment, while an exhibitionist who exposes himself or herself to people who want to watch would have a paraphilia but not a mental disorder requiring treatment. Some critics have argued that the term "paraphilia" is stigmatizing as well and should be done away with entirely, but the point is that the psychiatric establishment has come together to decide that having a nonnormative (atypical) sexual interest is not pathological in and of itself.

Further, the cultural phenomenon of *Fifty Shades of Grey* has opened up many eyes to the potential for types of sex beyond the vanilla norm (although it did pathologize Christian Grey's sexuality as arising from childhood trauma).

Despite all this, the number of BDSM-identified individuals has risen but still remains a small minority compared to the large numbers of folks who indulge (but only in their minds) in every taboo fantasy under the sun. It is still unclear what separates those who live the lifestyle from those who only dream about it, but we do have some clues that have merged in research on personality traits.

IT'S ALL IN THE CHARACTER

A number of recent studies have sought to compare the folks who identify as engaging in BDSM as a lifestyle with their vanilla counterparts. First, no single study has shown any correlation between BDSM and poor mental health, or pathology. One study back in 1991 claimed to show that paraphilic males were more likely to score high for neuroticism and low for agreeability and conscientiousness, but their sample seemed to include sex offenders (or those with paraphilic disorders) rather than a community BDSM sample.[36]

Another, more up-to-date study, however, showed quite the opposite. Dutch researchers in 2013 administered psychological testing to 902 BDSM participants and 434 control subjects and found that those in the BDSM group were less neurotic, more extraverted, more open to new experiences, and more conscientious than those in the control group.[37] The only negative was that they tended to be less agreeable. Other studies have shown similar results. Overwhelmingly, BDSM participants appear to be less neurotic and more open to new experiences than others.

So what does this all mean? And what do all these characterological categories signify? When research studies examine characterological or personality traits, they typically employ a construct called the five-factor model (FFM). These are the five personality traits that have been shown to be consistent throughout the human life span. These big five are: (O) openness to experience; (C) conscientiousness; (E) extraversion; (A) agreeableness; and (N) neuroticism. These letters spell out OCEAN, a convenient acronym for remembering the big five.

Let's go through each trait to see what they mean. This may not seem relevant for the moment, but have patience. I'll bring this back to sexuality soon enough, and we'll see how these personality traits play a big part.

Let's start with O, openness to experience. This trait is a measure of how much an individual is imaginative, creative, and curious.

C, conscientiousness, is a measure of how much an individual is organized, dependable, self-disciplined, and dutiful.

E, extraversion, is a measure of an individual's level of outgoingness, sociability, and assertiveness.

A, agreeableness, signifies compassion and cooperativeness.

And finally, N, neuroticism, is the tendency to experience negative emotions.

In the interests of brevity, I'm going to use the first letter to designate the personality trait moving forward.

Research shows that these personality traits are stable, appear early in childhood, and are at least significantly influenced by genetics. A study of 123 pairs of identical twins and 127 pairs of fraternal twins found that in descending order, 61 percent of O, 53 percent of E, 44 percent of C, 41 percent of N, and 41 percent of A are heritable.[38] Three other twin studies confirmed these results. A mean of the four studies showed that O comes in at the highest heritability at 57 percent, E next at 54 percent, then C at 49 percent, N at 48 percent, and A at 42 percent.[39] Over and over, it is O (openness to new experience) that research shows to be most determined by heredity, and it is this same personality trait for which BDSM participants scored the highest. If an interest in BDSM is completely environmental, how do we make sense of all this data?

To get a better understanding of the interplay of genetics and environment in the creation of personality, let's move our focus to child psychiatrist Stella Chess, who followed 133 children from infancy through adulthood and studied their patterns of behavior over time.[40] She and her associates found nine dimensions of behavior present from birth, which she defined as distinct temperamental traits:

- Activity level: how active the child is generally

- Distractibility: the degree of concentration the child displays when not particularly interested in an activity
- Intensity: the energy level of a child's response, either positive or negative
- Regularity: the predictability of a child's biological functions such as appetite and sleep
- Sensory threshold: how sensitive this child is to physical stimuli and external senses
- Approach/Withdrawal: the child's typical response to a new situation or strangers. Does the child eagerly approach new situations or people or seem hesitant and withdrawn?
- Adaptability: how easily the child adapts to transitions and changes, such as trying a new activity
- Persistence: the amount of time a child continues in activities in the face of obstacles
- Mood: the child's tendency to react to the world primarily in either a positive or a negative way

Chess took these nine temperaments and further divided them into three types of children: easy or flexible; difficult, active, or feisty; and slow to warm up or cautious. Most kids fall in one of these three buckets, while others may share attributes from all three.

Of the nine temperaments, some of them appear to easily lead into one of the five personality traits. For example, activity level and approach/withdrawal are clearly connected to E, extraversion; regularity with C, conscientiousness; adaptability with O, openness to new experiences; and mood with N, neuroticism. The point here is that our personality traits are stable across the life span and are about 50 percent attributable to heritable temperaments that we display right out of the womb.

It also appears that openness to new experiences and conscientiousness aren't attributes of only BDSM players. A recent unpublished study, for example, has found that both O and C are predictors in an interest in consensual nonmonogamy, such as polyamory (specifically, high O and lower C).[41] Indeed, organizations such as the National Coalition for Sexual Freedom (NCSF) serve both the BDSM and poly communities. Both of these groups clearly have their differences, but what research shows unites them are inborn characterological traits that predispose both groups to wanting new experiences as well as placing great importance on fidelity and consent.

A LOOK AT THE DARK SIDE

So, I hear you asking . . . can all these diverse forms of sexuality really be considered a type of orientation? Orientation is all about an attraction (or not) to a specific gender, right? Well, not really. And to make my case, we are going to take a little journey off the beaten path and look at another, darker, unpleasant and illegal form of sexuality that scientific research appears to conclusively show is an innate, biological orientation. Pedophilia.

Before we get started on this topic, however, I think it is important to make a few disclaimers. First, in no way, shape, or form am I condoning the act of pedophilia. Unlike the other sexual behaviors discussed above, it is nonconsensual (children cannot provide consent), and so it belongs within the jurisdiction of the criminal justice system when a crime is committed. (I would argue that preventative help for pedophiles who are struggling with their urges should be part of our mental health system [it is not], but that is a subject for another time.)

Second, most pedophiles never act on their urges; they simply struggle in silence, often too ashamed to even reach out for help. I think it is essential to differentiate between pedophiles who conscientiously refuse to act on their urges (virtuous pedophiles) and those who do act on them. We call the latter group child molesters. So pedophiles are not necessarily child molestors; far more often, they are not.

Third, I am approaching this topic from a scientific perspective. Really, this entire book is about my work as a clinician in the field of sexuality from a scientifically informed practice. As a result, if we want to truly understand human sexuality, we must approach it from a scientific, not moralistic, perspective. With that all said, let's take a look at the evidence and see how it applies to our discussion in this chapter.

First, let's get a better sense of who they are. There is no totally accurate way to gauge the number of pedophiles. Sociologist Sarah Goode claims that 1–2 percent of men are pedophiles, although "one in five of all adult men are to some degree capable of being sexually aroused by children."[42] About one third prefer boys, a third prefer girls, and another third are attracted to both, so pedophilia appears to operate independently from arousal to any specific gender.[43] Other research supports this. In fact, to date there have been a total of eight studies on this very topic. Five of them employed the PPG and found that from a high of 17 percent to a low of 1 percent of research subjects displayed pedophilic interests.[44] That's quite a range. The most recent study, a questionnaire of 531 undergraduate men, found that 7 percent admitted sexual attraction to "little children"; another 18 percent had sexual fantasies of children of any age, 8 percent masturbated to those fantasies, and 4 percent admitted they would have sex with a child "if no one found out."[45]

Canadian psychologist James Cantor has studied pedophiles for most of his career. His team at the Centre for Addiction and Mental Health in Toronto conducted MRIs on pedophiles who were convicted child molesters and found that they typically have less white matter—the tissue in the brain that carries messages to other parts of the brain.[46] In addition, Cantor has found that pedophiles are overwhelmingly male, tend to be shorter, are three times more likely to be left-handed, and in the aggregate possess IQs about ten or fifteen points lower than nonpedophiles. According to the research, Cantor concludes that "it's become harder and harder to explain pedophilia on just [early childhood events]. It's either purely biological or a mix of biological and experiential. But pure experience can't explain these data." Sound familiar?

But didn't child molesters typically experience their own child abuse growing up? Not so fast. Remember, not all pedophiles are child molesters. Psychologist Michael Seto has found that only about half of convicted molesters are indeed pedophiles.[47] The rest struggle with a wide assortment of mental disturbances ranging from psychopathy to psychosis and merely offend against children as a crime of opportunity, but they are not pedophiles. In other words, they have sexually harmed children, but they do not have a sexual attraction to children. If anything, sexual abuse in the past can make a pedophile more vulnerable to then also sexually abusing a minor, but it does not create pedophilia in and of itself.

In addition, a 2001 study found that 67 percent of offenders reported suffering from sexual abuse as children; however, only 29 percent were willing to claim they were abused when polygraphed.[48] The researchers concluded that offenders were highly likely to be motivated to portray themselves as victims in order to receive more lenient punishment. So what we are looking at is compelling evidence that pedophilia is not simply a deranged outcome of adverse childhood experiences but perhaps an orientation in its own right.

Let's pause here for a moment to put this into context. I understand that we are on rocky ground, since there is no way that lesbian and gay individuals would want their sexuality compared to pedophilia. I get that, and I am not at all implying that these two issues should be equated. Lesbians and gays engage in consensual, loving relationships just like straights, while pedophilia can never be considered consensual. End of story. Homosexuality is much like heterosexuality, not pedophilia. The first two are an orientation to gender, the last one is an orientation to age. But that does not mean that pedophilia is not also an orientation.

So this brings us back to a central question. The top minds in the world that study pedophilia conclude that it is an orientation of age, not of gender. Which means that orientation is much more complex and nuanced than we may have imagined. It doesn't refer only to gender but possibly to a myriad number and variety of sexual attractions. If pedophilia is an orientation that is not based on attraction to gender but on an attraction to some other aspect of the individual, such as age, then what attractions to other characteristics of an individual can be classified as orientations?

It is a provocative question, but remember, I am not asking it as part of some social agenda but simply building off the foundations that science has laid before us. Is it possible that attraction to sexual dominance or submission is another orientation? Can other features of the person be part of the orientation too? I think so far the research seems to indicate that the answers could be yes and yes. But remember, science is always evolving, and all we can do is try and interpret it to the best of our current knowledge base.

FINAL THOUGHTS

So we've gone through a long and winding journey to make sense of the origins of human sexuality. Let's recap a bit and form some conclusions.

starting with the aspect of sexuality that appears to be the most determined by physical (genetic, hormonal, and/or prenatal) origins—orientation. And as we've seen, orientation includes not just heterosexuality and homosexuality but other variations, such as bisexuality, asexuality, and quite possibly a whole bunch of "philias," such as pedophilia. Although epigenetics plays a role (not all identical twins of gays are also gay), it appears that the environmental influence (to whatever extent it is) occurs in the womb.

Next come those aspects of sexuality that are probably also mostly determined by genetics but with some enhancement or trigger due to environmental cues after birth. These include most of the fetishes, which seem to almost exclusively affect men.

Moving further along, we come to certain aspects of human sexuality that for some feel more like an orientation while for others more like a leisure activity or lifestyle. Here we are talking about BDSM, polyamory, swinging, and other forms of consensual nonmonogamy.

Let's start with BDSM first, since it is more likely to be identified as an orientation by its participants. For those who experience it as an orientation, I am inclined to believe that there is indeed something innate going on, which would explain why so many participants state that they became aware of their sexuality at a very early age. The age of first awareness closely mimics the age of awareness for gays and lesbians, supplying more credence to the possibility that BDSM is also an orientation for some. And remember, no evidence exists that this group has experienced more trauma than a non-BDSM cohort, so we are left trying to explain why BDSM cannot be an orientation as well.

For others who are strongly inclined to practice BDSM or other alternative relationship lifestyles, but only see it as one fun aspect of their sexuality rather than the core of their identity, innate factors such as temperament and stable characterological five-factor personality traits such as openness to new experience and conscientiousness play an exceedingly large part in explaining their activities. These core personality traits are disinhibiting factors that allow these folks to act on their fantasies (remember, these are the same fantasies that so many others have as well) and communicate their needs to their partners rather than suppressing them.

3

BE LIKE MIKE

Society's Incessant Demand for Social Conformity

In December 2014, U.K. antiporn advocates won a monumental and far-reaching victory when the U.K. government passed the Audiovisual Media Services Regulations 2014, in which a whole host of sexual acts are now banned from British porn, based on what the British Board of Film Classification (or BBFC) deems as "content that is not acceptable."[1] These acts included the following:

spanking
caning
aggressive whipping
penetration by any object "associated with violence"
physical or verbal abuse (regardless of whether consensual)
urolagnia (known as "water sports")
role-playing as nonadults
physical restraint
humiliation
female ejaculation
strangulation
facesitting
fisting

The final three listed fall under acts the BBFC views as potentially "life endangering." This legislation, which sparked protests in which women sat on the faces of men in the public square, came on the heels of a committed campaign by conservative British prime minister David Cameron to regulate and suppress Internet porn. Although female ejaculation was banned, for the moment, the male "cum shot" has been spared.

Avant-garde Yugoslav film director Dušan Makavejev created films in the 1970s focusing on the intersection between government, society, and sexuality. In his work, he raised a critical eye toward authority and its desire, or more like its incessant drive, to eradicate and suppress all freedom and dissent. For his efforts, he was persecuted and eventually blacklisted. As Makavejev so deftly shows in his films, the first line of suppression for any authoritarian government is one of the key sources of our human creativity, inspiration, and personal sense of freedom—our sexuality. History shows that as soon as an authoritarian government rises to power, one of the first things to go is human sexual rights.

Take a look around at the world, and you can see for yourself the crackdown on human sexuality imposed by authoritarian and dictatorial regimes—Egypt's gay community targeted by governmental crackdown,[2] Russia's institutional violence and discrimination toward gays,[3] Uganda's antihomosexuality legislation,[4] female circumcision (genital mutilation) in Iraq ordered by Islamic State in Iraq and Syria (ISIS).[5] Sadly, I could go on and on. What's the common factor? None of these are democratic governments. And? They all harshly cut down sexual freedoms.

We might think that we are much more free in the Western world. And compared to the above examples, we are, of course. But the 2014 British legislation brings to the forefront the sobering reality that we are not truly as free—especially sexually—as we think we are. As I'll detail in subsequent chapters, the United States, of all culprits, has a particularly bleak and dark history of sexual oppression, even to this day.

In fact, it's almost as if cultures absolutely need to suppress sexuality in order to function. I would argue that that is not a fatalistic determination. In other words, it doesn't have to be that way. But the course of history has shown that these two things—culture and sexual repression—go hand in hand. It's almost as if one has been mostly reliant on the other. But to understand why, we have to take a closer look at how culture is formed in the very first place.

IN WITH THE OUT CROWD: THE PSYCHOLOGY OF GROUP THINK

When we examine the roots of culture and of societies at large, we must invariably come to the conclusion that society consists of a collection of people. In other words, a society is one large group. So an understanding of societal mechanics is not possible without understanding also how groups operate.

In his book *The Science of Good and Evil*, science writer Michael Shermer points out that groups form by a twofold process—inclusion and exclusion.[6] Said differently, groups define themselves equally by what they are *and* what they are not. Shermer argues that morality forms within the context of this kind of group formation. In other words, we must not kill our neighbors, friends, family, or other members of our in-group because that will threaten the survival of the group. Killing those outsiders, though, well, that's OK. In this way, Shermer states, we develop what he calls a *provisional morality*. Morality is the order of the day, provided it is in relation to our behavior toward our in-group.

Group psychoanalyst Wilfred Bion categorized group formations into three different types, what he called "basic assumption groups."[7] According to Bion, these three groups are the *dependency*, the *fight-flight*, and the *pairing* groups. I'll go through each one in turn.

In dependency, the main aim of the group is to attain security and find protection for its members. This is usually done through identifying one true leader who may be viewed as omnipotent or omniscient. Hence, in order to survive, groups naturally seek out an authority figure—a chief, a sultan, a king, a dictator—and this leader typically derives his authority from an even higher source of power, such as a god or powerful spirit. The less a group is cohesive and the more its survival is at risk, the more doggedly it searches for a secure authority.

Examples of this group dependency dynamic can be easily found throughout history. As the rise of the Third Reich in Nazi Germany so unfortunately aptly demonstrates, when an entire country and its economy is destabilized, as Germany was after the First World War, a group consisting of millions of people rallies together to follow one powerful leader who holds all the answers, who holds the Truth. And one result for Germany was that millions of group outsiders—Jews, gypsies, invalids, and homosexuals—were sent to their deaths. This example plays out throughout history to various extents—anytime a country is destabilized and the masses are afraid, reactionary elements rise to power, promising absolute truths and moral safety. The rise of conservative governments in Europe demonstrates this trend most recently. And predictably, civil liberties fall, with sexual liberties the first to go.

The next assumption group that Bion identified is the fight-flight group, which acts to preserve itself by either running away from or fighting someone or something. In other words, this is a very vigilant and fearful group. This group needs to find enemies in order to justify its own existence. Indeed, the group would not exist on its own if it were not coalesced around engaging with some external enemy. As can be seen in the example above of the Third Reich, these external enemies can be multiple and varied, but one thing they share in common is that they are in some ways different from the in-group. These differences can be physical, ethnic, religious, or, often, sexual.

The final assumption group is the pairing group, whose main purpose is the survival of the group through sexual reproduction. I think it is this third assumption that may provide more clarity on why it is that sexuality is the first in line to be repressed. If a group is attempting to survive through pairing, then any form of sexuality that is not involved in reproduction (i.e., heteronormative) is dangerous to the integrity of the group's survival.

The main point in all of this is that groups function on all three assumptions, not one alone. It is part and parcel of the group process to seek survival through (a) finding an authority figure to satisfy its need for safety, security, and dependency, (b) finding an external enemy to pit itself against through either war or avoidance, and (c) prioritizing the continuation of the group through sexual reproduction. Taking all three assumptions into account, we can see developing groups (I will differentiate developing from developed groups shortly) as those which find stability in authoritarianism, conformity, and the confinement of sexuality to procreation.

I think this model holds some answers for why government authoritarianism, social conformity, and sexual repression inevitably always go hand in hand. They are all global aspects of the same core issue—a group attempting to ensure its survival.

In this way, we can view society as one big multifaceted and complex group process at work. And culture is the outward expression of that group process.

Social psychologists Jeff Greenberg, Sheldon Solomon, and Tom Pyszczynski developed a model for cultural expression that they called terror management theory (TMT).[8] The basic premise of TMT is that culture and everything it encompasses, such as values, beliefs, morals, institutions, art, and so on, exist merely to manage existential terror—in this case, the existential terror of group annihilation.

Everything from national identity (fight-flight assumption) to ideas around death and dying, to attitudes toward sex (pairing assumption), to religious values (dependency assumption), to privileging humans over animals is all part of our incessant need to deal with our existential terror of annihilation on a group level.

In some ways TMT may also explain the great ambivalence about sexuality that we experience as a society. On one hand, sex is extremely pleasurable. It can be experienced as creative, rejuvenating, connective, expansive. In other words, all things opposite of death and dying. On the other hand, all these positive aspects are experienced on a personal, individual, and subjective level and possibly on a small-group level but not on a societal or large-group level. (More on this in a moment.) Paradoxically, leisurely sex that is divorced from procreation threatens the death of the large group. This is the ultimate conflict that I believe this book is about.

ONCE THERE WAS A KING: HOW SOCIAL CONTROL HAS BECOME DECENTRALIZED

Somewhere around ten thousand years ago, human civilization moved from roaming packs of hunter-gatherers to agrarian societies, where landownership became a central focus of power and privilege. I'll spare the details, as they can be readily found in other sources, but the main point here is that agrarian societies were able to grow in size far beyond the limited scope of small hunting tribes.

Around this time, the group dynamics outlined above really became codified as social groups became larger and more complex. Anthropologist Robin Dunbar, while studying the relationship between primate brain size and average group size, concluded that humans are able to keep track of only 150 stable relationships at a time—what is now called Dunbar's number.[9] As a result, any social group larger than 150 requires stricter laws and rules in order to maintain social cohesion. In other words, the larger the group, the stricter it must become to stay alive.

Psychologist Christopher Ryan and his coauthor, psychiatrist Cacilda Jethá, in their book *Sex at Dawn*, conclude that early hunter-gatherer societies were much more sexually liberal and promiscuous than we have previously thought, especially imagining it from our modern, heavily civilized lens.[10] Taking a multidisciplinary approach, including evolutionary science, anthropology, biology, and primate studies, they conclude that it was in the best interests of an ancient tribal woman to have intercourse with as many of the tribe's men as possible in order to obscure paternity, thereby forcing all the men in the tribe to protect her and her children. In addition, the shape of the human penis appears to be conducive to "sperm competition"—pulling out competing male's sperm from the vagina through the suctioning vacuum created by the penis head. In short, humans (without the interference of society) were made for fucking, and lots of it, and all the time.

Obviously the times (and the standards) have changed, but the main point here is that larger groups mandated stricter group norms and more powerful dynamic forces involving the three group assumptions of dependency, fight-flight, and pairing. I believe it is not coincidental that the modern agrarian era also coincided with the rise of organized religious activity.

As I mentioned in chapter 1, the decline of the influence of religion in the 1800s (which started at the dawn of the Renaissance and picked up steam during the Industrial Revolution) required new ways of meeting societies' dependency needs. Sociologist Michel Foucault argued that in many ways scientific categorization and labeling replaced some of the ways of managing social order that was once maintained by religious decree.[11] (I would argue that this new rise of scientific dominance was ineffectual in meeting group dependency needs, as witnessed in the rise of numerous dictatorships in the 1900s, but that is a subject for another time and another book.)

At any rate, at the dawn of the twentieth century, most Western countries were in the midst of significant social and economic changes brought about by technological advances. Capitalism became the dominant economic force, replacing feudalism, as private ownership replaced serfdom and feudal lords. I think in many ways it is capitalism that holds the key to understanding where we are right now as a society when it comes to sex and where we may possibly end up. And it is with the intersection of capitalism and sexuality that we continue our understanding of why our culture is so sex negative and what it is that we can do about it.

The first thing that we must understand about capitalism, and the main area in which it differs from other economic structures, is that power is decentralized. Yes, power is still a big, big force in capitalism, even though business is conducted by private entities and controlled by free-market forces, largely outside of the limits of government control.

Granted, outside of tweaks to make the free market work better, such as consumer protections, antitrust laws, and the like, governments such as those of the United States try to let the free market operate independently to match supply with demand. But rather than central control by a powerful, sadistic dictator, individuals in this kind of setup are now controlled by their employers, who can be equally as powerful and sadistic as any other dictator, although on a much smaller level. And sure, you can go ahead and start your own small business, but now you are controlled by the same free market that can empty your bank account and take away your home equally as cruelly as the cruelest of power-hungry despots in the world.

Now I'm not saying that living in the United States is as oppressive as living in Uganda or Saudia Arabia. Obviously, that's not the case, and thank goodness for that. But what I am saying is that in many ways, freedom is as much a myth in the United States as it is in more oppressive countries. We may have more economic freedoms, and we won't be thrown in jail for our religious beliefs or social values, but unless we are born with a trust fund, we are most definitely not free. So despite the many benefits we experience living in the Western world, our society operates with the same basic assumptions as any other group that needs to survive—dependency, fight-flight, and pairing. (The recent upswings in the past twenty years of religious fundamentalism, conservative politics, and warmongering highlight these dynamics in action.)

Most importantly, what our economy (and hence our society) needs to function is a group of willing consumers who will keep the free market functioning. This is where power is diffused and experienced most subtly. Unlike a powerful centralized government that forces people to take on certain work or do certain things, market capitalism does not present itself as overtly coercive. Instead, it uses subtle manipulation and other psychological maneuvers to get people to buy into the system willingly, what linguist and social scientist Noam Chomsky calls "manufactured consent."[12]

To understand what this "psychological manipulation" may look like, first we have to consider what we as a society need in order to create a better free-market system, which is better consumers. And better consumers are those who spend more. And those who spend more are those who are more likely to feel like they don't have enough, like something is missing or lacking. In other words, people who are insecure. Insecure individuals are better consumers. So putting the logical equation together, our society needs to create and continue to foster an entire cadre of insecure citizens who are willing to spend their way out of their insecurities in order to maintain the economic system, and, therefore, social stability.

Now I'm not stating that we need to overturn capitalism or that I have devised a better system. Really, even with capitalism's warts and all, no better system has yet been created. As Winston Churchill once said about democracy, "Democracy is the worst form of government, except for all those other forms that have been tried from time to time," and I would extend the same sentiments to capitalism.[13] It is flawed, except in comparison to others. My intention here is not to advocate for a different economic structure but merely to point out how our current economic and social structures affect our experience of our sexuality. More precisely, the instilled insecurity necessary to socialize us into being better consumers also removes us from the experience of truly accepting and embracing our sexuality.

These two facets—mass consumerism and sexual insecurity and alienation—are completely connected and inseparable. How is this possible? Sexual messages are everywhere. Advertisements. Commercials. Porn. Everywhere. Aren't these things making us more sexual? Read on.

THE MEDIUM IS THE MASSAGE: HOW CULTURE AND SOCIAL INSTITUTIONS ENGAGE IN MYTH-MAKING

As I mentioned, free-market capitalism seeks to turn us all into better consumers to feed the beast. And boy does capitalism use a lot of sexual imagery to make its point. But here's the thing—it's not truly about the sex, it's about the *commodification* of sex. What am I talking about?

Cultural theorists use a term, "reification," to designate the process of transforming various human interactions into objects that take on a life of their own, independent from the original source. Philosopher Georg Lukács argued that capitalism attempts to turn all of humanity into commodities that can be bought and sold. [14] Let's see how this plays out in human sexuality.

Turn on the TV any weekend afternoon—there's usually a bunch of sports on—and lots of commercials during the breaks and halftime activities. Let's go through some typical commercials we might see during this time. An average Joe walks on the beach with his buddies, he pops open an ice-cold can of his favorite alcoholic beverage . . . and all of a sudden, a bevy of hot, well-endowed beauties in skimpy bikinis bounce out all around, looking for nothing but some good times and sexy fun. Damn, this guy is in heaven . . . he looks down at his beverage and thinks, "Thanks, Beer Light!" Clearly, drinking this can of beer has opened up new doors of unlimited pleasure and sexual fulfillment.

Now let's deconstruct this ad for a moment. Yes, this ad appears to be about sex, but is it really? No, the whole purpose of it is to sell beer. And to sell this beer, the marketers are making a few assumptions. First, the person watching this is a heterosexual male. Second, this guy is at least somewhat dysphoric (mildly depressed) and is displeased with his sex life. Sure, I highly doubt that the marketers expect the people watching the ad to take it literally, that if they drink the beer, their sex life will skyrocket through the roof. But we're not talking about literalism here; it's all allegory and coded language. In other words, even though it is not meant to be taken literally, it will be noticed on a deep psychological level by those people for whom the ad resonates. And there's only one group for whom this ad could possibly resonate. You know, depressed, sexually unfulfilled people. The same ones who make for good consumers.

Still doubtful about the insecurity that the media cultivates? Let's take a step back and look at other forms of programming, not just commercials. On any random week, go ahead and take a look at the selection of TV shows out there that have something to do with sexuality and see what you find. Luckily, I've already done this for you.

On this particular random week, I have found the following shows listed on the TLC channel: *Strange Sex* and *Sex Sent Me to the ER*. One of the hallmarks of *Strange Sex* is a focus on "strange fetishes." These include some of the most unusual varieties that more often than not portray the fetishists in a negative light. These include a "looner," or balloon fetishist, [15] a feeder who enjoys feeding his wife until she is so heavy that she is bedridden, [16] and another guy who loves to sniff dirty tennis shoes. [17] In yet another show, *My Strange Addiction*, we learn of a cast fetishist who enjoys wearing casts on his limbs even though they are not injured. [18]

These shows follow a similar format. The fetishist is shown as a social outcast. He or she appears to be completely defined by the fetish. His or her friends or acquaintances are interviewed and say that they find the fetish to be "weird" or "strange" but they've learned to somehow accept it. Sometimes the individual is set up on a date or some other social situation, only to be roundly rejected or dismissed by the other person. For example, the cast fetishist meets a woman at a bar, but she then tells the camera that she doesn't want to have anything to do with him. Sometimes, at the end of the episode, we see the individual going out to a social event with other like-minded individuals, to a place often represented as a social hangout for misfits. The locations are often poorly attended nightclub events with the underlying theme that at last this person has found a place where he or she (usually he) can finally be accepted.

I think this show represents the strange ambivalence that the media conveys about sexuality. On one hand, *Strange Sex* shows individuals who are trying to be understood and validated and seek out an accepting community. That's positive, and in other areas of the book I argue strongly in favor of community support as a means of self-acceptance and identity formation. On the other hand, the program shows people with fetishes as strangers and loners, individuals who are completely defined by their fetish and have difficulty getting along not only with the random blind dates but also with forming an acceptable peer group of friends. It's not only that the fetish is "weird" but that the individual himself is also inherently "weird."

The title *Strange Sex* sums up this contradiction. On one hand, I wouldn't be surprised if the producers saw themselves as progressives who were trying to shine a light on the plight of their unfortunate subjects, but on the other hand, the word "strange" implies that these people are not like us, they are somehow different, and so we must look at them like some oddities, as if they were from the circus freak show.

Sex Sent Me to the ER takes it to another level. Here, the act of sex isn't merely strange, it's downright dangerous. Or both strange *and* dangerous. In one episode, for example, a duo of ventriloquists end up in the ER when the male develops a painful condition on his penis called phimosis.[19] These folks keep gabbing it up and arguing with each other via their puppets as the exasperated physician attempts to manually massage the man's penis to loosen his foreskin. In another episode, a couple comes in with another penis injury, this time cause by the guy wearing a chastity belt.[20] The doctor tries to examine him, all while a bunch of female roller derby skaters look on and make jokes.

In yet another episode, a young man ends up in the ER after "breaking" his penis during some vigorous sex.[21] His church group appears in order to pray for his penile recovery. I'm not sure whether any of these are true events, although the show does claim they are real, but the implied message is that rough sex or kinky sex (with a chastity belt) is bound to get you in trouble. Let's break this down a bit further. First, it's worthy of derision and ridicule. Folks who wear chastity belts as part of sex play are in the same boat as those who carry on conversations through puppets. And it's completely a laughing matter anyway, as the exasperated grins and one-liners of the doctors are matched only by the silly editing and musical choices of the producers. And if you get too into it, too rough, well, you may just end up in the ER too, and even though the church group provided humorous relief, the implication is that this rough sex fucker is one big fucking sinner.

Another show, *My Strange Criminal Addiction*, profiles a sex offender with a foot fetish, focusing on the "strangeness" of his interest in feet rather than on the only salient point worth mentioning—that he was engaging in nonconsensual behavior.[22] The way the material is presented, it almost feels as if the foot fetish itself is as disturbing as his behavior. The first episode focuses on a frotteur (someone who finds sexual arousal by rubbing up against someone else's buttocks) who has been arrested fifty-three times for grinding against women in New York City subways.[23] Sure, he's out of control, but his deviance is tied into his compulsivity and nonconsensual behavior rather than his arousal at butt grinding. Interestingly, he has an identical twin who is also a frotteur; perhaps something innate is going on? To his credit, resident expert Dr. Mike Dow does remark, "It's not surprising that identical twins are engaging in such behavior . . . they share so much, they even share a womb, which exposes them to levels of hormones which have been shown to correlate with a disposition to gravitate towards fetishes." I'm not exactly sure of the source of Dr. Dow's citation, but doesn't this sound familiar?

I have still yet to see the show where people are experiencing their sexual interests as simply one (important) part of a larger whole, where other people may know of their sexual proclivities but no one gives a crap enough to make it the point of the entire discussion, where the person can socialize normally and be an included member of mainstream society without being alienated because of his or her sexual interests, and where kinky and/or rough sex lands you in relationship bliss rather than the ER. When we get to the point that these kinds of TV programming are also being offered, then I would say that our media play a lesser role in exploiting our native insecurities about sexuality.

But this also points the way forward. It is no coincidence that all the major social movements have occurred within the framework of free-market capitalism—women's suffrage, the civil rights movement, and LGBT rights. And I believe they could never have occurred if not for capitalism. Why so? The free market is amoral; it doesn't care whom it sells to. Sure, insecurity breeds more sales, but so do large blocks of affinity groups. Once groups of people with common identities, issues, or agendas become large enough to affect the economy, all of a sudden they start to matter. And all of a sudden they also garner political power. But economic power always comes first.

If women, for example, have enough economic clout that companies can advertise specifically to them, they also develop enough political clout to advocate for themselves. It is not coincidental, I believe, that according to historian Russell B. Adams Jr., Gillette's Milady Decolette was "the first razor designed and marketed specifically for women" and was billed in the extensive national advertising campaign as the "safest and most sanitary method of acquiring a smooth underarm" in 1915, followed by national women's suffrage in 1920.[24]

It is also not coincidental that, mainly due to urban migration, the annual income of African Americans increased threefold, from three billion dollars to ten billion dollars, attracting new mass-marketing efforts from the tobacco industry and many others into the "emerging Negro market," foreshadowing the civil rights movement of the 1950s and 1960s.[25] An article from 1944, for example, was titled "The American Negro—An 'Export' Market at Home."[26]

LGBT rights fall within the same framework. As homophobia recedes and same-sex marriages become the law of the land, marketers have been trying to figure out how to sell to the "lucrative gay market" for the past two decades, if not more.[27]

Within capitalism, economic power becomes political power. And it all happens within group formats. In other words, only groups can change other groups. Once small affinity groups bubble up and become large enough to affect the real source of power, which is the free market, they then win over other social and political concessions. Rather than isolated, atomized individuals, sitting on their living room couches waiting for the next bunch of sexualized sales pitches, much more sexual authenticity occurs off the couch, when people band together and create their own self-identities and thereby determine their own needs rather than succumb to the manufactured needs offered to them by the marketers.

I also do not believe it is coincidental that the past twenty years or so have brought us perhaps the greatest wave of new self-identified groups in all of history. We now have so many kinds of possible sexual identities, lifestyle choices, sporting activities to participate in, and forms of appearance to choose from. There's a little thing that happened in the early 1990s called the Internet, and it has revolutionized not only the way our economy functions but also the ways in which we communicate and identify ourselves, and hence the way we create groups and communities.

Some people may cynically refer to this as "identity politics," but in my mind, this is the only tried and true, historically proven way to effect change. When people create groups out of common identities, they create new economic markets, and through the process described above, that economic influence also brings with it social and political influence. Yes, the free market is all about social control when it comes to the alienated, atomized, and isolated individual. In many ways, it prefers things that way as it breeds better consumers. But there's a loophole in all of this. The free market doesn't account for blocks of cohesive, like-minded individuals banded into groups. In this situation, instead of creating markets, it serves these markets. And because it is interested only in profits, it serves all of them. And with the disruption of new technology, such as the Internet and social media, it is easier than ever to influence and affect the system.

In conclusion, social restriction is created, indeed required, by group dynamics. But, paradoxically, it is only through group dynamics (of smaller, more cohesive affinity groups) that these restrictions can be eased and social and political freedoms gained through increased economic influence. Indeed, if true personal authenticity is suppressed by group dynamics, it can also only be recovered, on larger scales, also through groups. And new technology has made this easier and more possible than ever. In this way, technology is also a powerful tool in helping us foster sexual authenticity. I'll write more about how we can connect to appropriate groups in the final chapter, but for now let's briefly survey all the ways in which sexuality has been repressed in our society to date.

4

LAW AND ORDER

I Fought the Law and the Law Won

On a bright sunny morning, June 26, 2015, the citizens of the United States awoke to a new state of the union. That morning, the Supreme Court ruled that sex-same marriages were indeed constitutional by a narrow vote of 5–4. But as much of the nation celebrated legal progress, this success also underscored the legal shackles that have historically, and still do, restrain and repress sexual expression.

In the previous chapter, we covered the reasons why societies, and particularly large and complex societies, have sought to control sexuality as a means of group survival. We surveyed the myriad ways in which group processes are at play in societal development. In this chapter, we'll take a brief survey of the "how," not "why." As we'll see, the "how" of repression has transformed through the centuries, moving from the realm of priests and religion to the legal and criminal justice system and finally to the realm of medicine, and, yes, psychotherapy. But let's not get ahead of ourselves and, for the moment, take a more careful look at the intersection of sexuality and the law.

THE TROUBLE WITH BUGGERY

Perhaps no other sexual issue has been the focus of law enforcement as much as homosexuality. Specifically anal intercourse, or sodomy—buggery, if you will—but it was usually never enforced with heterosexuals. The oldest such law comes from the Assyrian Law Codes of 1075 BC, which instructed that any man engaging in homosexuality in the military be turned into a eunuch.[1]

A common misconception exists that the ancients enjoyed a much more casual and liberal view of sexuality. Yes, the ancient Greeks did encourage sexual relations between older male adults and their younger mentees, but historical evidence appears to indicate that adult homosexual relations were frowned upon (particularly on the passive recipient) and female homosexuality had no place, as women's role was to serve their husbands within the patriarchy.[2] Same thing in ancient Rome.[3]

Homosexuality didn't even exist as a word until 1869, when it was coined by Hungarian journalist Karl-Maria Kertbeny.[4] He was also one of the first to view it as an inborn sexual orientation rather than something done due to vice or "wickedness." Prior to that, there was no reason to use a term for orientation because it was unthinkable that someone could naturally have desire or love for the same sex; the only thing that mattered was the behavior, and it could be explained away only through moral failings.

Even though homosexuality was frowned upon, it was not really criminalized in legal doctrine in the Western world until King Henry VIII of England introduced the Buggery Act of 1533, making sodomy punishable by death.[5] This law, which lasted on the books until 1861, could also be used to condemn any other sex act deemed to be worth punishing, as sodomy was defined only as an "abominable and detestable crime against nature." In Germany, sodomy didn't even refer to anal sex—it was the term for bestiality.

That's not to say that the state of affairs was good for homosexuals in medieval times. In thirteenth-century France, for example, first-time offenders would lose a testicle; the second time around would lead to dismemberment; and three strikes, you were out—you would be burned alive.[6] This punishment wasn't only for men; women engaging in same-sex behaviors would also be mutilated and killed. No matter the nature of the complaints, things are definitely not so bad as way back when.

The Enlightenment brought a bit of a respite, a turning of the tide. In 1786, Pietro Leopold of Tuscany became the first ruler anywhere in the world to abolish the death penalty for sodomy,[7] and this was then followed in France by the Penal Code of 1791, which took the height of the French Revolution as an opportunity to decriminalize homosexuality.[8] Napoleon then extended this code in 1810, effectively decriminalizing homosexuality in most of continental Europe (which had already been conquered by France).

Things didn't fare so well in the states, however, as sodomy was punishable by death in most states.[9] Thomas Jefferson tried to make things a bit better by changing the punishment to castration, but this law didn't fly with the Virginia legislature.[10] If castration was viewed as a step forward, I think we can safely conclude that America wasn't a good place to be practicing buggery.

Prior to 1962, sodomy was a felony in every single U.S. state, usually punishable by a lengthy prison stay.[11] In fact, by 1970, only Illinois had decriminalized what they called "consensual sodomy" (although "soliciting" for sodomy would still get you a rap sheet).[12] Really, it was only in 2003 (yes, 2003!), that sodomy laws were struck down all over the United States with the Supreme Court decision in *Lawrence v. Texas*, in which the court ruled that sexual behavior done in private was protected by the U.S. Constitution.[13] At the time of the ruling, someone convicted of sodomy in Idaho would face a life sentence,[14] while a person convicted in Michigan would get a maximum of fifteen years for the first time and a life sentence for repeat "offenses."[15] In fact, prior to the Supreme Court ruling, Michigan was one of thirteen states that had still not legalized same-sex marriage.[16] Talk about a "blue state."

THE RIGHT TO BE SILENT: HOW SOCIETY TAKES AWAY THE RIGHTS OF SEXUAL MINORITIES

So now we come to the conclusion that we are living in a country where (at least for the past decade or so) it is perfectly legal to practice whatever (consensual) sex act we please without fear or threat of negative consequences or persecution, right? Not so fast. According to a 2008 survey by the National Coalition for Sexual Freedom (NCSF), which interviewed 3,058 BDSM participants, 1,146 (37.5 percent) stated that they had either been discriminated against or experienced some form of harassment or violence due to their sexuality.[17] Some 22.5 percent of those discriminated against stated they suffered some form of "persecution," such as denial of participation in some club or activity, while 20 percent stated they had lost a job due to their sexual preferences. Surprisingly, 30 percent of the respondents who were discriminated against stated they were discriminated against by a professional or personal service provider, such as a medical doctor or mental health practitioner (see chapter 5).

A typical example of a job denial that made national headlines is the case of Vancouver resident Peter Hayes, who was denied his application for a chauffeur's permit due to allegations that he was involved in a "cult-like relationship . . . based on a master/slave dynamic."[18] Apparently, an angry ex-girlfriend exposed him as both a BDSM enthusiast and a pagan (which apparently is where she got the "cult-like" reference from).

Hayes's lawyer countered, "His identity as a BDSM lifestyler means that he not only participates in BDSM activities, but that BDSM practice is a core part of his identity and being. His intimate relationships must include this and his most fulfilling relationships are with those who not only participate in BDSM but are also lifestylers themselves." The case was dismissed in 2010. Even though the court declined to rule on whether BDSM should be protected from discrimination under British Columbia's Human Rights Code, it did state that it "assumed, without deciding, that BDSM could constitute a 'sexual orientation' protected by the Code."

In England, Operation Spanner was a police sting operation carried out in Manchester in 1987 aimed at the gay S&M scene. This led to a conviction of a group of gay men for assault that "occasioned actual bodily harm"—in other words, S&M. The case went up to the House of Lords and in 1990, the *R v Brown* ruling determined that consent was not a valid defense for "wounding and actual bodily harm."[19] What makes this case particularly puzzling is that in other similar cases, such as *R vs Wilson* (which involved human branding) and *R vs Slingsby* (in which a man inadvertently killed his sexual partner by inserting his entire fist into her vagina and anus while wearing a signet ring), consent was viewed as a valid defense.[20] To say that consent is used inconsistently in the English high court would be a huge understatement.

One other major area in which societal sexual stigmatization and persecution occurs is in child custody cases. In an article in the *Journal of Homosexuality*, sexologists Marty Klein and Charles Moser describe a child custody case in which the mother's visitation rights were severely limited because she was involved in an S&M relationship, even though there was no child abuse and nothing sexual was ever done in the child's presence or in its awareness.[21]

The NCSF's Incident Reporting and Response (IRR) program was created in 1997 to assist those who are struggling with discrimination based on their sexual practices. They have been tracking the success rates of those who have contacted them for support with highly interesting results. First, every year since 2009, the numbers of those who request help with child custody/divorce issues has been decreasing, and in addition, the percentage of those whose custody was not removed because of their sexuality has also dramatically increased.[22]

Specifically, in 2010, only 12 percent of those who sought help from the IRR were able to prevent their custody from being removed; the number rose to 23 percent in 2011, 53 percent in 2012, and 89 percent in 2014 (the 2013 numbers were unavailable). In other words, between 2010 and 2014, the chances of retaining custody for those in alternative sexual lifestyles went from slim to likely. NCSF director Susan Wright credits this to more general public awareness as well as changes in the DSM that depathologized kink.

I've compiled some sample comments from the 2008 NCSF "Survey of Discrimination and Violence against Sexual Minorities" as it relates to family court proceedings as examples of the type of discrimination respondents faced:

> "A judge granted my former husband supervised visitation on the basis of two pictures of me bound with rope that happened to be over 10 years old . . . my former husband didn't have to prove anything."

> "Loss of custody and supervised visitation ordered because I was deemed to be in a 'Perverse' sexual lifestyle 'outside of the confines of the social moral norm' . . . no kidding . . . that's what the judge said."

> "Social Services removed my children because they said I was a sexual deviant even though my interest and participation in the bdsm lifestyle was not why they were removed. It was because of a spiteful ex boyfriend."

"The state's child services is 'concerned' that my children might grow up to be into the same things I am into. They want to try to find a way to prevent this. So they have family therapists 10 hours a week in my home, an individual counselor for me, one for one of my children and one for family therapy. They also claim they are concerned as to the degree of exposure my children see of my lifestyle (which is NONE, I do not do any kink in front of my children), so then they are concerned if they are being adequately cared for if I go outto scene. . . . Then they are concerned well, is the person u meet following you home, which could endanger your kids. Seems just anything they can think of."[23]

Fortunately, as mentioned, due to advocacy efforts, folks are much less discriminated against in family courts in recent years.

WORKIN' 9 TO 5: CRACKING DOWN ON WORKING GIRLS

Perhaps nowhere else is the government regulation of sex more apparent than in the area of sex work. By sex work I mean literally any kind of work that involves the exchange of money for displays of sexuality. Much of sex work doesn't involve sexual intercourse, as strippers, cam girls, and dominatrixes can all be considered sex workers. However, much of public policy and legislation surrounds prostitution, so I will focus much of the research data on this particular issue.

Before we get started, I think it's important to make a few disclaimers about why I'm addressing the issue of prostitution in this book. First and foremost, I am not advocating for prostitution or trying to assert that it's a wonderful profession that should be pursued by all the young women in our society. I'm also not saying that it has no negative consequences, that all women in the trade have equal experiences, or that seeking out prostitutes for sex cannot be disruptive to relationships, marriages, and careers.

What I am saying, though, is that a government crackdown on sexual behavior prevents the possibility for an honest and open discussion on what sex work means for its participants and how society can provide appropriate resources for those who do choose sex work. The research we have shows that a wide variety of different types of sex workers enter the field, that they do so for a number of reasons, that almost none of them are coerced and many enjoy their work, and that they would be much safer if prostitution were legalized or at the very least decriminalized.

When it comes to sex work, what we are really talking about is women's sexuality. And specifically, I'm talking about the double standard in our society between men and women when it comes to sex. Women who have lots of sex and like it are called sluts and are subject to slut shaming. (Men get shamed too, but it's usually in the context of a committed relationship—see the discussion of sex addiction in chapter 5). I see this issue of slut shaming come up a lot in my work with sex workers. Most sex workers are women, and because it is assumed there is no way in hell that women like sex, it must be also assumed that these women are somehow oppressed or coerced to do what they do.

Of course, there are unfortunate people who fall into some kind of human trafficking scheme, and I don't want to minimize that, although I must say I'm not sure how accurate the alarmist headlines are. It's important to note I'm not talking about street prostitution here, in which the women are often engaged in survival behavior and are often afflicted with various addictions, but rather indoor sex work, which accounts for a majority of it and is legal in most developed countries, including Canada.[24] (More on that in a moment.) For example, in a 2005 State Department report, an antiprostitution advocate made claims about women and girls being trafficked to work in strip clubs but could find only six such cases in seven years of research.[25]

In my experience, sex workers do sex work because they love sex. And because it is flexible and pays well for the amount of time they do it. Yes, they enjoy what they do. And they are more concerned about law enforcement than about sexual exploitation. I think it's a mistake that people make to assume that strong, confident feminist women view sex in some sort of negative light. They often confuse feminism with the Andrea Dworkins and Catharine MacKinnons of the world. However, a large contingent of pro-sex feminists advocate female empowerment through sexuality, and the clash between these two rival factions is now known as the "feminist sex wars."[26]

Sex-positive feminism is a big movement with numerous conferences, both nationally and internationally, in which attendees discuss such key issues as the decriminalization of prostitution and feminist pornography. Yes, feminist pornography. There is so much stigma around sex work that in order as a society to truly understand it, we need to put aside our cultural biases and take a look at what the research evidence truly shows. And when it comes down to it, those who think that all or even most women have a problem with pornography or prostitution in which all parties participate consensually and through self-agency, well, they live in a sheltered cave.

Speaking of pornography, a recent study in the prestigious Journal of Sex Research found that many women in the pornography industry actually have higher self-esteem, a better quality of life, and are more spiritual than their nonporn cohorts.[27] The researchers concluded that the "damaged goods" theory about sex workers was unfounded.

Recently, the Australian government ran a research project, interviewing about two hundred indoor prostitutes. This is what they found, according to Ronald Weitzer, a George Washington University professor:

> A study by the Australian government reported that half of the 82 call girls and 101 brothel workers interviewed felt their work "was a major source of satisfaction" in their lives; two-thirds of the brothel workers and seven out of ten call girls said they would "definitely choose this work" if they had to do it over again; and 86 percent in the brothels and 79 percent of call girls said that "my daily life is always varied and interesting."[28]

In addition, sociologist Tanice Foltz found that the escorts she interviewed not only enjoyed their work but also saw themselves as superior in some ways to other women.[29] According to Foltz, "They consider women who are not 'in the life' to be throwing away woman's major source of power and control, while they as prostitutes are using it to their own advantage as well as for the benefit of society." Psychologist Sarah Romans conducted a study comparing indoor sex workers and a community sample of similar women who were not sex workers. She found absolutely no differences between them in physical or mental health, self-esteem, or the quality of their social networks, which backs up the other study cited above that found that porn actresses are not "damaged goods."[30]

The point is that anyone who assumes that any woman engaging in sex work is somehow damaged is practicing social injustice. Taking away a woman's kids because she does sex work is social injustice. For that matter, I'll go the next step and say that in my opinion, based on longitudinal outcomes, the criminalization of most sex work is in itself a social injustice because it exposes these women to unnecessary dangers.

First of all, most prostitution happens indoors. It's hard to get exact numbers, but the estimate from a variety of surveys is that only about 20 percent of prostitutes work on the street.[31] Those who work indoors tend to feel safer, report less victimization, and enter the field for a number of reasons that have nothing to do with coercion or oppression. A study by Stephanie Church found that while 27 percent of street prostitutes had been assaulted, 37 percent robbed, and 22 percent raped, only 1 percent of call girls had been assaulted, 10 percent robbed, and 2 percent raped.[32] Clearly, indoor work is much safer and as a result attracts a different kind of worker. Studies show that, compared with street prostitutes, indoor workers have lower rates of childhood abuse, enter prostitution at later ages, and are more educated.[33]

In those countries where prostitution is legalized, such as the Netherlands, Australia, and New Zealand, women report an even greater sense of safety. A 2004 study by the Ministry of Justice in the Netherlands found that the "vast majority" of sex workers in the red-light districts "often or always feel safe."[34] In another study, 97 percent of Australian sex workers felt working in a legal brothel was more safe and secure.[35] In New Zealand, decriminalizing sex work increased the workers' willingness to make police reports and "increased confidence, well-being, and a sense of validation."[36] According to the same government study, "decriminalizing prostitution made sex workers feel better about themselves and what they did." And for those who would argue that legalizing sex work would lead to an increase in prostitution, the same New Zealand report found that the number of sex workers did not increase after decriminalization but in fact decreased by more than half in the subsequent five years.

About 15 percent of my practice consists of sex workers of one type or another. These include strippers, escorts, dominatrixes, and porn performers. All women. Often, they refer one another to me because they know I will not judge them for the work they do. The kinds of issues they come in for are usually run-of-the-mill kinds of stuff, usually revolving around themes dealing with relationships and career transitions. My experience echoes that of the results from the *Journal of Sex Research* study on porn actresses described above. Those who have spent some time in sex work say that it has increased their self-esteem and has given them a range of opportunities, from financial to travel, that they would not have had otherwise.

Rather than psychological pathology, what I think is the common factor in all my sex worker clients is that they, more often than not, come from lower socioeconomic backgrounds. Really, I don't think it's a big stretch to compare blue-collar work for men to sex work for women. As a result, they are often denied the same kinds of educational opportunities that individuals from higher socioeconomic backgrounds possess. They may often come from families that don't privilege college educations, don't have the money for college even if they desired, and don't have the luxury of engaging in unpaid internships that build résumés like their more entitled peers have.

Participating in sex work allows them to make enough disposable income to use toward school, contribute to the family, or take care of dependents such as children. The kind of money that can't be earned working at McDonald's or some other job that doesn't require a college education. Sex work keeps them afloat and helps them plan for a different kind of future if that is what they want. Many, however, enjoy it enough that they stay with it until they can no longer continue, usually due to age. It is at this point that they often may look to transition out, at which point they may seek counseling for support throughout the process.

When it comes to relationships, the problem is usually with the partner and his (or her) lack of acceptance for the lifestyle rather than with some deep-seated psychological issues that prevent the woman from entering into a relationship. It is at these times that she may also look to leave the field as a means of appeasing the desires and insecurities of her partner.

When I think of this scenario, one of my sex worker clients, Debbie, comes to mind. Debbie is a voluptuous blonde in her late twenties who moved to New York City from Tampa, Florida, to get serious with a guy she met while he was visiting her strip club on a business trip to Tampa. He had promised her the moon and the stars if she came to live with him in New York, but the reality of the situation was much different. She dropped everything in Tampa—after all, here was a guy who would text and call her every moment, say they had a future together; it was all very romantic, and best of all, he didn't seem to care about her strip-

ping. In fact, he said it turned him on, that here were all these guys that
wanted her, but he was the only guy who could have her, that she came
home to.

So she moved into his apartment in Hell's Kitchen and easily found
another stripping gig on the West Side. Things were fine and dandy at
first, but the problem started, as is so usually the case in these situations, when (in this case) the guy started developing deep feelings, and
all of a sudden those views about how cool and hot it was to have a
stripper girlfriend evaporated. Instead, jealousy replaced arousal, contempt replaced desire, and a once cool and edgy woman became tainted
goods.

So it was in the midst of this situation that I first met Debbie.

"Listen Doc, I gotta get make some changes. Get out of the business. Stripping isn't working for me anymore. My boyfriend Rick, I
can't lose him."

"Why would you lose your boyfriend?"

"He wants me to quit dancing. He says he stays up all night waiting
for me to come home, imagining all the guys at the club leering at me.
He doesn't want to touch me anymore."

She pauses and I let her collect her thoughts for a moment.

She continues, "I really don't know what to do. I love him. But I also
don't want to quit. Dancing has been good for me. It's all I know and I
don't really want to depend on him financially, you know?"

"I do. But let's take a moment to figure out what is the best move for
you. Maybe that involves quitting, and maybe that involves staying with
it, or maybe there's some in between. But the most important thing is
that you don't lose yourself in this process."

That's a bit of a summation distilled from many months of work. But
the main point is that Debbie's struggle wasn't with her dancing. It was
with others' attitudes about it. And that pretty much sums up the main
issues that sex workers struggle with, which is their acceptance in mainstream society. This also highlights a very important point—most sex
workers resist changing their occupations, even when pressured by romantic partners. To do so would undermine their independence, self-
esteem, and sense of self that they have actually developed and enhanced *through* sex work.

Of course there exist victims of human trafficking, but those accounts that position all sex workers as victims are no more than a mani-

festation of sex panic and the resulting media circus that ends up poking at our most insecure spots and basest emotions (see chapter 3 on the role of media and advertising in intensifying fear and insecurity).

The United States is one of the few Western countries that has outlawed prostitution on a national level. Our neighbor to the north, Canada, does outlaw brothels but legalizes other forms of indoor prostitution, such as escorting. One such escorting service, Toronto Cupids (based out of Toronto, obviously) also reimburses a percentage of its employees' college tuition once they have worked a certain period of time.[37] As a result, the agency attracts young women who are seeking to leverage sex work to achieve other aims in life that are beyond their socioeconomic ability.

As we did in the previous chapter, let's also take a look at how the media plays a part in all of this. *Sex Slaves: Polk County* is a documentary on MSNBC, which follows the working of Polk County, Florida, Sheriff Grady Judd in his dogged pursuit of prostitutes and their johns.[38] Judd and his law enforcement personnel entrap both unwitting sex workers (by posing as prospective clients) and unsuspecting would-be clients by placing bogus sex ads online. In the episode I watched, they captured two young African American women and promptly interrogated them about whether they were trafficked slaves, abused, or at the very least coerced in some fashion. The women, initially terrified, then seemed to relax and took a cavalier attitude, denying that they were doing anything that wasn't consensual. The female producer undauntingly badgered them with more questions that seemed to try to steer them toward admitting to their victimhood, but the women refused to take her up on it. One woman said that she was looking to leave the business but that she had no regrets about what she did since she was able to make money and buy nice things for herself.

In the end, we are left with the uneasy feeling that, while it is true these women could probably benefit from more education and could do greater things with their lives than meeting complete strangers in motel rooms for sex, their stories are not being accurately captured by the television cameras. Instead, when they are prompted by leading questions to fill some preordained narrative, they are being as objectified by the television production and law enforcement portrayed in the program as much as by anything the johns are accused of doing. Except that in this case, the objectification is not about sex, but about crass commercialism and political gain. Despite watching numerous filmed raids, not once did I actually see them interrogate a "sex slave."

When these women are portrayed as "slaves" because they have sex for money instead of as individuals capable of making their own choices and for their own reasons, they end up losing their humanity primarily because of their sexual behaviors and choices. By calling the show *Sex Slaves* instead of the more appropriate term "sex work" and trying to fit each story line into this narrow narrative, the show is implying that there is no way that women would ever make the choice to have sex in exchange for money unless they were enslaved into it. Like the other shows I discussed in the previous chapter, this program isn't about prostitutes or sex workers at all. Rather, it's about the portrayal of non-normative sexuality as sexual deviance (in this case, male sexual deviance and female oppression).

THE PATH FROM CRIMINAL TO CRAZY

In summation, in this and the previous chapter, we have covered the many ways in which culture uses both coercive force through law enforcement and the court system as well as manipulative propaganda-like techniques through the media to control threats to social group cohesion. However, I have purposefully left one key coercive strategy out, which I will cover in great depth in the next chapter—the medicalization of sexuality.

What do I mean by "medicalization?" Sex has gone through various phases of coercion that may or may not sometimes overlap.[39] Initially, sex that was considered nonnormative was viewed through the lens of religious dogma and considered "immoral." Then, around the time of the Industrial Revolution, science began to phase out the dominion of religion, and moralization of sexuality was replaced by the criminalization of sexuality and enforcement through the criminal justice system. And finally, what was at the time considered criminal then became pathological, as in the case of mental illness and disorder, to be treated by the medical field, namely psychiatrists and other mental health personnel. In this way, sexual "deviance" migrated from the realm of priests and clergy to prisons and finally to psychiatric institutions and psychologists' offices.

That is not to say that these are all distinct phases that exist in completely separate times and eras. In fact, they often coexist simultaneously, as we'll see in the next chapter. But the main point is that, for the most part, when we as a society want to deal with people whose sexuality we don't like, we've typically sent them for psychotherapy and mental health treatment for the better part of this and the past century. And as a psychotherapist myself, it pains me greatly to know that this is the area where much of sexual oppression occurs today.

Psychoanalysis, historically and in particular, has taken a strong interest in changing people's sexualities, as the many volumes of written work about the treatment of homosexuality and "perversions" attest to. However, thankfully, very few therapists now practice this kind of "conversion" therapy for homosexuality except for some conservative and dogmatic counselors operating more on faith than science. However, sexual oppression still exists openly in the therapy world. And it has a very specific name. Sex addiction.

5

FEAR AND LOATHING

How to Create the Perfect Consumer

John was a successful surgeon in New York City. The day of his first session, he entered my office, carefully looked around the room, and sized me up.

"I am mortified at what I have done, and I hope you can help me," he said after a few hesitant moments. "I am a sex addict and if I don't get some help, my wife will leave me."

Often, when I first see clients (and I prefer to use the term "client" versus "patient," as I see my work with them as a collaboration, not a medical procedure) who identify as sex addicts, they've just reached rock bottom and feel frightened, confused, and distraught. John informed me that he was not a good person and required severe punishment. He needed to be placed on the strictest possible regimen, complete with three intensive therapy sessions a week, weekly behavioral reports, and monthly lie-detector tests. He couldn't have sex or masturbate for six months. Or so the inpatient sex addiction program where he had just spent thirty thousand dollars and a month of his life had told him.

Over the course of our hour-long consultation, John provided me with a more detailed picture of his difficulties. For five years, he had been married to a very loving, caring woman who nine months earlier had suddenly decided to stop all sexual activities with him. When I asked John why his wife insisted on a sexless marriage, he responded, "I guess she has body image problems."

John had never once cheated on his wife, but the lack of sex was beginning to get to him.

And then a younger, high-spirited female colleague who respected John for his intelligence invited him to a medical conference in San Diego, which promised to be both fun and relaxing. She e-mailed him the details, ending her sentence with "It would be great if we could get together," followed by a smiley face. John responded, "That does sound nice." But it never went further than that. John's wife somehow found this e-mail, and all hell broke loose. All of her suspicions were true. John could not be trusted; he was a liar and a cad. He had betrayed his wife, shamelessly carrying on an emotional affair with another woman. How dare he send smiley faces through e-mail to another woman?

Divorce was the only option. Either that or treatment, since John was obviously sick. He could not go through another divorce; this was his second marriage, and the first divorce had been very costly. He had spent years building his practice. How could he have it all thrown away like this? John got on his hands and knees, begging his wife for forgiveness. He told her he was weak; he had given in to temptation. If she could only forgive him, he would find the help he needed. He would punish himself, as he so rightly deserved. If only she would give him another chance.

That night, he went online and searched for sex addiction rehab centers. None existed in New York City, but he found a bunch of them in Beverly Hills, Los Angeles, which seemed like a heck of a lot nicer place to go than Mississippi. The description on the website promised intensive treatment, permanent results, and happy marriages. It wasn't cheap, but it seemed worth it. He quickly called the 800 number, booked his reservation, and called his travel agent to take care of the arrangements.

During the course of his stay, he worked daily with a therapist, both individually and in a group. He discussed his childhood need to be validated, to be loved. He talked about his lust, his awful desire to look at attractive young women passing by on the street. What was wrong with him? He should only have eyes for his wife. He watched porn twice a week; this was feeding into the addiction. How could he desire those beautiful bleached-blonde women with those perfect bodies that he saw in porn when his loving wife was sleeping in the next room, snoring softly? It was all just too awful to think about what he had done. He had jeopardized his marriage due to his sex addiction.

The first few days went by quickly, in a blur. Talking about his childhood brought up strong memories. He was instructed to draw and paint what he imagined himself like as a child. The emotions poured in. If only his father had been more present, he would not have sent that e-mail to that seductive woman. John cried. He pounded the walls. He was not going to let his addiction control his life.

After his stay, he was given an aftercare program. He must provide his wife with a weekly account of all of his behavior and submit to random polygraph tests. He must join a twelve-step group and start treatment with only a certified sex addiction therapist (CSAT) as well as a therapist trained in working through childhood trauma. And he must stop any form of sex, including masturbation, for at least six months. There was no other way to achieve sobriety. You must quit cold turkey. Not even a thought. That would be considered lust. And lust feeds the addiction.

At no point in his stay did anyone ask John why his wife stopped having sex with him. No one seemed to wonder or care what a healthy adult man should do if he was deprived of sex for nine months. No one bothered to get more information about the nature of John's relationship with his wife. No one even asked about his relationship with his colleague or what the e-mail was all about. And no one asked why John identified himself as a sex addict. No one cared. And why should they? John was calling them, asking for a service, with check in hand. Who were they to turn him down?

John didn't come back for a second session. I told him that I did not think he was a sex addict. That was not what he wanted to hear. Most likely he called another therapist and found one who would gladly give him the service he wanted for the right price. And so John will continue on his course of treatment, abstaining from sex indefinitely, under the strict observation of his wife and team of therapists. He will be told that he is sick and that he needs to continue to pay for his expensive treatment if he has any hope of recovering and saving his marriage. And so his identity as a sex addict will continue to strengthen, always to be used against him. Nothing in his relationship will change.

John's situation is not unique. Like countless others, he is a victim of dubious quack therapies—like sex addiction treatment and reparative therapy—that financially and emotionally exploit vulnerable and fearful people—people who are afraid of losing their relationships and their livelihoods, but also people who are afraid of sex and, ultimately, themselves.

SEX SELLS: HOW THE MEDIA MUDDIES THE SEXUAL WATERS FOR PROFIT

The voice on the other end of the line crackled with an indistinct European accent. Franz, a television producer, was calling to get an expert opinion for an upcoming German documentary about sex around the world. The segment about the United States centered on sex addiction, and Franz wanted to find out what the deal was with Americans and sex addiction. No one in Germany, he explained, had even heard of sex addiction before the show *Californication* hit the airwaves in his homeland. Hank Moody, the self-obsessed main character, seemed to be a truly American creature, absorbed only with himself and getting laid, and nothing else.

"What's the deal with you Americans and sex?" Franz wanted to know.

Without realizing it, Franz had asked me one of the best questions I've ever gotten. The truth is, sex addiction is an American disease. Many people of other countries have never even heard of sex addiction, or maybe only vaguely through American media. While sex addiction treatment is a booming, profitable business in the United States, it is unheard of in the rest of the world. Why is that? I struggled with this same question while trying to give Franz a good response.

The answer came to me through one of my clients. The German documentarian had asked whether he could interview one of them, and my thoughts immediately went to Dougie, one of my most animated and outspoken clients. If anyone were truly a sex addict, it was Dougie. He had struggled with almost every single kind of sexually compulsive behavior that one could imagine—voyeurism, exhibitionism, transvestitism—you name it, he had done it all. The issue wasn't the behavior itself but that his behavior had been escalating and he couldn't get it under control. Things came to a head when he was arrested for public lewdness. Facing several years in jail, Dougie decided to seek help. I asked him whether he would be gracious enough to appear on camera and, unsurprisingly, he eagerly agreed.

While we were talking about his compulsions, I asked him what he would like to tell the interviewer. His response was a little surprising, even for a wildcard like Dougie. He said, "I just want these Germans to know that I would not have been so screwed up with my sexuality if I was ever taught by my family or society that sex was okay. I was never told anything, and then I would be punished. It made me just want to rebel and see what I could get away with. See how crazy I could get."

What Dougie seemed to be saying was that negative messages about sex had contributed to his out-of-control, conflicted, and painful sexuality.

I thought again about Franz's question, and the answer became clear. The United States was the only country in the world that idealized individuality so much yet sent so many mixed messages about sex. This was the country that invented celebrity culture, that pioneered the use of sexual messaging to sell beer and cars yet stigmatized so much of sexual behavior.

I think back to numerous celebrities—actors, athletes (we know who they are)—whose drama illustrates this conflict so well. First, the public loves these celebrities, loves them enough to buy all the stuff they hawk on television. But the fawning fans quickly turn on a dime when the crap hits the fan and all the sexual affairs come to light. The same fans that once loved the celebrity now love to hate him. The media jumps in, poring over all the reasons for the sudden fall from grace. Maybe this celebrity is a sex addict? How else to explain how a young, rich athlete or actor, with dozens of young females throwing themselves at him, could lose control and actually have sex with them? Clearly something must be wrong with him. To like fame and power and sex so much. Especially the sex part. Only a sex addict would have sex with so many women.

And so these celebrities go to rehab and come out changed men (and it is almost always men). And the fans are there to accept him back into the fold. He is now rehabilitated and would no longer be having sex. At least not with more than one woman. And the tabloids blast the news of him becoming serious with another woman. Here now stands before us a rehabilitated man. But there is usually still some drama. Will he stay rehabilitated, or will the diabolical sex addict come out, rearing his ugly head, and tarnish yet another woman's chaste reputation?

This is how our culture works. We elevate to cult status the successful individual but harshly punish that individual for being human—in this case, for having sex. It leads to self-absorbed, self-obsessed narcissistic people who, at the same time, hate themselves for their human desires, sex included. People who strive for the type of personal perfection found in magazine advertisements that always remains elusive. People who compare themselves to celebrities and despise themselves for not living up to some impossible vision the media pounds into their minds from every outlet possible. People who have become the ideal consumers. From these ashes, the sex addiction industry rises.

But it's not just sex addiction. Sex addiction is just the latest incarnation of a cultural hysteria centered on controlling and limiting sexual expression. For years, the hysteria focused on sexual "deviants," which mainly referred to homosexuals. Homosexuality was considered a mental disorder by the psychiatric establishment until 1973.[1] Yet even to this day, mental health professionals can be found around the country specializing in "curing" homosexuality. And they have thousands of vulnerable clients, ashamed of who they are, filling the professionals' offices and wallets. In many ways, the sex addiction and ex-gay industries share a lot in common. And some of the same folks are involved in both.

EXPLOITING SHAME: GAY REPARATIVE THERAPY

L.I.F.E. Recovery International, a Christian ministry based in Lake Mary, Florida, is one of dozens of typical organizations that one may find in both the sex addiction and ex-gay industries.[2] On their website, they write, "Sex addiction is a growing epidemic that is reaching our youth through the media. This world view of 'sex is okay,' combined with hormonal changes, creates a ripe environment for sexual activity." They advocate a program called "Sexual Integrity for Young Men," which basically means abstinence. In an advice column found on their site, a representative of the organization writes to a woman who is worried that her son is gay: "Two common threads exist among those who struggle with homosexual tendencies. First, does your son exhibit any signs of childhood molestation or incest? If you suspect this is the case, seek help from a local Christian counselor."

So what kind of treatment could this boy expect from his local Christian counselor? The answer: reparative therapy. Spearheaded by psychologist Joseph Nicolosi, reparative therapy aims to cure homosexuality by fixing childhood traumas of parental neglect.[3]

The advice column continues, summarizing the beliefs of the ex-gay reparative movement. "Then look at the father/son (and for girls, the mother/daughter) relationship. Does your son feel accepted by his father? . . . The father holds the key to affirming a boy's manhood. Without that blessing, a gaping hole is left in a young man's life. . . . Some young men attempt to 'cannibalize' other men through homosexual actions to fill that void."

Reparative therapy has been discredited by every single leading psychotherapeutic organization—including the American Psychiatric Association (APA), the American Psychological Association, and the National Association of Social Workers—but is still widely practiced in certain circles throughout the country, despite absolutely no proof that it works.[4] In a recent study, the APA determined that not only was reparative therapy not effective, it also ran the risk of making patients more depressed, anxious, and even suicidal.[5]

Despite this, well-meaning parents have for decades taken their sons who were not interested in girls and sports to wise therapists to cure these boys of their effeminate ways. Money has poured into research to develop more powerful therapeutic techniques to rid the world of the "disease" of homosexuality. In the 1970s, psychologist Ivor Lovaas and George Rekers, who was then a doctoral student, conducted what was later called the "Sissy Boy" experiments at UCLA.[6] These experiments were designed to test a new behavioral approach to stopping homosexuality—by literately beating it out of little boys. Boys in the study were rewarded for "masculine" behaviors and severely beaten for anything resembling effeminate behaviors.

Later, Lovaas and Rekers published an article calling their treatment a fabulous success, using the case of a little boy, Kirk Murphy, as evidence of the transformation of a soon-to-be-homosexual into a healthy heterosexual young man. The article was titled "Behavioral Treatment of Deviant Sex-Role Behaviors in a Male Child." In 2003, at age thirty-eight, Kirk Murphy tragically committed suicide—a gay man still traumatized by the treatments he received as a child and overwhelmed with his sexuality.[7] George Rekers, one of the leaders of the study, was himself outed as a homosexual in 2010 when he was photographed with a male escort.[8]

That one of the leaders of the antigay movement was discovered to be gay himself might appear stunning on the surface but should come as no surprise. Many of the loudest homophobic voices out there have turned out to be gay, including various religious and political figures such as megachurch pastor Ted Haggard and former senator Larry Craig.[9] Numerous psychological studies have shown that homophobia is most intense in those who are worried or confused about their own orientation.[10]

Internalized homophobia is in fact one of the most common sexual difficulties I see in my office. Often, these individuals have first turned to reparative therapy for answers but only became more depressed and anxious. Though overwhelming research shows that sexual orientation is innate, for many the process of fully accepting their sexuality is a long and difficult journey.

Psychologist Vivienne Cass created a six-stage theory of the process of coming out.[11] This is a powerful tool to help understand where anyone is in the process. I use it all the time with my clients. I will go into more detail about this model in chapter 6, but for now I will focus on only the first stage, which is often the most problematic.

In stage 1, *Identity Confusion*, individuals experience intense internal confusion and turmoil over whether or not they could possibly be gay. Most experience this in early adolescence, or most likely even earlier, but with proper affirmation the individual can quickly get past this stage and move forward. Unfortunately, many get stuck in this stage and never can get past it.

David, a financial analyst in his late twenties, was in the midst of this struggle when he called me one evening to schedule an appointment. On the phone, he told me his problem was so embarrassing that he could tell me only in person. In my office, he still couldn't bring himself to tell me the problem, except to say that he believed he was a sex addict. Otherwise, his life was pretty good. He had a nice apartment, a pretty, young girlfriend, and lots of friends.

And, oh, David finally slipped in, he couldn't stop watching gay porn. And sometimes he went on Grindr, a smartphone app that helps locate nearby men, to hook up with guys in the area. Often he couldn't get hard with his girlfriend and had to visualize gay porn to get off. All of his sexual fantasies involved men. But don't I or anyone else dare call him gay.

By the time he came in, David was already an expert on all the ex-gay, reparative therapy information out there on the web. To him, all of that stuff just seemed to make sense. He never experienced the love of his neglectful father. His father was weak and distant, preoccupied with his small business. And all David was doing by hooking up with other men was trying to find the warm embrace and acceptance that he never received from his father. If only he could fill that gaping hole, David would be cured of his homosexual yearnings and would be free to live his life as the man he was intended to be. A straight man. This is the story David told himself.

David initially didn't come in complaining of his fears of being gay. He described himself as a sex addict who happened to struggle with gay porn as one of his addictions. This is a common situation. In my experience, most men whose main struggle is internalized homophobia come into treatment as self-described sex addicts. Homosexuality to them is just one other perversion, such as sadomasochism or pedophilia.

Homophobia and sex addiction coexist in the same ecosystem. One of the most popular sex addiction twelve-step groups, Sexaholics Anonymous (SA), forbids any gay activity among its members.[12] According to them, any homosexual activity is considered "acting out." Many of my clients struggling with their orientation have been members of SA. To them, unwanted gay thoughts were equivalent to sex addiction. To make matters worse, as of this writing, sex addiction organizations such as the Society for the Advancement of Sexual Health (SASH) refuse to condemn SA or remove its banners from their sites.[13]

In working with someone like David, I knew the work had to be very slow and presented in small, manageable doses. If I told David right off the bat that he might possibly be gay, he would simply walk out the door and never come back. And he could possibly wind up in the hands of a reparative therapist. And he would never be helped and instead be traumatized further.

The first step with David was building an alliance, which I accomplished through "joining" with him. By joining, I mean that I initially took his side and showed him that I understood his worldview. So just because he spent his entire life consumed with gay sex, of course this didn't mean he was gay. And because he had to pretend that his girlfriend was a man in order to have sex, of course this was because he was looking for his father's love.

This may seem counterintuitive, but with someone so dug into his position, this is the only way to build enough trust to slowly start changing the person's mind. After a few months, I presented him with the possibility that maybe he was constantly looking for gay content as a way of testing whether he would respond to it. In other words, because he was so afraid of being gay, maybe he was constantly checking his "gayness." Checking to see whether he would respond to gay material in a "gay way." This is often a very successful gateway into taking a closer look at the actual homophobia. If I can get the client to take on an air of curiosity about his (or her) homophobia, we are on our way.

I will often phrase it like this: "If the homophobia is causing you to act so obsessively, even as a straight man, doesn't it make sense for us to tackle this homophobia once and for all?" Or, "If this homophobia is causing so much pain in your life, imagine how much your life would be better if we could finally just get rid of it?"

I've never had a client who wasn't able to buy in with this kind of appeal. So then we start taking a look at the homophobia. By doing so, we externalize it. It is no longer only experienced as an internal situation, but because we have named it and can examine it, it now feels like there is something we can do about it.

At this point, I provide a lot of psychoeducation. I challenge clients' beliefs about gay relationships. I usually hear stuff about gays being unable to maintain long-term relationships, myths about HIV, AIDS, and other STDs, and other assorted antigay propaganda that the client has bought lock, stock, and barrel.

Once clients begin to challenge their misconceptions about homosexuality, though, they inevitably start to reflect again on their own sexuality. Suddenly the doors have opened to reexamine the possibility that they may in fact be gay—or bisexual at least. At this point, the client begins to accept the possibility of being gay.

Once homosexuality is destigmatized, the need to hold onto fear and shame disappears. Homosexuality begins to become a viable identity. The individual starts to wonder how he can learn more. He may ask himself, "Maybe I've been gay all along. How do I continue to find out who I really am?" At this stage, he may come to accept that he is most likely gay and may look for other similar individuals as a way to find out for sure.

In David's case, he is still unsure about being gay but has wrapped himself around an identity as a bisexual. He has come out to his girlfriend about his sexual interests in other men, which was a lengthy process in therapy of working out the best way for him to do so, but to his surprise, she was not only accepting but also enthusiastic about exploring her own bisexuality. Since then, they have included other partners in their sex life, both male and female, and David reports that they are closer than ever. He no longer spends hours on gay porn or cruises for guys online. He still, though, does have some difficulty staying present with his girlfriend in bed. Maybe he is bisexual. Maybe he is gay. Who cares? I allow my clients to define their own sexualities. It's their particular journey of discovery. But along the way, it is my goal to help them eliminate any of their internal sexual shame that gets in the way of their truly experiencing a joyful life.

And, oh yeah, David is no longer a sex addict.

NEVER ON A SUNDAY: THE SEX ADDICTION INDUSTRY

Let's now take a closer look at what the sex addiction industry is all about. The first thing to know is that even the phrase "sex addiction" is controversial, more accepted by the media and the public than by mental health professionals. We've all seen the media headlines about various public figures caught with their pants down, from New York governor Eliot Spitzer's escapades with high-priced call girls to Anthony Weiner's crotch shots on Twitter.[14] When people think of sex addiction, the thought often conjures images of out-of-control, narcissistic, powerful men or shady old perverts in trench coats. However, the entire idea of sex addiction is relatively new, less than forty years old, rising to its current popularity in only the past decade.[15] No one disputes that sexually compulsive behavior exists, but the entire controversy explodes around viewing sexual behavior as a potential form of addiction.

The diagnosis of sex addiction does not exist in the latest version of the *Diagnostic and Statistical Manual* (*DSM-5*), psychiatry's reference bible.[16] The phrase "sex addiction" was added to the *DSM-III* (1980) and then removed "because of a lack of empirical research and consensus validating the sexual behavior as a bona fide behavioral addiction."[17] Every single attempt so far to include sex addiction as a mental health diagnosis has been turned away for lack of evidence and scientific basis. Yet thousands of people around the country continue to be diagnosed as sex addicts every year and submit to expensive, unproven treatment methods.

The industry is booming, fueled by celebrity culture and inpatient rehab centers. Alexandra Katehakis, founder of the Center for Healthy Sexuality, a sex addiction treatment center in Beverly Hills, has publicly stated that there was little market for her services until celebrities stepped out publicly to embrace their identities as sex addicts.[18] Now, as of this writing, six inpatient sex addiction centers operate in Beverly Hills alone.

Absolutely no proof exists that the sex addiction treatments offered by inpatient centers or by certified sex addiction therapists (CSATs) have any effect.[19] UCLA researcher Rory Reid agrees, saying that there have been only a handful of studies, none of which have been conclusive.[20] In addition, and most damning, many of these centers take in folks who are not even compulsive (but perhaps feel ashamed about their sexuality) and lump them into the same cohort with others who are truly more out of control. Leading sex addiction authority Robert Weiss has shared with me personally that moralists and conservatives take this issue and extend it into nonclinical areas of treatment.[21] This is the aspect that I refer to as the "sex addiction industry." More on that in a moment.

Therapists who have achieved the title of CSAT are not required to have any training in sexuality whatsoever. Requirements for certification include 120 hours of classroom training and thirty hours of supervision from a certified CSAT supervisor.[22] These 120 hours consist of four week-long modules. The promotional literature advertising these trainings states that attendees will learn about "the recovery zone," "the grievance story," "the legacy table," "addiction interaction," and "twelve-step principles." Nowhere in their marketing do they state that they provide any kind of training or education in sexuality. This becomes an issue when a client shows up with complex sexual difficulties, which can be understood more than one way, and that individual gets lumped in with everyone else as a sex addict. To my knowledge, II-TAP's stance was that they assumed folks, as licensed therapists, were getting sexuality training elsewhere, which is rarely the case. In addition, I've heard that they are now starting to integrate more sexuality diversity training, and I hope that is true.

CSATs use a self-administered test called the Sexual Addiction Screening Test (SAST) to determine whether someone is a sex addict.[23] This test consists of twenty-five true-false questions about various possible sexual behaviors. Sample questions include:

- Have you subscribed to or regularly purchased/rented sexually explicit magazines or videos?
- Do you often find yourself preoccupied with sexual thoughts?
- Do you look forward to events with friends or family being over so that you can go out to have sex?
- Have you ever had sex with someone just because you were feeling aroused and later felt ashamed or regretted it?

A score between 1 and 3 means sex addiction is an area of "concern." A score of 3 to 10 requires meeting with a trained professional, and anything higher means the person is a full-blown sex addict. Most of the questions on the list are things that most people have experienced at some point in their lives. So basically, everyone will score at least a 1 and should be concerned about being a sex addict.

Let's take a look at each of these questions one at a time, starting with the viewing of porn and having sexual thoughts. Studies have shown that virtually all, yes *all*, males in the United States have at one time or another watched pornography. One of these studies found that, on average, single men watched porn for forty minutes, three times a week, while those in relationships watched once or twice a week for about twenty minutes.[24] By far, most of the porn use happens in religious "red states," Utah leading the way with the highest rate of Internet porn subscribers.[25] (By the way, states in which respondents agreed with the statement "I have old-fashioned values about family and marriage" were much more likely to be states with higher porn use.) A psychological study of 283 students, using tally counters, found that men think of sexual acts an average 34.2 times a day (the women's average was 18.6).[26] Are all these men sex addicts?

For the third question, people with a healthy sex drive commonly may look forward to excusing themselves from boring events or social obligations to do something that feels more interesting, pleasurable, and fulfilling—like sex. A survey of 3,300 men and women found that more than half the individuals (1,743) had experienced one-night stands, often with complete strangers, and that 80 percent of men and 54 percent of women specifically categorized it as a positive experience.[27] So 80 percent of these men were really glad they had sex instead of doing something probably more boring that they could have been doing instead.

The fourth sample question is whether one had ever had sex while aroused and later regretted it. Remember that 20 percent of men in the study reported a negative experience from a one-night stand. However, almost half of women reported negative experiences, specifically mentioning regret and feelings of "being used" or "degraded" as reasons for negative outcomes. Based on this data, it seems that a lot of people have had sex with someone while aroused and later regretted it. Are they, too, all sex addicts?

It's not that sexually out-of-control people don't exist. They do. I see them in my consulting office every single day. But most people caught up as patients in the sex addiction industry are normal. There is nothing wrong with them, and that's the problem.

One of the first tasks that mental health clinicians learn in their training is what's called "differential diagnosis." This refers to the ability to understand slight differences in the origins of psychological problems, even if on the surface they seem similar. For example, someone who constantly cheats on his spouse may really feel out of control or may merely feel entitled. So, the reasons behind the behavior are totally different, even if the behavior looks the same. The ability to conduct a differential diagnosis is a necessary requirement for any therapist and requires both clinical and life experience and a flexible, open mind.

The famous therapist Abraham Maslow once said, "If you only have a hammer, you tend to see every problem as a nail," and this rings true for the sex addiction industry. Many of its members come from very religious, evangelical backgrounds, which would not be a problem if it did not bias their judgments. There is nothing wrong with religion, but treatment can be harmed when therapists make decisions based on religious or moralistic, rather than clinical, reasons. The code of ethics of most mental health organizations states that therapists must not push their own views on clients; this code, sadly, is rarely followed.

Let's take a closer look at the idea of labeling sexually compulsive behavior as a kind of addiction. It's going to get a bit technical, but don't worry, it won't last long. The idea of sex addiction is modeled on the symptoms of chemical addictions. This is known as the "addiction model." Patrick Carnes, an addictions specialist, first connected sexual behavior with the addiction model in his book *Out of the Shadows* (1983).[28] The addiction model views compulsive sexual behavior as a disease, which has helped to legitimize it as a medical issue, like alcoholism or drug addiction.

The *DSM 5* lists seven criteria for a diagnosis of substance dependence (addiction).[29] The two most important for our purposes are tolerance and withdrawal. "Tolerance" means the need for more and more increasing amounts to have the same effect. "Withdrawal" refers to an intense physical reaction when something the body becomes used to gets taken away. Unlike chemical addiction, sexual behavior has never been shown to lead to increased tolerance or biological withdrawal. The most current research can be summed up with these three conclusions:

- It has not been shown that you need increasing amounts of sex to get the same effect, which is the case with drug addiction.
- Though it may involve risk-taking behavior, there is not strong evidence that the risk taking escalates as it does in other forms of addiction.
- Though it can be difficult or impossible for people to stop compulsive sexual behavior, there is no proof that they suffer from actual withdrawal.

Clear differences exist between the biological addiction of chemical dependence and the sex addiction described by the sex addiction industry. All the facts go against the entire idea that sex can be an addiction in the same way as alcohol or drugs. But comparing sex with alcohol or drugs is not accidental. It has a specific, political purpose.

The best way to understand this is to take a look at other things we consider addictive. Besides alcohol and drugs, lots of possibilities are out there. Gambling, eating sweets, drinking sodas, playing video games. The list goes on and on. What's the connection? These things are all bad for you. They are either illegal or unhealthy and must be used in moderation. And so it is the same with sex. Sex is bad; it's dangerous. At best, it must be done in moderation. Or so the sex addiction industry wants you to believe. That kind of fear is merely another form of social control.

So who are the people in my practice who are genuinely struggling with getting control of their sexual behavior? First, they are actually a very small percentage of the number of people who are unofficially diagnosed as sex addicts every year. These are folks with emotional difficulties who use sex to cope with painful emotions. They are not addicted, but they do make bad choices. They may crave the thrill of the chase or the validation of being desired, but really it's not about the sex. They have sex to feel better, to escape their inner pain. My clients who are truly sexually compulsive have emotional problems, not sex problems.

They often come into my office convinced that they are sex addicts. They've heard about sex addiction on TV, or their wives or partners have accused them of sex addiction. By calling themselves sex addicts, they may feel like they are joining an exclusive club of high-profile people they see on TV. I usually use the same terminology of "sex addiction" with them in the first sessions because this is what they understand. But slowly, as we build our relationship, I help them to change the way they label themselves. They learn that they are not addicted to sex. They just happen to use sex in harmful ways.

I am reminded of Jacob, a successful advertising executive. He came into treatment after his wife discovered his encounters with high-priced escorts. Despite his career success, Jacob would constantly criticize himself, calling himself "worthless" and "hateful." Jacob's father was a harsh disciplinarian who praised Jacob only for perfection. When Jacob felt weak or vulnerable, he learned to keep it hidden inside so that he would not disappoint his father. Jacob learned that his only value came through what he accomplished, that his real self was not worth loving. And so, in his career, he drove to succeed with laser-like focus, but nothing was ever good enough to chase away his inner demons.

Jacob often felt fraudulent, like his outward success did not match his inner self. If only people knew who he really was, everything would come crashing down. Every wrong look, every slight criticism was felt as deep hurt. His self-esteem was a house of cards, ready to fall at the slightest disturbance. But Jacob never learned the tools to cope with his fear and pain. He had to do anything in his power to restore balance. He just needed to feel good again.

His relationship with his wife had become strained. Too much resentment had built up from the past. How could he let her in on his fears and worries? She would only turn it back on him, he thought. There was no one he could trust, nowhere to turn. He needed to feel in control, desired, and powerful again. And so Jacob looked online and found an ad for a woman promising the time of his life. And so he went. And paid. And it felt really good. He told her what he wanted, and she did it with a smile. She didn't judge him. And she didn't make any demands. It was all about him. And that's the way he wanted it.

Jacob kept this up for a few years, until his wife discovered one of his e-mails. As soon as the whole mess hit the fan, he stopped cold turkey. No more prostitutes. He was going to try and make this marriage work. Anything but divorce. You see, he wasn't addicted. He could stop at will. It was a choice. He simply felt like taking the easy way since it felt so good—and besides, how would his wife ever find out?

My job with Jacob was to help him understand his own inner emotional life. I didn't even talk about the sex. It was only a distraction from the real work needing to be done. I needed to help him identify his emotions as they were happening, understand their historical nature, and give him tools he could use to make better choices. In the end, the success of the work lay in helping Jacob to honor himself in a way that did not depend on external accomplishments.

If caught up in the sex addiction industry, Jacob may have been required to stop all sexual behavior for six months. He would go to meetings where he would proudly announce to other members that he had stayed sober for yet another week. He would wear his badge of sex addiction like a scarlet letter: Once a sex addict, always a sex addict. But none of his real problems would have been resolved. That's the tragedy of the sex addiction industry. It doesn't solve anything because it's looking in all the wrong places.

The sex addiction industry sees pathology everywhere. It often turns normal behavior into sickness. In short, the industry bases its entire philosophy on these three main wrong assumptions:

1. Sex and sexual desire are dangerous.
2. There's one "best" way to express your sexuality.
3. Relationship sex that enhances intimacy is best.

In other words, if you're not married or at least in a committed relationship, you probably shouldn't be having sex. And if you are having sex, it should always be about feeling closer to your committed partner. And God forbid you do any of that kinky stuff.

Without any clear definition of sex addiction or how to measure it, without extensive training in all aspects of human sexuality, and without any proof of successful results, the sex addiction industry is built on sand. This does not stop its therapists, though, from creating a billion-dollar industry, with trainings, workshops, videos, audiotapes, recruiters, and pricey, unproven inpatient retreats. The sex addiction industry is in the business of selling fear, and it is very profitable.

I KNOW IT WHEN I SEE IT: PORNOGRAPHY AND SOCIETY

No discussion of sex addiction can be complete without touching on the whole hubbub about porn. Antiporn crusaders have been at it full force for decades. In a perverse twist, their icon is the sexual serial killer Ted Bundy, who, while awaiting his execution on death row, blamed his rapes and mutilations of dozens of women on violent porn he watched as a kid.[30]

The war on porn seems to consist of three main strands. The first is the whole addiction angle, where the viewing of sexual material supposedly stimulates a dopamine rush through the reward circuitry in the brain, much like heroin or similar drugs.[31] That may be true. But so does having a delicious slice of chocolate cake. Dopamine rush. So does looking at a beautiful vista of the Golden Gate Bridge. Dopamine rush. I don't see anyone looking to ban photographs of the Golden Gate

Bridge. Anything that feels exciting and exhilarating will release a chemical reaction. So what?

The entire chemical addiction argument about porn addiction either uses bad science or takes real science out of context to make the case for a slanted agenda. For example, researchers from the United Kingdom recently announced that a study of nineteen self-described porn addicts showed increased activity in a part of the brain called the *ventral striatum* that is involved in processing pleasure.[32] A control group also had activity in this area but lit up a bit less than the addict group. Both groups' brains lit up. This research comes in the wake of British prime minister David Cameron's proposal to use the government to block Internet porn. However, this study doesn't exclude for other preexisting factors, such as libido and/or sensation seeking, so no conclusive causality can be established.

In 2013, researchers at UCLA conclusively proved that porn was not addictive. In a study published in the *Journal of Socioaffective Neuroscience and Psychology*, they compared the brains of self-described porn addicts and the brains of regular folks while both watched porn, and they could not find any difference at all in brain activity between the two groups.[33] None. If anything, the only difference in brain response was in those who described themselves as having high libidos. The scientists concluded that "degrees of sexual compulsivity did not predict brain response at all." In other words, porn addiction does not exist.

In fall 2015, another groundbreaking study came out. Joshua Grubbs, from Case Western University, studied 3,055 men and women from three different universities on a number of dimensions, including amount of pornography use, perceived addiction to pornography, and personality traits, as well as a host of emotional and psychological components.[34] Grubbs and his team found that emotional factors such as anxiety and depression had absolutely no correlation with porn use but much to do with one's self-perception of being addicted to porn. A representative sample was followed up with a year later. Again, results were identical. The research team concluded that labeling oneself as a "porn addict" was the one surefire way to develop distress around porn. One more time, this time with feeling: In other words, porn addiction does not exist.

Again.

Case closed.

The second strain of porn condemnation centers specifically on masturbation. Masturbation is a solo activity, the argument goes, that prevents men from fully engaging in intimate relationships. Of course there are men who prefer porn to actual sex with their partners, but in my experience it is most often the case that these men use porn to escape their relationship rather than finding themselves ensnared in a web of sexual visuals that prevent them from getting into it with their partner.

The whole issue with masturbation has a long history dating back centuries. Back in the 1800s, it was called degeneracy theory. Degeneracy theory stated that sexual "perversions" escalate due to growing desensitization of the individual, who needs greater and more perverse stimulation to achieve intense arousal.

Degeneracy theory has its roots in the Victorian era, when masturbation was viewed as immoral, serving as a gateway to even more deviance and debauchery.[35] As part of this antisex crusade, Anthony Comstock, a special agent of the U.S. Postal Service, formed a committee on the suppression of vice and lobbied Congress to pass a law enforcing extreme forms of censorship on what he viewed as obscenities.[36] Obscenity, as he defined it, meant anything impure and suggesting "libidinous thoughts," especially in young men.

Abstinence crusaders such as the Reverend Sylvester Graham, the maker of Graham crackers, and John Harvey Kellogg, the creator of Kellogg's Corn Flakes, took up the mantle of degeneracy theory in the United States.[37] This duo believed that food, fitness, and abstinence were the pillars of good health; Kellogg specifically created his corn flakes to reduce "carnal desire." Kellogg may have been the world's greatest antimasturbation advocate in all history. As a physician, he advocated sewing up the foreskin of boys with silver wire and circumcision without anesthesia to prevent masturbation; for girls, burning off the clitoris with carbolic acid was the antidote. For his own health, he slept in his own bed without ever consummating his marriage. Presumably, his followers thought this was why he lived to the ripe old age of ninety-four.

Let's put this issue with masturbation to bed right now. Masturbation is healthy. It is the way that individuals learn about their sexualities. Masturbation helps us to learn what we want sexually and communicate that to our partners. Masturbation often uses fantasy, which allows us to get more in touch with our internal psychologies. Yes, masturbation can be excessive. But in that case, it's just another form of escape. The problem there isn't masturbation, it's the emotions that masturbation is used to detach from.

The third argument against porn revolves around the issue of violence against women. This is where Ted Bundy comes in. The detractors have their slogans out in full force.

"Look at the serial killers in our country that were raised on porn."

"Porn degrades women as objects."

"Porn promotes violence against women."

And so on, and so on. Now let's look at the facts. We have real science behind us to help answer the question of whether or not porn increases violence. And we have lots of it. Researchers in *many* countries have actually taken a look at this. And the results are conclusive.

In every country studied, sex crimes have fallen inversely with the legalization of pornography. Yes, you read that right. Porn up, sex crimes down. This research, spanning over twenty years, covers three continents and dozens of countries, including the United States, Croatia, Finland, Sweden, Denmark, Germany, the Czech Republic, Japan, and Shanghai and Hong Kong in China.[38]

In 2007, Professor Todd Kendall of Clemson University stated that based on his extensive research, "Potential rapists perceive pornography as a substitute for rape . . . pornography is a complement for masturbation or consensual sex, making pornography a net substitute for rape."[39] Let's take a look at this statement a little closer. Professor Kendall is saying that people who are thinking of rape actually choose to watch porn instead of going out and acting out on their urges. And that pornography merely leads to masturbation or consensual sex.

That about sums up my experience as a sex therapist as to how I address porn with my clients. For many, porn is their first introduction to new sexual activities and experiences that they were never aware of before. For many couples, watching porn is the fuel for mixing things up and adding variety to their stale sexual lives. For many men, porn provides the sexual variety that they crave without feeling like they need to get that variety outside their relationships. For most, porn is a source of inspiration, creativity, and new possibilities. Yes, for some it is a refuge from life and relationship problems. But that doesn't mean porn should be banned. And, in the big scheme of things, porn helps society by reducing sex crimes.

Next time someone warns you of the dangers of porn, remember this simple slogan, backed up by decades of scientific research: Porn up, sex crimes down.

II

Lives Reclaimed: Embracing Sexual Freedom

6

CH-CH-CHANGES, TURN AND FACE THE STRANGE

How the Process of Change Occurs

Now that we've spent the first part describing how and why we have been separated from our authentic sexual selves, the rest of this book describes in great detail what you can do about it and specifically how I, as a sex therapist, help my clients work through these issues.

The first thing that anyone going through the journey of reclaiming his or her sexual authenticity must understand is that it is never easy and will usually require facing some level of anxiety. This has to do with the process of how change happens, which I will review in the next few pages.

OUTSIDE THE COMFORT ZONE: LEARNING TO APPROPRIATELY TEST THE LIMITS

Feeling anxious is normal. It's a healthy and even necessary part of the process. Let's take a look at what this process of change involves. Imagine a circle and that everything in that circle includes all the things you know and love, the things you are used to doing, the things that are habitual—basically, the things you are already most comfortable with. Let's call this your comfort zone. And everything inside it doesn't make you anxious. Most people stay in this comfort zone their entire lives and rarely, if ever, venture outside. This is a great strategy for reducing discomfort but a terrible one if you ever want to grow.

When we are talking about expanding our potential or experiencing new things, we inevitably must face the fundamental issue of stepping outside this inner circle. And so, by definition, doing so will feel a little uncomfortable, perhaps a little awkward, and it will often cause at least a moderate level of anxiety. That is all fine and to be expected anytime we seek to expand our comfort zone.

Let's take a look at figure 6.1 to illustrate this concept as well as to lay down the steps necessary to grow the circle outward.

As you can see, right outside the inner circle are two additional layers—the learning and panic zones. We'll get to them in a moment. But again, as a review, everything inside the comfort zone includes all the things we are used to and feel comfortable with. Having sex in the

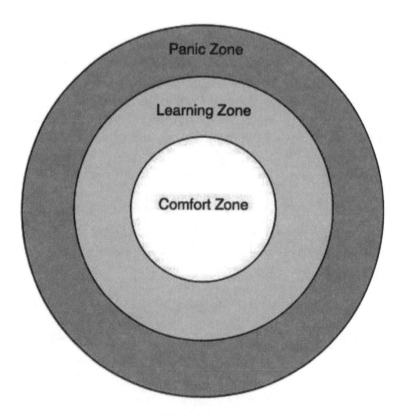

Figure 6.1.   Comfort, Learning, and Panic Zones

missionary position with all the lights out may be the only kind of sex in the comfort zone for some people. Group sex parties may be in the comfort zone for others. However, if you are looking to expand your sexual comfort zone, I imagine that you are probably somewhere in the first part of the spectrum. And that's OK. For some, that is where they will stay, and that's fine if they are happy with that. For others however, who are looking to overcome society's social inhibitions, this section will be most valuable.

Now let's look at the two concentric circles outside the inner circle. You can imagine these circles as lines demarcating how far outside the comfort zone you have ventured. The middle circle, the learning zone, represents activities that are outside the comfort zone but that do not produce enough anxiety to cause great distress. The outer circle, the panic zone, represents activities that are so far out of the comfort zone that they would produce high enough levels of discomfort to flood the person with anxiety.

When we explore new things, we want to stay in that middle circle and stay out of the furthest one. In other words, we want to go only so far outside the comfort zone to stimulate moderate enough levels of anxiety that can be tolerated without overwhelming us. If we venture too far into that outer circle, not only will we be confronted with too much anxiety, but we most likely will simply run back to the comfort zone and vow to never venture out again. In other words, when we jump too far, not only do we not learn anything, but the experience is also counterproductive by traumatizing us from trying again.

If you never step outside the comfort zone, it never expands, and you stay the same your entire life. That's why evolving sexually requires stepping outside your comforts, which inevitably requires some level of anxiety. The key here is how far outside the comfort zone you venture. Often, folks may have had early negative experiences with sexuality that frightened them from ever experimenting again. It doesn't have to be that way.

I always tell my clients that real growth can only occur when we expose ourselves to moderate levels of anxiety that are low enough for us to tolerate. When we are able to stay with the anxiety and see that we are able to master the situation, the anxiety falls away and we have expanded our circle of comfort. In this way, we expose ourselves to higher and higher levels of anxiety, inching our comfort zone further out in graded steps.

Usually at this point I work with my client to identify appropriate next steps that would allow the individual to expand his or her comfort zone but with minimal or tolerable amounts of anxiety. Before we determine these steps, though, I think it is essential for the person to really have a clear understanding of what he or she is trying to accomplish. Specifically, before we put the wheels into motion, it is important to first get a sense for where each person is starting out. It is not so simple usually as just pushing oneself through anxiety. There is also the little issue of motivation, which leads us to an important concept we must first consider before moving forward—the transtheoretical stages of change model (pictured in figure 6.2).[1]

As you can see, the first stage of the change process is called *Precontemplation*. In this stage, the individual typically isn't even aware of having a problem. These folks typically don't show up in therapy, but if they do, it is usually due to pressures from others such as partners, an employer, or the court system. They are therefore resistant to change and place responsibility for their problems on others.

Next comes *Contemplation*. In this stage, the individual has a dawning experience of realizing that something is wrong. This may be the first time the person acknowledges having a problem and may start looking for solutions. It is in this stage that I often see my clients first show up. They are tired of feeling a certain way, but at the same time, they may not have enough insight or commitment to really tackle the issue, so they may often defer and procrastinate on doing hard work or finishing assignments. It is not uncommon for contemplators to tell themselves that some day they are going to change but then show no sign of taking concrete steps in the present. In other words, they experience a high level of ambivalence.

As a result, they may experience a lot of fits and starts, making some progress and then falling back into old habits. This is OK! It's part of a process, and the last thing we want is for individuals to become so down and self-critical that they give up. The key is to stay with it.

Third is the *Preparation* stage. In this stage, most folks start making concrete plans to take action and change their behavior. In addition, their thinking is clearly marked by directing their thoughts more toward the future than the past. They have not yet fully resolved their ambiva-

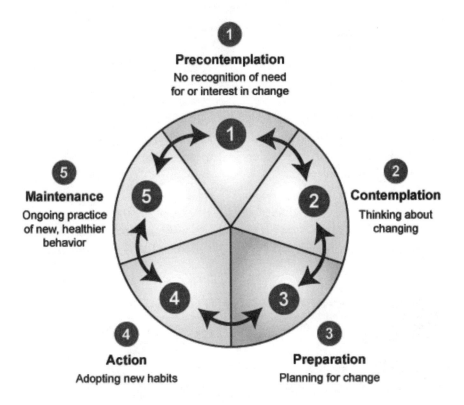

Precontemplation
No recognition of need
for or interest in change

Maintenance
Ongoing practice
of new, healthier
behavior

Contemplation
Thinking about
changing

Action
Adopting new habits

Preparation
Planning for change

Figure 6.2. **Transtheoretical Stages of Change.** *Courtesy of James Prochaska*

lence, but they are more strongly in touch with the part of themselves that is actively seeking change.

Next comes the *Action* stage. In this stage, people overtly modify their behavior and their surroundings. Because people are putting their plans into movement, this stage requires the greatest commitment of time and energy. Usually in the beginning, change is more visible to others.

And finally comes the *Maintenance* stage. Change never ends with action. Without a strong commitment to maintenance, there will surely be relapse, usually to the precontemplation or contemplation stage.

Remember the model for the stages of coming out that I described in chapter 5? Let's take a moment to revisit this model here briefly because it coincides so well with the transtheoretical stages of change model. The model for the stages of coming out was initially created to illustrate the experiences of LGB individuals coming to terms with their orientation.[2] However, I believe it can be applied to anyone who is coming to terms with any aspect of his or her sexuality, so I will adapt this model for our discussion here. Take a moment first to familiarize yourself with the six stages, pictured in figure 6.3.

The first stage is called *Identity Confusion*. The most common quest here is "Who am I?" This stage begins with the person's first awareness of gay or lesbian thoughts, feelings, and attractions. The individual typically feels confused and experiences turmoil. This stage coincides with *Precontemplation*.

As we've seen in earlier chapters, being exposed to society's sexual prejudices inevitably produces feelings of alienation and isolation. Individuals at this stage are not consciously aware of their sexual desires; they cannot describe what is wrong. They may hide their feelings from

Figure 6.3.   Cass's Stages of Coming Out. *Courtesy of Joe Kort*

themselves and others, suffer low self-esteem and depression, and communicate their conflict only through behavioral problems.

The second stage is *Identity Comparison*. Individuals move into this stage when they can finally acknowledge their desires, which is the first developmental task of this stage. That may mean simply acknowledging a confusing sexual thought or fantasy without fully understanding or labeling what that means. They may often think, "Maybe this does apply to me."

Once the feelings have been identified, the next task is telling someone, a vital function in beginning one's self-acceptance. The confidant's reaction has a powerful impact. If negative, it can confirm old prejudices and lower self-esteem. If positive, it can counteract old prejudices and permit individuals to begin accepting their sexual feelings and increase self-esteem. This stage spans the *Contemplation* and *Preparation* stages.

The third stage is *Identity Tolerance*. Here, individuals come to an understanding that they are "not the only one" and may often look for additional resources to continue their journey, such as community and role models. This stage straddles the *Preparation* and *Action* categories.

Common tasks in this stage are to develop interpersonal skills to meet and socialize with others having the same interest and to build a sense of personal attractiveness and sexual competence through their sexual relationships.

Next is *Identity Acceptance*. In this stage, people move toward self-acceptance and realize "I will be okay." Although these individuals are more self-accepting, they may still compartmentalize aspects of their sexuality. At any rate, they are becoming more identified with their sexual needs. This stage coincides with the *Action* stage of change.

The fifth stage is *Identity Pride* and also correlates to the *Action* stage. At this stage, individuals are focused on letting others know of their new identity. The main thought here is "I've got to let people know who I am!" The challenge here is that sometimes individuals can get so lost in their pride that they experience disdain for the larger, more normative aspects of society.

And finally, *Identity Synthesis* is a stage that dovetails with *Maintenance*. People integrate their sexual identity with all other aspects of self, and sexual orientation becomes *only one aspect* of self rather than the entire identity.

I've taken a look at these two models side by side to illustrate that the process of coming to terms and accepting one's sexuality firmly follows the stages of change model that describes all other change activities. Now that you've read through these change models and have perhaps identified where you are in the process, let's now look at specific steps we can begin to make to move forward in this journey, using my client Olivia, who came in at the most common entry point, *Contemplation*, as a case study.

BACK TO BASICS: UNDERSTANDING YOUR RELATIONSHIP TO SEX

Olivia, a divorcée in her late thirties, called me right after the ink on the divorce papers had dried. She had been married for seventeen years, since her early twenties, and so most of her sexual experience was with one man. Unfortunately, as the marriage wore on it became apparent to both of them that they were just not suitable for each other. Her husband wasn't that much interested in sex, but Olivia, well, she felt hemmed in and ready to explore.

Most importantly, and typical for the folks who contact me, she wasn't sure whether her desires were normal or, to put it in her words, "weird." See, toward the end of her marriage, Olivia found herself looking online for a specific kind of erotica. She fantasized about being tied up by a rough stranger, someone who would take control of her body and use it any way he pleased for his own pleasure. Someone who would rip her clothes off, throw her on the bed, and then smack her buttocks with his powerful, bare hands. Basically, someone who was comfortable with his own sexuality, unlike her husband. Olivia was looking for her antihusband.

She had started looking at online personal ads but felt too timid to respond to any of the countless e-mails she received. This is the part that I would like to freeze-frame and discuss a little further before going back to Olivia's story. This is the point where I suspect many readers may find themselves as well—coming to terms with a certain awareness that there are parts of their own sexuality that have yet to be explored, but at the same time too nervous and anxious to move forward.

Here's a specific exercise that I have found to be very helpful. Take a sheet of paper and draw a line down the middle, making two columns. Label the first column "What I Learned" and label the second column "What I Want." We are obviously talking about sex here, so we can leave that part out. In that first column, start writing what it is that you learned about sex growing up. Make it a list of bulleted items. For example, here are some entries from Olivia's list:

- Sex is dirty.
- Sex is something you give a man to control him, but girls aren't supposed to enjoy sex.
- Girls who enjoy sex are sluts.
- Sex should be done in the dark and under the covers.
- Sex is basically intercourse; anything else is perverted.
- Sex should be done only in the context of a serious, committed relationship.

In Olivia's right-hand column, she wrote the following:

- I want to have no shame when it comes to sex.
- I want to have sex with whomever I want, whether in a relationship or not.
- I want the focus to be on my pleasure as much as his.
- I want to try new things or at least feel uninhibited enough to try them if I choose.
- I want to feel spontaneous, not rigid or too planned out.
- I want to have sex with someone who is interested in finding out about my sexuality and how to please me.
- I want to feel free.
- I want to feel sexy.
- I want to have the confidence to go out and initiate the kinds of experiences I want.
- I want to be with a guy who enjoys sex as much as I do.
- I want to be with a guy who can't keep his hands off of me.
- I don't want to be like my mother.

Making this kind of a list is an important first step. I often have my clients take the list home and reflect on it in the days between sessions.

They can then add more stuff, cross out other stuff, and generally continue to clarify where they are coming from and where they want to go.

I'm a big believer in taking specific actions to change our thoughts and feelings—we can sit in the pose of Rodin's *Thinker* for ages and try to change our emotional state that way, but nothing, absolutely nothing, replaces changing our behavior.

As you can see, Olivia's list focuses much more on the present and future rather than the past. This is typical. When I ask people to think about these items, they usually focus on two particular things: identifying how they want to feel and on describing situations that are opposite from their current one. They usually don't know what they specifically want but are really good at determining what they don't. However, knowing what we don't want is often an important step in realizing what we do.

Taking into account the discussion above about comfort zone and anxiety, my client and I pick out one item—only one—from the right-hand column and agree on a specific behavior that would address that item. Also, we want to start with the low-hanging fruit to make our first steps feel even easier. For example, in Olivia's list, having the confidence to initiate new experiences is probably more of a low-hanging fruit than larger and more vague goals such as "I want to feel free," or "I want to feel sexy." Those will come with time, but we want to focus on the things more within our reach at the moment.

Here's another very good process exercise. Remember the comfort zone and anxiety diagram above? First, make a list of all the sexual things that fall within that inner circle, the comfort zone. List everything that comes to mind. The positions, the specific body parts, everything. Now consider the middle circle, the learning zone. What would you consider doing that's new but that would most likely be something you would do since it doesn't feel too far "out there" (the outer circle, panic zone) for you at the moment?

So what would "initiating a new experience" look like? Well, for one, it doesn't have to directly lead to sex right away either. Initiating a new experience at this stage could be as much as going out and buying a new outfit or starting with a workout regimen. Usually when it feels hard to initiate something in one area, it feels hard across the board. Later we can talk about more specifics when it comes to sex, such as specific fantasies and desires, but for now we want to be as concrete as possible to establish a feeling of forward progress and momentum. In Olivia's case, she identified that making some online contacts and going to a sex shop to look at toys and fetish gear was something that wouldn't be too provoking.

I'm a big believer in putting things down in writing. I often have my clients keep a journal where they work through certain assignments or put down their thoughts and feelings in a stream-of-consciousness kind of style. Numerous studies have shown the benefits of journaling.

For example, research has shown that journaling helps in externalizing problems so that individuals feel more of a sense of self-agency, a feeling of having more internal control.[3] Psychologist James Pennebaker has studied journaling, or expressive writing, extensively.[4] His studies have shown that journaling helps with a wide variety of human factors, such as bolstering the immune system, lowering blood pressure and stress, and improving sleep.[5]

Once we have done this kind of writing, this is a good time to take a look at what it takes now to convert the contemplation into action, in other words, to start making necessary behavioral changes. At this point, we have moved toward the *Preparation* stage.

One of the most common issues here that contributes to a feeling of ambivalence is the fear associated with change. It often blocks folks from making the leap from contemplation to preparation. It's one thing to think about changing, but doing it, well, that's a whole 'nother story. I have often found that making the leap is easier when we have a better understanding of the nature of our fears. As a popular twelve-step slogan goes, "Name it to tame it." So to stop letting our fears manage us and to instead learn to start managing our fears, we want to understand what these fears are and where they come from.

VISUALIZING A NEW YOU: LETTING GO OF FEAR

For simplicity's sake, I will break down fears into the three most common types that I see my clients struggling with. These are, in no particular order, (1) the fear of failing, (2) fear of the unknown, and (3) fear of emotions. These are all quite ubiquitous but can create devastating effects, and so I would like to briefly touch on each one in turn. And although they are uniquely different, they also have much in common.

Let's start with fear of failing. This fear is so common, it has a word to describe it—"atychiphobia." In the older heyday of psychoanalysis, a common way of seeing clients who were struggling to make progress was that they were simply resistant. This viewpoint assumes a kind of oppositional stance, with the client somehow working or fighting against the therapist to make change or progress. Rather than trying to push up against this so-called resistance, I take what I call a "pro-symptom" approach, which basically means that I want to try to understand what the benefits are of holding onto these problems or symptoms rather than discarding them at once. Rather than try to push someone into something he or she is not yet ready to do, I like to explore some incremental changes we can make without necessarily destabilizing things too rapidly for the client.

I often come across the fear of failing as a root cause of the kind of "stuckness" that folks can sometimes feel mired in. This is where people may typically experience the strongest sense of ambivalence—a part of them wants to get going and put things in motion, while another part feels it cannot move forward. It is this second part, the paralyzed part, toward which I want to address my interventions. Again, rather than seeing this part as resistant, I view it as a part that is trapped in fear, and as is often the case, it is the fear of failure. So when someone simply cannot get the wheels in motion to start on a new journey, invariably a fear of failure is underlying the ambivalence and feeling of being "stuck." This type of fear often comes up as performance anxiety. The fear of public speaking, the fear of test taking, or, yes, the fear of not being able to perform sexually often belies a more powerful fear of trying and failing, along with the shame that potentially comes from that failure. So the fear of failure is often tied into fears of feeling shame, which I will get into more in the next chapter.

Which leads to the second type of fear—the fear of emotions. A common root cause of diffuse anxiety that we cannot explain often lies in trying to suppress uncomfortable emotions, such as shame, grief, and anger. It is this suppression of emotions that may cause the symptomatology of anxiety. Here's a good way of understanding this: Let's say you are driving down the highway and somebody suddenly cuts you off and it feels so annoying. What might you do? You might honk your horn, yell, and/or make some comments. I'm not saying you should do these things, but these are things that you may conceivably do, and you probably won't feel any anxiety about doing so. But what if you were at work and your supervisor had just given you a bad performance review that you felt was unfair, and now you have to sit in a prolonged business meeting with this supervisor and a bunch of other people? What you really want to do is tell your boss how angry you are, but you can't allow yourself to do it because there will be repercussions—your job is on the line, you might not get that promotion, and so on. So what might you do? You might feel uncomfortable and grit your teeth, clench your fists, and tap your feet, trying to suppress your angry feelings. What does it look like? Yes, that's right—anxiety.

Anxiety doesn't necessarily have to be about negative feelings. It could be about positive feelings too. Folks who have undergone a lot of trauma may not trust in positive feelings because they've had the rug pulled out from under them one too many times, so they may start to feel anxious when they realize they feel fine. It may feel like "waiting for the other shoe to drop," and in these situations, the individual may self-sabotage in order to get the anxiety out of the way. This kind of chronic anxiety about emotions may play out with difficulties in interpersonal relationships and in achieving the feeling of intimacy and closeness with a lover or partner. Sometimes out-of-control behavior or performance issues are (unintentional) means of regulating levels of closeness.

Which finally leads us to the last fear, the fear of the unknown. Making any kind of personal changes exposes us to an element of the unknown, even if the change is for the best. What would it be like to be so vulnerable with another person? Well, we may be rejected or abandoned eventually; we simply don't know what to expect. This is the fear of the unknown. This fear may also contribute to the aforementioned feeling of "stuckness." A part of the individual may want to change, but that subjects the person to the unknown, to thinking, "Who will I be once this metamorphosis is complete?" It is a very scary thought.

The main point is that often when it comes to a feeling of being "stuck," somewhere lurking is one or more of the three main types of fears I have outlined above. By understanding the dynamics behind that feeling of anxiety, ambivalence, and paralysis, we can start to take some steps to make progress in spite of the fears that haunt us.

A moment ago I mentioned shame, and it truly is an iceberg, as it contributes significantly to that feeling of "stuckness" and anxiety and may even paralyze us from taking any action at all. I find that it is this process of understanding and coming to terms with emotions that may take the longest, but is often the most crucial part of the journey, a part that must be traveled through. As a result, I'm going to spend the entirety of the following chapter covering the work that my clients and I do to get through the emotional stumbling blocks and to the authentic sexual self, waiting on the other end.

BRIEF RECAP

The process of change overlaps with the process of coming out into our sexual identities. We go through distinct stages, often marked by anxiety and ambivalence, but that is normal and to be expected. During this discovery process, it helps to take an inventory of your beliefs and your desires while also taking stock of the specific types of fears you encounter.

7

THE AUTHENTIC SELF
Resolving Internal Shame

I am going to focus this chapter specifically on the core emotion of shame, since it wreaks so much havoc on all aspects of our lives, but in particular our sexuality. Shame can be highly nefarious, as it is one of those emotions that can become internalized as part of our identity. To understand why, let's take a look at the difference between two words that are often used interchangeably but are actually quite dissimilar—guilt and shame.

Guilt is an emotion that we experience when we feel bad about something we did. Shame, in contrast, is an emotion that is experienced as feeling bad about who we are. This self-identity aspect of shame makes it into a potentially highly problematic emotion. This is because sexuality, whether we are speaking about gender, orientation, or specific interests or behavior, is often experienced as a central, core aspect of one's personal identity. If we also experience a great deal of shame, since it touches upon our self-identity, it inevitably also affects the way we experience our sexuality. For this reason, folks struggling with any aspect of their sexuality also frequently struggle with the emotion of shame.

For many, shame is a very difficult emotion to experience head on, and so it is warded off so as to not have to be dealt with. And if we are not aware of it but it is still affecting us nonetheless, we may often find ourselves frozen or unable to move forward and have no idea why. As a result, I often find it helpful to bring the feeling of shame to conscious awareness so that we have access to it and can try to transform or mold it. But it's not only shame. In my experience, a lot of people struggle with identifying any emotions, let alone shame.

I often use a variety of specific techniques to help my clients understand their internal emotional world better. To do so, I primarily focus on individuals' somatic experience (experience of their body) in order to gain a better understanding of their emotional state.

Psychologist Silvan Tomkins, in his research on human emotions, identified nine main categories of affect, what he called his "affect theory."[1] According to him, these emotions were biologically driven and existed on a continuum from mild to severe. Later, researcher Paul Ekman, building on Tomkins's theory, identified specific facial expressions that accompanied each emotion.[2] These are the nine affects, listed with a low/high intensity label for each affect and accompanied by its biological expression.

Positive:

- Enjoyment/Joy—smiling, lips wide and out
- Interest/Excitement—eyebrows down, eyes tracking, eyes looking, closer listening

Neutral:

- Surprise/Startle—eyebrows up, eyes blinking

Negative:

- Anger/Rage—frowning, clenched jaw, red face
- Disgust—lower lip raised and protruded, head forward and down
- Dissmell (reaction to bad smell)—upper lip raised, head pulled back
- Distress/Anguish—crying, rhythmic sobbing, arched eyebrows, mouth lowered
- Fear/Terror—frozen stare, pale face, coldness, sweat, erect hair
- Shame/Humiliation—eyes lowered, head down and averted, blushing

Ekman later revised this list, adding more emotions, such as guilt, pride, relief, and amusement. Nevertheless, this list is a good starting point for anyone looking to gain a better sense of his or her emotional landscape. These nine affects are building blocks, like primary colors. The primary colors of red, yellow, and blue combine to form secondary colors. For example, red and blue combine to make purple; red and yellow make orange; and yellow and blue make green. The secondary colors then combine to make tertiary colors, and so on. Emotions are the same way. We obviously have many more than these nine emotions, but the more complex ones are built from these nine foundational ones.

If you take a look at this list, the first thing you'll recognize is that there's a heck of a lot more negative emotional possibilities than positive ones. Let's focus a bit more on these negative ones, since it is the negative emotions that cause the brunt of our difficulties, not the positive ones. Let's start out by eliminating a few of them—dissmell because it is contained to a specific context, and disgust because it is similar enough to anger/rage. What we are left with are four key emotions—anger/rage, distress/anguish (grief), fear/terror, and shame/humiliation. These four affects create the majority of our emotional havoc.

One important thing to remember about these emotions is that they are evolutionary—they are there to serve the purpose of helping our species survive. For example, anger helps us to assert ourselves, fear triggers the fight/flight response and serves to help us run away or defend ourselves, grief allows us to bond even closer after the loss of a loved one, and shame prevents us from hurting those around us. However, these feelings may often be instilled in us separately from any immediate purpose and block us from truly operating under our own free will.

Another crucial aspect about emotions and one that is also conveyed in the above list is that all emotions also inhabit our bodies. So, as an example, someone who is experiencing happiness smiles. A smile is simply an automatic contraction of a particular group of muscles in and around the face and lips. It is immediate, unconscious, and completely predicated on experiencing the emotion of joy. On the other hand, when we are sad, we frown; when we are angry, we may grit our teeth and clench our fists. And so on. These are only a few examples of the somatic component of our emotions.

Having an understanding of the connection between emotions and our bodies is essential, especially when it comes to the area of sexuality. Because the experience of sexuality is primarily an experience of our bodies and because our bodies are so closely aligned with and affected by our emotions, I have found that working through issues of sexuality often requires addressing important emotions that come up or stand in the way.

This is a chart that I hand out to my clients and ask that they fill out several times a day until the next session.

Let's start with the far left-hand column, "Situation." For this one, randomly check in at various points in the day and describe the situation in the moment. For example, you may be in the shower, preparing for a business meeting, driving to work, stuck on the train, whatever. Doesn't matter. Just capture the moment, and if you can't write it down that instant, remember it and write it down at the next opportunity you have.

Next is "Emotion." Use the list of the emotions Tomkins identified as a guideline. For example, if you feel annoyed, that is not an emotion on the list; the most appropriate synonymous emotion would be anger/rage. Really, most words we use to identify our emotions are euphemisms instead—annoyed, disappointed, frustrated, and other such words are all ways of describing low-level anger. If you don't feel anything, don't try to make it up to fit it into the emotion list. Writing "none" is fine.

The next column is "Physical Sensation." Here, write down whatever you happen to feel physically in the moment. This could be some sort of physical pain somewhere in the body or other sensations such as an itch, temperature sensations on the body, or signs of anxiety, such as "butterflies." Again, if you can't identify a sensation, don't force it; write "none" instead.

And finally, in the last column, write down your anxiety level from one to ten, with one designating no anxiety at all to the highest level of

Table 7.1.   Chart for Keeping Track of Feelings and Physical Sensations

Situation	Emotion	Physical Sensation	Anxiety (1–10)

ten. Fill out these columns without trying to figure out a connection. There is no right or wrong answer. Just do your best. At this point, I typically end with these exercises for the time being, without adding more homework, since I don't want to overload my clients. I only want to see them try it so that we can discuss it at the next session.

What I commonly find is that this is a deceptively difficult exercise for most. The reason is that most folks have no idea what they are feeling emotionally or in the body. And there's a specific reason for this. In order to cut ourselves off from our sexuality, we inevitably have to cut ourselves off from our feelings and our bodies. As a result, many of us walk through life as disembodied versions of our true selves. Whenever I work with someone who is experiencing a lack of sexual desire, difficulties with performance, or an inability to experience pleasure, assuming medical causes have been eliminated, there is often a strong element of the problem related to this kind of disembodiment.

A MOMENT OF ZEN: LEARNING TO BE MINDFULLY AWARE

At this point (typically in the next session or two), I introduce a few additional exercises that help people to gain greater self-awareness. The first one is called "grounding." Grounding is a mindfulness exercise that helps individuals to isolate awareness in each part of their body. Let's go through this step by step.

First, place yourself in a comfortable seated position with both feet planted firmly on the ground. Focus your attention on your feet. What do you feel? If you are wearing shoes, do you feel your feet inside your shoes? What do the inside of your shoes feel like? Do you feel the bottom of the floor? Is it hard or soft? Wood or carpeted? Do you feel any other sensations, such as heat or cold, dampness or dryness? Now move up your legs. Do you feel them on the inside of your pants? If your legs are exposed, what is the sensation of the air around your legs? Now your knees. Are they propped up at a ninety-degree angle to your feet? Do you feel any sensations there, any pain for example? And so on.

In this way, you make your way up to the very top of your head, moving through your waist and core, up your stomach and chest, through your arms and shoulders and on up through your neck and head. Take your time with each body part. The idea is not to rush. By doing this exercise, you are learning to focus your attention on your body and slowly develop more awareness of each area of your body.

By practicing this exercise several times a week, you will start to develop more full awareness of your bodily experience and sensations. Now let's take that somatic awareness and connect it to our emotions. Once I explain the grounding exercise to clients, I may ask them to go back to an earlier experience and feeling state from the grid (above). I will ask them to describe the situation again, asking questions at certain points to clarify for further detail. Once the individual is emotionally back in time to the past event, I'll ask them to describe what they feel.

They will then respond by stating an emotion such as anger or sadness. I'll ask, "How do you know?" This often brings up stumped expressions, followed by "What do you mean, how do I know?" It seems like a silly question, like the answer is obvious, but that's simply not the case. Typically clients will answer that they know because their brain is telling them so (or something like that).

I then respond that what they are describing is their *cognitive* awareness of their emotion, but can they identify what their emotion feels like in the body? So for example, if they say they are feeling anger, I ask "Where is it in the body?" Often, the person will say it's somewhere in the chest or neck or some other part of the upper body. "What does it feel like?" "Tight." Now we are getting closer.

Emotions are experienced in three distinct ways: (1) cognitively—you can think about and discuss the emotion; (2) somatically—you experience the emotion in the body; and (3) impulsively—you have a gut instinct to do something, such as punch someone if you are angry. An impulse is not cognitive because it is more like an urge rather than a thought process involving language.

I like to use the example of holes in a boat. Imagine that you have three holes, and water is spouting out onto the deck. The three holes represent cognition, somatic feelings, and impulses. If you cover up one hole, what happens? The water spouts out more strongly in the other two open holes. What if you cover up two holes? That's right, water just gushes forth from the one open hole. When we do not have access to all of our emotional experiences, we are likely to struggle too much with the remaining areas of emotional experience. For example, if we are disconnected from our bodies, we are much more likely to feel cognitively preoccupied (obsessive) or impulsive.

Here's another technique I use to address the cognitive piece. It's based on the psychological idea of *schemas* and the recent psychological research on *memory reconsolidation*. (I'll get to what that means in a moment.) A schema is literally defined as a "representation of a plan or theory."[3] Psychologically, this refers to the set of internalized beliefs, values, thoughts, and emotions associated with a particular situation or experience. These beliefs and thoughts and emotions are all bundled up so tightly together as to be indistinguishable, and so they all feel virtually automatic when a person finds himself or herself in the exact scenario that would trigger that schema.

Let's take a look at a specific schema as an example, one that extends beyond sexuality in order to provide a broader understanding. My client Gary came in for sexual anxiety but soon found out his anxiety was more global in nature. He had a very unstable childhood. His mother was erratic and most likely had an undiagnosed mental condition such as bipolar mood disorder and borderline personality; his father was never around. Gary's mother's erratic behavior meant he never knew what he could expect next, and he was always hypervigilant to prepare himself for the possibility of the rug being pulled out from under him at any moment. One time, for example, Gary's mother announced that she would be taking him to the town fair, but once they had all gotten into the car and were on their way, suddenly she found a reason to cancel her plans and return home, blaming it all on Gary. In young Gary's mind, he had no idea what had happened or what he had done; he only knew that once again, what he was counting on the most was destroyed on a whim by his mother.

This recollection came forth when Gary and I were discussing the anxieties he automatically experienced whenever he found himself trying to do something new, like start a new work project or a construction project at home. It didn't make sense to Gary that he would get anxious about these things; he excelled at work and was confident in his ability to perform most activities he set his mind to. But it was only when I brought up the concept of schemas that he was flooded with memories about his erratic mother. This train of thought resonated with Gary. It now made sense that he was met with a wave of anxiety every time he tried something new. It wasn't because he wasn't capable; it was simply because he had internalized a specific set of automatic thoughts and feelings that were reinforced every time he had to entrust his emotional well-being in doing something new with his mother.

To get to the exact belief system encapsulated by the schema, I ask my client to finish a sentence. In this case, I asked Gary to finish the following sentence "Trying something new is scary because_____." Without hesitation, Gary responded, "Because I know that somehow the rug will be pulled from under me." This statement implies a whole bunch of other beliefs including the following—"people cannot be trusted," "the world is an unsafe place," and "better not to expect anything so as to not be disappointed." It was easy for Gary to uncover these foundational assumptions after reflecting on the memories from his childhood that were triggered by our conversation.

In a moment, I'll get to how I help my clients to overcome and change these schemas, but for now I want to take this train of thought back to the realm of sexuality and take a look at the kinds of sexual schemas that I commonly see in my practice and that interfere with my clients' enjoyment of sex and their sexual functioning. For those of you following along by doing the exercises suggested within the book, you may have already uncovered some of these schemas through the exercise in chapter 6. A typical schema, for example, is the one written down by Olivia on the left-hand side of her sheet as the first thing she learned about sex, that sex is "dirty."

What do we mean by "dirty"? Just as in the schema described above, multiple implications are associated with this term. For one, dirty implies impurity; therefore, sexuality is somehow impure and so immoral. Because it is immoral, it may also be dangerous. Part of being immoral or dangerous is that it is also something that is just plain bad, maybe even evil, hardly something that one can or should enjoy. These are all beliefs that people may take with them into sexual encounters, especially if they've experienced sex-negative messaging from culture or particularly from their families.

Along with these foundational beliefs comes a set of automatic emotions, such as anxiety, guilt, fear, or shame. They are often experienced as so automatic as to be indistinct from the beliefs that create them. Earlier in this chapter, we took a look at how we can identify these emotions. But now we will examine how we can change the underlying beliefs on which they are built. To do so, however, we are going to take a slight detour and examine the latest developments in some ground-breaking new psychological research in the field of memory reconsolidation, which I alluded to earlier.

Memory consolidation refers to the process in the brain in which short-term memories are converted into long-term memories, which are then stored in the region of the brain called the hippocampus.[4] This is where our schemas, the very scripts from which our life's path is written, are contained. Because they are held in the regions of the brain that hold long-term memory, these schemas may feel ingrained and unalterable. The process of memory reconsolidation aims to retrieve these long-term memories and then reorganize them with new inputs so that these long-held schemas are reconsolidated again but in a different form from before.

This may all sound too technical or scientific, but it can better be understood with a simple example. Let's go back to Gary, who, as we saw, has been struggling with a schema in which the world is an unstable and dangerous place. By retrieving the old memories of his mother's erratic behaviors, we are able to add something else to them, perhaps another viewpoint or way of seeing things, so that when they are reconsolidated again, they are slightly altered by these new inputs introduced by the therapist. For example, if Gary were able to wrap his mind around and deeply understand that his mother's erratic behavior was not representative of all other people, these memories would then be reconsolidated not as examples of the sins of humanity but merely as examples of one person's (his mother's) struggles and limitations.

Joseph LeDoux, a psychology professor at New York University, and his colleagues conducted an experiment in which they showed that reactivating fear memories in humans allows them to then be updated with nonfearful information and then reconsolidated in a way that the fear response is eradicated.[5] They showed research participants a visual object and then paired it with mild electric shocks, conditioning the subjects to associate fear with that particular object. Then they reminded the subjects of the fear the following day but this time presented information that the object was safe. The researchers found that this was superior to classical extinction (which is the common exposure process most people are familiar with) because the fear completely disappeared, while it was merely reduced with extinction techniques. In other words, rather than focusing on exposing subjects to the feared object as a means of overcoming fear, they found that they could completely eliminate the fear by focusing instead on the *memories* of the object.

In another experiment, LeDoux and associates created fear responses in lab rats by associating certain sounds with electric shocks.[6] They then retrieved the fear response a number of days later by playing the sounds again, but this time they injected a chemical called anisomycin, a protein-synthesis inhibitor, that prevented the brain from reforming new memory connections after retrieving them. Those rats that were injected with anisomycin no longer experienced the fear response. In other words, this research demonstrates that long-term memories are somehow broken down during the retrieval process, which makes them more labile for new information. When the anisomycin blocked the formation of new memories associated with the electric shock, the rat's memoires were reconsolidated without the previous fear response.

I don't mean to get too technical here, but my point is that cutting-edge psychological research shows that old beliefs and schemas can be changed during the sensitive process of bringing up old memories to the forefront. Let's examine how this process can be used for psychotherapeutic benefit and then specifically to help break free of old and unnecessary psychological dogmas that prevent us from truly experiencing sexual authenticity.

To this effect, psychotherapist Bruce Ecker expands on the nascent psychological insight of memory reconsolidation research by introducing some new psychotherapeutic techniques that he calls *coherence therapy*.[7] In coherence therapy, Ecker seeks to introduce contradictory information at the very moment that old, long-standing memories are recalled. In this way, he is trying to create a dissonance between the old memory and the new information that would force the client's mind to choose the option that reestablishes internal congruence.

In Gary's case, the technique may look something like this. At the moment that Gary recalls an example of his mother's erratic behavior, I may ask him whether he ever remembers an example in which his mother carried out something she promised. If Gary can bring this to recollection, then it can change the fundamental belief that his mother was *always* unstable and erratic. Acknowledging this would force Gary to challenge his conclusions about his mother and, most importantly, challenge his underlying schema that since his mother was always untrustworthy, it means all people are always untrustworthy.

Another way that I could use coherence therapy techniques is to directly address the schema itself. So, for example, I may have Gary remember times in which new events or people were experienced as fun and pleasurable rather than bogged down in anxiety. I may have him create a new statement such as "Sometimes new experiences are fun and pleasurable" and then have him write it out on an index card. Then I would have him recall the negative memory while rereading the index card, forcing his mind into a cognitive dissonance. It may also work the other way around, whereby Gary would write down the schema he is trying to change on the index card and then bring it out at the moment he experiences events in his life that contradict that schema.

And here is the important essence of this exercise. New learning is guided by several distinct psychological processes, most notably selection bias and reinforcement. I will go into greater detail on this in a following chapter, but the main point is that we form our conclusions about life from a limited array of experiences and then ignore all other experiences that disconfirm our original beliefs. Through the process articulated by Bruce Ecker in his coherence therapy, we attempt to alter long-held beliefs by introducing disconfirming evidence at the moment that the old memories we are trying to influence are recalled.

Let's take these principles to the sexual realm. Gary has learned to challenge his global beliefs about the uncertainty and dangers of the world. He can now apply the same thought process and techniques to his sexual experience. In addition to everything else, he has learned that sex is unnatural and unsafe, so he has to hold off from enjoying sexual pleasure. When he can remind himself of instances where he has indeed experienced sex in a safer or more neutral way, he can begin to contrast these experiences with his negative learned schema. Sometimes it's necessary to create new experiences in order to have the lived experience with which to confront pathogenic beliefs.

SOMATIC INTERVENTIONS

In my experience, combining memory and physical (somatic) experiences can be a very powerful intervention. Let's examine what that may look. In the case of Gary, he has specific troubling memories from the past as well deep shame about his sexuality in the present. Going back to shame, this emotion is often one of the core difficulties that prevents us from experiencing authentic sexuality.

Psychologist Peter Levine developed a psychotherapeutic intervention called somatic experiencing, which he modeled from his examination of animals in the wild.[8] Levine started by asking himself the following question—why is it that animals in the wild never develop posttraumatic stress disorder (PTSD) symptoms like humans or domestic animals? It's a profound question because if any creature should logically develop PTSD, it is a wild animal because it is constantly fighting for its survival. It's the law of the jungle—eat or be eaten. So wild animals must constantly be on the vigil, looking out for predators. And if they do survive an attack, why is it that they are seemingly able to carry on without any noticeable disturbances from their near-death experiences?

Levine found his answer by reviewing tapes of animals that had just survived predator attacks. What he found was that once the animal is in the clear, free from any imminent dangers, it goes into what looks like convulsions. The animal literally shakes out its fear until it has gotten the emotion out of its system. In one poignant video that can be seen on YouTube, a polar bear that was running away from researchers, who had shot it with a stun gun, goes into a full convulsion once it awakes and then moves on with its life as if nothing had happened.[9]

Conversely, humans and domestic animals never have the opportunity to do so. In other words, they internalize their emotions, and the painful, disturbing emotions remain lodged in the body. Indeed, research on trauma suggests that PTSD symptoms are mitigated if an individual has a chance to move his or her body during the traumatic event rather than feel immobilized in one place.[10] Some trauma researchers believe that many witnesses of the crumbling of the Twin Towers during the September 11, 2001, attacks were spared from the worst of the trauma due to the feeling of self-agency of being able to run away.[11]

This process appears to be confirmed with research on the beta blocker medication propranolol, brand name Inderal, which is used to combat high blood pressure and heart rhythm disorders. Propranolol is often used off-label by performers, speakers, and other individuals who may face performance anxiety due to its ability to dim the nervous system.[12] In other words, someone who takes propranolol is going to experience a reduction in nervous system activation, to the point where it becomes impossible to experience the typical performance anxiety jitters such as shaky hands and trembling voice.

Anyway, propranolol has been tested with war veterans that had just experienced a traumatic event. When it was administered immediately after the traumatic event, the veterans experienced a significant reduction in future PTSD symptoms.[13] In another study, eleven patients were administered propranolol after trauma and studied for several months, with a marked decrease in PTSD type symptoms.[14] In addition, other studies have found that propranolol helps deal with traumatic memories even for those folks who have experienced trauma for a number of years.[15]

Why I bring up the discussion of propranolol is that it gives us some very concrete evidence that trauma originates in the body. In other words, because propranolol reduces nervous system activation, and hence the body's response to fear, such as shakiness, trembling, and so on, this may suggest that PTSD doesn't have a chance to gain a foothold because the body is shielded from the brunt of the fear response. This ties back into Levine's animal studies in which animals that are able to shake out the fear response don't develop PTSD. So we again come back to the body and the way it handles emotions, in this case specifically, fear. If it can't discharge the fear, then as research suggests, perhaps we can combat PTSD by preventing the body's response to fear in the first place.

I am introducing all these ideas as a means of illustrating two key concepts—(1) that emotions are stored in the body and (2) that we can start to gain some sense of mastery of these emotions by addressing our interventions toward the body. So what does such a typical intervention look like?

First, what I want to do is help my client bring up a memory that will elicit the chosen emotion he or she is struggling with or looking to work on. We want the emotion to be real, as much in the room as possible, rather than a thought experiment or intellectual exercise. This is where I combine the emotional, somatic, and memory (see above) components in my work. A most important consideration here is to ensure that the memory is within what's called the *window of tolerance*. In other words, the memory has enough emotional valence that it brings up the required emotion, but the emotions produced are not intense enough to overstimulate the individual.

Let's take my client Neil, for example, who came to me with a desire to explore bisexuality with his wife but was unable to do so because of his great shame about his desires. In one of my initial sessions with Neil, I asked him to come up with a memory of the first time he remembered becoming aware of his bisexuality. Sometimes these memories are fuzzy, sometimes razor sharp. In Neil's case, he remembered being twelve years old and surfing the web, finding himself drawn to pictures of naked men as well as women. In this case, his memory was one of curiosity and excitement rather than shame, and that's very typical. Indeed, shame is never something that's created in a vacuum; shame is something that is done to us. It takes an outside source to shame us. And as a result, shame is often mixed with anger due to feeling violated by the persons or institutions that shamed us.

I asked Neil to hold that memory of his excitement for a moment. To check in with his body to see how it responds to the memory. This is the "grounding" exercise I introduced earlier in this chapter as a building block. Neil said he felt a surge of energy moving up his spine and a tingling sensation indicative of nervous excitement. I asked Neil to imagine the energy coursing up his body and then to check in with his body language, his posture. When he felt the energy rise up, what is his body's natural inclination to do? Neil said he felt expansive, like he wanted to lift his chin and open up his shoulders. That's good, I said, let's just stay with that for a moment.

I let a few minutes pass. At this point I simply want Neil to be comfortable associating certain physical experiences with specific emotions. I then ask Neil to remember a time where he felt uncomfortable, perhaps shamed by his sexuality. The memories rush in. One specific memory came to the forefront. In his mind's eye, Neil is changing in the locker room. He remembers vividly that this was a time where he was just entering puberty and was starting to sprout some hairs around his genitals. There were some older boys in the corner of the locker room, about sixteen or seventeen years old. They were just starting to undress and were taking their time, socializing and talking about whatever but not really undressing yet. Neil was very curious to see what their penises looked like. Were they full of a thick patch of pubic hair? How big were they? Were they uncircumcised?

Neil went slowly, poring over every detail. It was as if the vision was happening right before us, in real time. I asked Neil how he felt. He said he was still in touch with that nervous anticipation from before. Neil took his time getting dressed, always peeking over his shoulder to see if the older boys were naked yet. Damn, it was taking so long. Finally, Neil peeked around one last time as one of the boys was just about to pull down his underwear. The boy noticed Neil, and as their eyes locked, an angry scowl appeared on the boy's face. Neil turned around quickly in sheer embarrassment and shame, finished dressing hurriedly, and rushed out of the locker room without turning back. I could see Neil's face turn crimson as he was describing this, his shoulders hunching over with every wince.

I let him sit with these emotions for a short while, but not too long, as I want to make sure that the memory is not overstimulating. So, to that effect, I observe his body language and his breathing patterns to gauge where he is in his internal experience. And then I ask Neil what he is experiencing in the moment. "Shame, so much shame," he says. "I was found out," he continues, "I feel so creepy and dirty."

"Okay, you have comingled shame with your early experiences of your sexual desires," I say. "And now what we are going to do is start to disentangle the two."

I ask Neil how he knows that he is experiencing shame. He says he feels a sinking feeling in his chest. I remark that he indeed does feel sunken in—his chin and shoulders have collapsed inward. I reiterate that this not meant as a judgment, simply as an observation in which we are both working together to remain curious and understand his subjective experiences.

At this point, I ask Neil to remember that feeling of excited energy flow that he experienced earlier in the session. That state of energetic arousal in which he found himself in excited anticipation of sexual discovery. If you went back to that feeling, I ask, what changes would you make in your body posture. He seems confused for a moment, but I coach him along. "Remember you mentioned that energy flow up your spine, well what were your head and shoulders doing in that situation?" I ask.

Neil looks around at both of his shoulders and cracks a knowing smile. "Well, for one, I would lift my head and roll back my shoulders," he chuckles. "Good. Let's roll back our shoulders together," I say, and I make the shoulder-rolling motion with him. We are in this together.

"Now how do you feel?" I ask.

"Better, much better," he replies.

"Good, now hold that feeling. What is it like, do you still feel that sinking feeling in your pit?"

"No, it's gone."

"That's right, it's impossible for your body to be expansive yet sinking at the same time."

I can see the wheels turning in Neil's mind. "What are you thinking?" I ask.

"This is just wild. I had no idea I could start to change the way I feel so quickly."

"We want to hold on to this feeling," I add. "Just stay with it. Stay with it a while. There is no rush. When you are ready, I want you to start to reintroduce your shameful memory. But slowly. And as you do it, I want you to make a point of keeping your body language as open and expansive as it is currently."

Neil takes his time and in a few minutes he tells me he's back in the memory. Back in that locker room. Now I ask him to replay the memory again, but this time staying in touch with his expansive physical self. This time as he goes through it, the memory feels different. Less passive. Less victimizing. And less shameful. In fact, there is a boldness that Neil begins to feel as he is sitting right there in the stall at age twelve.

"There's nothing wrong with being curious about those boys' genitals," he says. "The problem wasn't with me. It was the way that boy made me feel. He was the one with the problem, not me."

That's the first step in decoupling sexuality from shame.

AWARENESS

As you can see, self-awareness is a great part of this process. To that effect, I often trumpet the importance of mindfulness to my clients in helping them to resolve a number of sexual difficulties. For most, it's not easy to put a mindfulness or meditation practice into effect because there are so many obstacles and distractions that get in the way during the course of our busy lives. In addition, many people give up prematurely because taking out time throughout the day to put a meditation practice into place feels like hard work, without any concrete results or metrics to be able to point to at the very beginning. Indeed, it takes a while to see specific results, and by that time, many people have already moved on. It is well known by meditation teachers that dropout rates (for sticking with it long term) are quite high.[16]

As a result, I am constantly scouring for more resources that would allow my clients to experience a more seamless introduction to mindfulness. Here, I'm going to introduce a few basic tools, and then I want to explain in a little more detail what the quality of our focus and awareness specifically has to do with sexuality. I have learned that if my clients better understand the how and why, it helps them to dive in with a renewed sense of purpose.

One of the best tools out there is a completely free app called Headspace.[17] It was developed by a former Tibetan monk, Andy Puddicombe, and takes the user through a guided ten-minute meditation each day. It is both sequential (it builds on the previous day) and motivating (Andy's voice is both upbeat and soothing), so users have the feeling of having the personal touch of individual guidance. Like I said, the app is completely free, as are the first ten days of sessions, but then individuals have the choice of paying a nominal fee for more content that will guide them through a whole year's worth of sequential training.

In my experience, some people really take well to this app, while others still struggle to stay motivated. For those who specifically need more immediate feedback and metrics to stay on point, I recommend the intervention of new technology, specifically an EEG (electroencephalogram) headband called Muse. This headband, when connected to its accompanying meditation app, records brainwaves while the user meditates and gives instantaneous feedback when the mind starts to experience tension by producing the noise of howling winds and choppy waves.[18] While the mind is calm, the user hears the sounds of a soft breeze, rolling waves, and chirping birds. At the end of the exercise, users can see the results of their session, specifically what percentage was spent calm as opposed to anxious. Muse will set you back three hundred dollars, but I think it's an excellent tool for those who need more feedback and metrics to stay consistent. The one thing about Muse, though, is that it doesn't train you to practice mindfulness but rather more of a focused meditation, but I would still highly recommend it.

Now let's get to one of the main issues I want to discuss—types of focus and awareness. While researching EEG technology, I discovered the work of Les Fehmi, a pioneering psychologist in the area of neurofeedback. He was conducting research on techniques to stimulate the production of alpha waves (the kind of electrical activity generated by the brain when relaxed) and stumbled on a certain state of consciousness that immediately sent the brain into alpha wave production, which he termed "open focus."[19] To grasp the concept of open focus, we must first understand the four kinds of focus that Dr. Fehmi uncovered. These types of focus exist on two different continuums and when combined create a type of grid consisting of four distinct awareness states. Let's take a look at the illustration below.

The first continuum of focus types is narrow versus diffuse. When we are in narrow focus, our attention is placed on small details, while in diffuse focus, we are able to soak in a broader spectrum of senses. The best way to understand this is to visualize the difference between a zoom and a wide-angle camera lens. While looking through a zoom lens, we see clear details of the object of our attention, but everything else in the background is blurry and obscure. While peeking through a wide-angle lens, both foreground and background are clearly visible, although we are not seeing depth of field.

Next we have objective versus immersed focus. While in objective focus, we are outside the object, and we are analyzing it like a specimen that is foreign to us, outside our subjective experience. While immersed, we are inside the experience, feeling merged or "at one" with the subject of our awareness. So in summary, narrow versus diffuse can be better understood as zoom versus wide angle, while objective versus immersed is more outside of versus merged with.

By combining these four focus types into a grid, we get four categories of awareness: narrow objective, narrow immersed, diffuse objective, and diffuse immersed. In brief, narrow objective is when we are narrowly focused on some small detail or item of study (for example, studying for a test); narrow immersed is when we are still focused on something specific but we feel more immersed in rather than separate from the object of focus (riding a bike); diffuse objective is when we are more holistically focused on an object (observing a painting or panora-

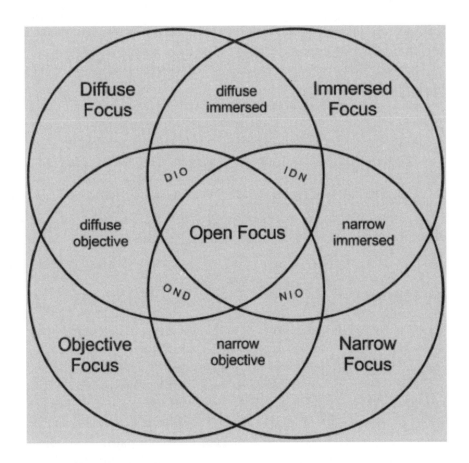

Figure 7.1. Fehmi's Styles of Attention. *Courtesy of Kurt Vega*

ma); and finally diffuse immersed is when we are completely engaged with all of our senses (orgasm, religious ecstasy, etc.).

Dr. Fehmi argues that most of our waking lives we are stuck in narrow objective. Indeed, we are almost trained that way by society—go to school, study for tests, specialize in a certain subject area, attend to specific performance metrics, and so on. This is where we also get stuck in a number of maladies, specifically somatic and anxiety-related complaints. When we are trained to go through our lives in narrow objective focus, it is hard to switch that off. And one of the areas that we get the most stuck in is the area of sexuality. Inevitably, when someone is struggling with some sexual issue, that individual is approaching sex from a narrow objective focus. Specifically, that individual, while engaging or thinking about sex, is preoccupied with a narrow set of issues (erections, for example) and spectating (observing in a detached manner) one's performance while having sex. It's a recipe for disaster.

The awareness exercises we have discussed train us to enter into more of this kind of "open focus." As I've detailed in this chapter, I provide my clients with exercises to expand their focus to the entire range of their immediate experience. In short, what mindfulness aims to accomplish is to help individuals switch from a narrow objective focus that distances them from connecting to their sexual selves to a more diffuse immersed focus that allows them to merge more fully with their entire spectrum of sensations.

So far we've been contemplating and preparing. Now let's put all of these principles into action!

BRIEF RECAP

Shame is one of the most primary problematic emotions. All emotions also reside in the body. The way we interact with the world is through a complex interweaving of thoughts, feelings, and beliefs—what is called a schema. Through mindfulness exercises, we develop a closer aware-ness of our bodies as well as our thoughts and emotions. Once we are aware of our schemas, we can utilize the visualization, body-based, and cognitive exercises discussed in this chapter to diminish their intensity.

8

GET YOUR SEXY ON

Exploring New Horizons

Now that we've covered the internal blocks of our thoughts and emotions, it's time to ready ourselves for action. But as we've seen in our study of the stages of change, often we are still met with an internal resistance that prevents us from moving forward. In this chapter, we'll take a look at the different interventions we can utilize to get our asses in gear and out of a place of "stuckness."

But first, let's take a quick recap of what we've covered so far. In the previous chapter, we introduced the idea of the schema, the mix of thoughts, emotions, and beliefs that we have about any particular situation. Let's visualize what this looks like and then add in the central topic of this chapter, behavior (actions), to see how they relate to our schemas.

Imagine three layers (figure 8.1), in which the core holds the emotions, the middle layer is our cognitions, which includes both thoughts and beliefs, and the outer layer is behavior.

In this model, emotions are always at the core. That's because emotions are more foundational to our experience of humanity than thoughts or behaviors. Why do I say this? Well, let's take a look at a little newborn baby. How does the baby communicate? Through its feelings. In other words, it cries when it is sad, tired, wet, or hungry, and it smiles when it feels content. A caregiver gets to understand what a baby is trying to communicate through the vocal intonations of the

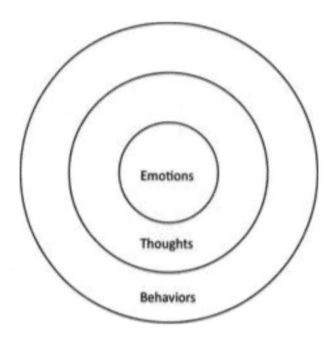

Figure 8.1.   Connection between Emotions, Thoughts, and Behaviors

baby that convey its emotions to the caregiver. So we are wired to connect with others through our emotions from day one.[1]

Thoughts, on the other hand, come later because they require language.[2] Here's an experiment to illustrate this point. Try to think of something, let's say, for example, make a to-do list in your head about things you need to do tomorrow. Good. Now how did you create that to-do list in your thoughts? What language did you use? Were you able to construct your thoughts without the use of language? If you try this experiment, you'll discover that thoughts exist only within the context of language. No language, no thoughts. No, we may still have ideas, we may have impulses and instincts and so on. Babies have instincts. And animals have instincts. But neither babies nor animals have thoughts because they don't possess the language in which to think. Okay, maybe some animals have a form of language, such as dolphins, but you get the point.

So going back to the illustration, emotions lie in the center, then thoughts, and I've placed behaviors as the outer layer, because that's the low-hanging fruit. What I mean by that is that typically our behaviors are influenced by our emotions and thoughts. You will most likely do very different things if you wake up feeling happy and optimistic versus sad and pessimistic. Heck, you might not even get out of bed if you feel too sad. So that's a clear example of emotions and thoughts influencing behavior, not the other way around. (But behaviors can also influence thoughts and feelings. I'll get to that in a moment.)

The reason I call behaviors the low-hanging fruit is that since they are usually a by-product of deeper internal processes, they are the most amenable to change. In other words, it's easier to change one's behavior than one's thoughts or feelings. Not easy, just easier.

So in this model, the internal layers influence the outer layers. But the exact opposite also is true. Changing thoughts can change emotions, and changing behaviors can change both thoughts and emotions. In this way, one change in the system can change the other parts of the system as well. It's merely most commonly the case that influence rolls from the core outward, but with mindful intentionality, the exact opposite can also be true.

This has been demonstrated numerous times through controlled research experiments. Let's take a simple behavioral change, such as pushing oneself to smile even if one doesn't feel happy. In one study, researchers at the University of Kansas asked 169 participants to hold chopsticks in their mouth in a way that simulated either a neutral expression or a smile while engaging in stressful tasks; those who smiled exhibited lower heart rates and increased positive feelings.[3]

In another study, twenty-five females, half of whom were administered a botox injection that prevented frowning, took a depression and anxiety questionnaire.[4] Those who were unable to frown reported feeling happier and less anxious even though they did not feel any more attractive, suggesting that their mood was lifted due to smiling more often. A third study found that individuals who frowned during unpleasant painful procedures were more likely to experience more pain.[5]

My point in all this is that there's never a right time to take action or make a move. We don't have to wait until our emotions have been worked through and our thoughts are aligned. In fact, the opposite is true. Often, we continue to evolve in our thoughts and emotions based on the behaviors that we choose. It is this intentional behavior that may often lead us to a "corrective emotional experience" that brings us the most transformative change.

DIPPING A TOE IN: OVERCOMING INITIAL ANXIETY

So you are ready to get started. You've identified your beliefs, comfort levels, and anxiety points as part of a process of contemplation. You've learned to work through anxiety and shame that can prevent you from moving into action. But, but . . . wait, something is still wrong. No matter what, you can't seem to be able to just let loose . . . and "let go." I'm sure anyone reading this book has heard someone close to them say (or has said it himself or herself) something like, "I just need to let go."

At this point you may tell yourself, "I could have the greatest sex and finally be me . . . if I could just let go."

If only it were that easy.

As a therapist, I know that many of my clients can relate to that idea. Let's face it, though—in our modern society, it is very difficult to "just let go." We are constantly driven by myriad pressures, both internal and external: the need to succeed, the need to compete with others for social status and gain, the need to pay bills, the need to save money, the need to raise kids, and so on. All train us into a constant state of vigilance and pressure. It never ends. And we can't let go.

And of course, as we've learned in the first part of this book, society is set up so that we are incentivized to not let go, no matter how strongly we may desire to. And, as you may have already noticed, this idea of letting go or not is also closely tied into that recurring bogeyman, anxiety. At its root is an element of "holding on" that I think is a fundamental aspect of anxiety.

When I ask highly anxious people about what they experience, they'll often mention that their anxiety feels almost like a much-needed friend, as if it were their one last firm grasp on reality, that their anxiety helps them feel alive, and that if they abandoned the anxiety, they would "fall apart." In this way, anxiety, like glue, is the one thing that keeps them intact. For folks who are constantly "holding on," learning to "let go" or "surrender" is a key component of mental health (and sexual) recovery.

Just as society at large prohibits us from letting go, a number of social institutions exist at least in part as a means of providing individuals with a structured and safe means of letting go, or "surrendering." Think of religion, for example. For Evangelicals, it is not enough to believe in God; one must also accept Jesus as one's savior.

SURRENDERING INTO OUR SEXUALITY: ON THE IMPORTANCE OF LEARNING TO LET GO

Let's take a closer look at that for a moment. From a psychological standpoint, appointing a personal savior is akin to shifting responsibility, agency, and choice onto that other entity, the savior. In effect, it absolves the individual from the anxiety of living in a world predominantly consisting of gray areas and self-agency. There is no longer a need to "hold on" when one has a savior—all the angst is now on the shoulders of the savior—and the individual, by "surrendering" to the savior, is able to finally now "let go." I think this is a big aspect of the appeal of organized religion for many folks.

Same thing for twelve-step groups. One of the first steps is to surrender to a higher power. Step 1 is to admit powerlessness; step 2 is to believe that a higher power can bring the individual to sanity; and step 3 is to turn one's will and life over to the higher power. Sounds a lot like surrender. No conclusive studies attest to the efficacy of twelve-step groups, but it is very clear that many folks are highly drawn to these concepts and feel a tremendous sense of relief from going through these initial steps.[6]

I think that these concepts of "holding on" and "surrender" are highly instrumental in understanding the connection between sexuality and psychology. Folks who enter treatment with sexual difficulties such as erectile dysfunction or delayed ejaculation often have difficulty with letting go, especially in the presence of another person. Individuals who struggle with sexual inhibition experience much of the same. I often explore concepts such as what it means to be vulnerable, to be exposed with another human being.

In many ways, to enjoy sex and achieve orgasm, we have to be able to let go and surrender in the present moment. To surrender to whatever may come next. To surrender to another human being. It can bring up a lot of anxiety, but that's something that needs to get worked through in therapy. Through role play, some folks can mindfully explore these psychological elements during sexual exploration. I'll get more into that in the next chapter. For example, to liven things up, some couples may incorporate blindfolds or light bondage to play around with these areas that touch on core issues of trust and vulnerability. When blindfolded or tied, we consensually place ourselves in a position of dependency from which we can explore the feelings that arise. How does it make one feel to depend on one's partner? Does it feel thrilling? Terrifying? Are we able to let go in the moment?

Or for others, sexual surrender is not a means of experimentation but a tried and true way to finally actually let go. Maybe it is their only way of letting go in the world. With bills, kids, relationships, and career all intruding on serenity, sexual submission may be the only way they readily have of surrendering to the moment and just letting go.

Some things to think about. "Letting go" is a big issue for many. We all need to be able to sometimes "let go." Sexual expression is one of the few areas that we can practice, experiment with, and test our psychological limits. For many, it is a means of establishing mental equilibrium through the mindful exploration of consensual surrender. But to surrender, we need to change our thinking.

To this effect, one of the first things I want to do to help my clients is to help them identify their thinking patterns. We've talked about schemas in the previous chapter. Here, I'll look at a specific aspect of thinking that may paralyze us from taking steps to move forward, what I call "outcome-oriented" thinking versus "process-oriented" thinking. Outcome-oriented thinking is literally what it sounds like . . . when we get ahead of ourselves and focus exclusively on the outcome. This is the default for folks with anxiety, and it's never a positive outcome that's in mind. And it only makes the anxiety worse. This kind of outcome-oriented approach is what results in performance anxiety and other sexual hangups.

Think about a time when you got anxious about having to make a speech or presentation or perhaps a sports experience where the outcome of the game depended on your next move. If you were to take an outcome-oriented approach in that situation, what might you do? You might, for example, think about how embarrassing it would be if you messed up; how the crowd or audience would laugh at you or judge you internally for your failings. They might not say so, but they won't think very highly of you once you are done. Sound familiar? This kind of outcome-oriented thinking always leads to a spike of anxiety that we continue to reinforce by dwelling on the outcome.

Process-oriented thinking, on the other hand, focuses more on the minute-to-minute process of completing the task rather than jumping the gun and going right to the outcome. Rather than focusing on what the audience thinks, an individual with a process-oriented approach would instead be thinking about the material more closely. The individual, for example, might think about what kind of audience will be listening, what their learning needs are, and what kind of message the individual wants to broadcast. The focus would be on learning the material and considering how it could be conveyed in a way that would be most readily digested by the audience. These are all examples of process-oriented thinking. This kind of approach serves to lessen, rather than intensify, feelings of anxiety because it bypasses the usual catastrophic thinking and instead immerses the individual in his or her present-moment experience.

Moving this into the sexual arena, an individual with an outcome-oriented approach would be thinking about the end game only—things like erections, orgasms, and the like—and usually imagining worst-case outcomes, such as shame and humiliation. Instead, I help my clients take on a process-oriented approach by focusing more on pleasure than erections, connection over orgasms. If an individual is enjoying the process, the rest will often take care of itself without the need for prompting.

Another stumbling block is that a lot of sexual advice out there urges us to be very mindful of the needs of our lovers, to be empathic, selfless, and attuned. If we can only satisfy all of our partner's needs, good sex will take care of itself. It's all nonsense. Sexuality actually requires a high degree of selfishness and ruthlessness to make it work. This is an issue that confuses many because it goes so much against the grain of what we are taught about human relationships.

Yes, making a relationship work requires attunement. It requires selflessness. If we want to make our partner feel special, we may wake up early in the morning before them to make breakfast. To make them feel understood, we will listen with an empathic ear, ask questions, provide comfort. We make them feel valued when we remember important dates and anniversaries. We make sure to compromise in some ways and give in in other areas that are more important to the other person.

All of that needs to disappear in the bedroom.

Folks who struggle with their own sense of sexual self often find themselves preoccupied with the needs and thoughts of others. That is wonderful in most relationships. It's a killer in the bedroom. There is probably nothing less arousing than having a partner who is constantly wondering whether they are "doing things right." There is equally nothing less arousing than a partner who is too afraid of asserting his or her sexual needs for fear of offending or hurting the other person. Sex is not for the timid.

Good sex occurs when both partners are focused on getting their needs met. Their needs. Not the needs of their partner. But by focusing on their own needs, an amazing and counterintuitive thing happens. The other person gets more of his or her needs met as well. Yes, when both people are selfishly and ruthlessly pursuing their sexual needs, fireworks happen. Often, the other person gets more aroused by seeing his partner totally caught up in the moment, and that is a motivator for getting his own sexual needs met as well. It becomes a virtuous cycle, in that each person feeds off the other's sexual intensity, each collaborating to selfishly pursue their sexual pleasure.

I often have to teach and nudge my clients to learn to be a little bit more sexually selfish in the bedroom. Indeed, in this sense, selfishness is in itself the act of letting go. They have often been taught to be mindful and respectful of the needs of others. They have been taught that it is wrong to be selfish and self-serving. They may have grown up worrying about hurting others or how their actions may affect those around them. And that is all great. Outside of the bedroom. Worrying about the needs of others kills sexual desire. Sex is the one area of life where I encourage my clients to become ruthless. And they find that rather than hurting their partners, they are actually helping them by showing them that they too can get their needs met in the bedroom.

GET YOUR ACT TOGETHER: MOVING TOWARD PLEASURE

Let's start to put this all together. On one hand, we have the anxieties that pose a block to moving forward, and on the other hand, we have the need to prioritize our desires, to get in touch with what drives us to be ruthless in going after our sexual needs. I find a very helpful framework at this point to be a therapeutic approach called acceptance and commitment therapy, or ACT. ACT was developed by psychologist Steven Hayes in the 1980s as an alternative to more dominant cognitive approaches such as cognitive behavioral therapy (CBT).[7] By combining mindfulness and Eastern philosophical traditions, ACT aims to accept uncomfortable thoughts and feelings rather than challenge or combat them. In addition, it aims to help an individual get in touch with his or her values and desires and move in that direction.

In describing this to clients, I compare it with the poles of a magnet. We all know that the magnet has two poles—negative and positive. I compare the negative pole with the uncomfortable thoughts and feelings that arise when we try to step outside our comfort zone (chapter 6). When we succumb to these feelings, we live in our fears, and our behavior becomes marked by avoidance, the avoidance of pain. The positive pole, however, is hedonic. It represents the pursuit of pleasure. Numerous studies show that mental distress is often correlated to experiential avoidance.[8] Indeed, as I've discussed at numerous points earlier in this book, one of the most important ways of changing how we feel is to take concrete steps toward pleasure, even if it is as seemingly small as practicing cracking a smile.

Remember Olivia's list from chapter 6? Let's revisit it here for a moment. What we are doing by making such a list is to clearly differentiate between these two poles—the pole of fear and avoidance and the pole of pleasure seeking (hedonism). When we notice that discomfort arises when we take a firm step forward, we simply want to notice it and realize that it is simply a thought or a feeling and not an absolute truth. Then we turn our attention toward making contact with our desire for pleasure. Remember, we've already done a lot of mindfulness work in simply noticing and becoming aware of what we think and feel. This is where it really becomes handy. By doing all of this groundwork, we have gradually developed a relationship with our internal selves, whereby we have the choice to soothe, tolerate, or discard our thoughts and feelings rather than feel controlled by them. This sense of control of our thoughts and feelings rather than avoidance I describe as a "leaning in" that I will go into in further detail in chapter 9.

As we bring our attention toward the positive pole, toward pleasure seeking and hedonism, we want to imagine what this pleasure may feel like, what it is that will motivate us to drive forward. Here we get in touch with our deeper values, our deeper identities, the things that hold the most meaning for us. This is a good time to continue the journaling. For some, this may come easier, as they find the exercise of noticing anxious thoughts and feelings but diverting attention to pleasure very liberating, unleashing a current of creative desire. For others, that creative drive has been suppressed so long that they still need a little help, a little push to be able to wrap their mind around seeing themselves as hedonic, pleasure-seeking beings. They may have developed a self-identity or narrative that blinds them from even being able to imagine themselves in such a way.

A NEW NARRATIVE

Truly, we do need to feel spontaneous and flexible enough to try new things, to be experimental, and to do so requires us to discard unnecessary dogma that may keep us feeling stuck and rigid. And what it all comes down to at the core is that all of these traits are simply different facets of a larger concept that I mentioned a moment ago—creativity.

I realize that creativity exists on a continuum. Some people have less of it, while others possess it in spades. But I'm also not referring to creativity in the artistic sense but rather as a conscious decision to open ourselves to something new. New ideas, new behaviors, new experiences—basically, stepping outside of one's own narrative, which we may often without awareness experience as rigid and confining, and letting go of story lines and expectations.

Here's a specific example that illustrates this particular meaning of creativity. Let's say a woman, we'll call her Sarah, has always had sex with her partner initiating. As a result, she has learned to expect the same and has even come to identify her sexuality with this level of passivity. She may tell herself, "Yeah, I never initiate sex, that's just not me." So she has now created a story line in which she never initiates, this story line has become a core part of her identity, and to do something different wouldn't even be a consideration since she would need to challenge her very identity to do so.

Without realizing it, Sarah has become so attached to her narrative that her sexuality has taken on a rigid quality, lacking all spontaneity, flexibility, and experimentation. In other words, her sexuality has lost all creativity. Sometimes the most important work I do with my clients is to help them identify their narrative and examine it closely. They don't need to change it, they don't need to do anything with it. But I at least want them to be able to identify it. Really see it. And then, since it is clearly and transparently on the table, decide whether it still works. Maybe it's outlived its expiration date. Maybe some of it still holds true but other elements of it need to go. Or maybe it works just fine. But fundamentally, folks need to understand that they are far more than the person they have defined within the boundaries of their story line.

We can all step outside of our narrative sometime and in this way create a new one. A more flexible and authentic one that corresponds more closely with who we really are. Let's go back to Sarah for a moment. Let's say one day she says, "You know, why don't I try something new, why don't I try to initiate sex this time?" And she initiates, and to her surprise, it works and it's great. Through her act of trying something new, of introducing creativity to her life and to her sexuality, she now has an experience that defines her in a new way. She has essentially now redefined herself.

In this way, by examining our own old assumptions and personal narratives and challenging them through playful creativity and experimentation, we are no longer controlled by old dogmas that have outlived their utility. We are no longer helpless before our fixed identities to experience choice and self-agency. We can identify any way we choose in the moment that suits us, or rather, not adopt any identity at all.

So let's see some examples of interventions I use to help my clients create new narratives using the techniques of narrative therapy. Narrative therapy was developed by psychotherapist Michael White as a means of modifying his clients' self-identities through the means of *externalizing*.[9] By externalizing, what I mean is that the individual begins to see the problem or difficulty not as an inherently internal core aspect of his or her humanity but as an external challenge, something that does not dwell within.

So, for example, what I might do with a client who struggles with depression is to externalize it by instructing the client to give the depression a name, Charlie, for example. And then I discuss the depression—Charlie—as if he is an unfortunate, pesky character that sometimes visits my client, like an annoying uncle at family gatherings. Often folks who are stuck in some negative pattern overly identify with their problems. They label themselves. Or others label them. Or both.

So a client who is depressed may say, "I'm a depressed person," instead of "I struggle with depression." In sexuality, the person may say internally, "I am a sexually shameful person," rather than "I sometimes feel shame in sexual situations."

So I'll say, "Let's change our relationship to this shame so that we can do something about it." I'll ask the client to give shame a name. For this example, let's call him Shamus. So I instruct my client, "When you feel shame, instead of identifying yourself as shameful, call it out and call it by its name—Shamus."

So, I ask, "What would you say to Shamus when he [or she] visits you?" Maybe it's a friendly "Hi, Shamus" (making friends with your enemies) or a playful "Not you again!" (making light of the situation), or maybe you are really mad and annoyed, so you might be very direct and blurt out, "Leave me alone, Shamus." Or even better, "Leave me the *hell* alone, Shamus."

Sometimes it's not a disturbing emotion that visits us but an internal identity that has become rigid and crystallized that we want to amend. Take, for instance, the rigid identity I discussed above of Sarah, who never initiates sex; she's "not that kind of woman." Keeping this exercise in mind, I may say to Sarah (if she is open to and interested in challenging this narrative), "You say you are sexually passive, that's who you are, but you also feel like there's a part of you that wants to take some risks, do something different." I continue, "So it's not that you are completely passive. There's a part of you that feels passive but another part of you that feels adventurous. When you identify yourself as passive, you shove down that part of you that is adventurous." I then conclude, "Would you like to get in touch with that more adventurous side?"

Assuming that Sally is at least in the contemplation stage, I will dive into the narrative therapy intervention and say something like, "Great, so let's take a look at that passive side of you, let's give it a name, since it's really not you, and only a mere part of who you are. What shall we call her?"

At this point, I'm looking for something easy to remember. If Sally doesn't come up with a name, and that may happen since even this kind of a discussion may feel a bit destabilizing, I'll suggest something like, "Well, she's passive, so let's call her something like Patty, Passive Patty, so that it is easy to remember her."

And we are off and running. From here on out, instead of allowing her to make excuses and complain that "That's the way she is," I'll always bring it back to Passive Patty who is now visiting Sally and robbing her of her assertiveness and sense of adventure.

At this juncture, I would like to make a few points. The intervention I just described combines several types of therapies, specifically narrative and ego state therapies. Ego state simply means "different parts of oneself." Another therapy also exists, called internal family systems (IFS), that also utilizes working with these ego states.[10] I have found that using ego states, especially along with narrative techniques, can be a very powerful combination.

Additionally, the act of always going back to Passive Patty, Charlie, or whatever name is chosen is called *anchoring*. Imagine a ship that drops anchor. The anchor prevents the ship from being sent adrift, even in the worst currents. Similarly, an anchor is something that allows my work with my clients to be centered; in other words, we can always come back to the same place without getting lost in the old habits of, for instance, "Woe is me, I'm just not that kind of a woman." We'll come back to this idea of anchoring later in this chapter.

All the techniques described in this chapter are helpful for a number of reasons, but what they all have in common is that they address an individual's resistance to making concrete actions toward change. In trying to take initial steps, folks often first need to get in touch with that little devil on their shoulder that is actively and covertly working against progress. Call it what you will, ambivalence, resistance, but it's that little voice, that little character that we've exorcised to the surface in the narrative therapy techniques we've explored.

But the problem is that waging that constant war between the part that is leaning toward growth and change and the part that is trying to stay mired in the past can be very tiring. It can sap our energy, our strength, and our motivations. In effect, sometimes we may find ourselves losing our willpower. But the wonderful news is that willpower has been studied, and we know a heck of a lot about it. And as a result, through research, we've found ways to preserve our willpower precisely when the going gets to be the toughest.

HARNESSING WILLPOWER: THE IMPORTANCE OF CREATING SYSTEMS

Roy Baumeister, in his bestselling book *Willpower: Rediscovering the Greatest Human Strength*, states that willpower is a finite energetic resource.[11] The more we use it, the more it is depleted. So when we are tired, sleep deprived, hungry, or have spent a full day making tough decisions, we are less able to come up with the willpower to push through more difficulties. Most interestingly, Baumeister found that willpower can be developed. Specifically, those individuals with the most willpower had found simple systems that allowed them to preserve their energies.

Instead of always having to decide, for example, between chocolate cake and broccoli, folks with strong willpower simply set up their lives so that they would rarely be exposed to the temptation to indulge in chocolate cake. In other words, they didn't waste their energy on fighting urges, constantly making decisions, or pushing through to do something that they didn't enjoy. Instead, they set up systems to help them conserve energy so that they had the willpower they had to have when they most needed it.

So what does this have to do with sexuality? Tons. Remember the stages of change, specifically contemplation? Well, the most powerful agent that saps us all of the willpower needed to move into action is ambivalence. And remember, ambivalence often comprises complex emotions such as shame as well as a large dose of anxiety. These difficult feeling states are energetic drains; they rob us of willpower. So in order to push forward into action, we need to preserve our willpower and circumvent the obstacles.

This is where Baumeister's work comes in. Using his model for our purposes, we see that somehow, in order to overcome ambivalence and preserve the willpower to move forward in our journey, we need to put some shortcuts, some systems in place. And these systems need to be automatic so that we don't have to put much thought or attention toward them once they are in place.

So what does such a system look like? Let's take a look at a few examples from my practice and tie them into the earlier process, the writing exercises we discussed in chapter 6.

As you recall, Olivia contacted me at a point in her life when she was experiencing a dawning, a slow realization of her sexual interests, but with a ton of past emotional sexual baggage and shame and no idea what to do with her fantasies and desires. If you recall, we first made a list of her learned, inhibiting beliefs and then created a diagram of all the aspects of her sexuality that fell within her comfort zone, all the aspects she was interested in but that fell in the slight anxiety circle, and all the aspects she was interested in but that fell in the high-anxiety circle.

Next, and here we come to the integral component of systems, we mapped out some small steps Olivia could make to dip her toe into the slightly anxious circle that fell just outside of her comfort zone. Olivia was fantasizing about BDSM and bondage scenarios, so a small step for her would have been to join a kink online educational site, such as kinkuniversity.com or kinkacademy.com. If that felt too intense, she might have made a plan to watch a mainstream Hollywood movie that depicted bondage, such as *Secretary*. Often, going in person to an educational event or socialization gathering, such as a munch (a dining social where individuals interested in kink get together in "vanilla" settings such as a diner to discuss common interests), although helpful, may feel overly anxiety producing or overstimulating to folks who are just beginning the process of self-discovery.

In Olivia's case, she joined an online social network called Fetlife.com and made a plan to join several online discussion groups within the site every week in order to follow along and acclimate herself to the verbiage and in-group cultures. So making a to-do list that feels reasonable, such as "I'm going to research and join three online groups each week for this month" is an actionable step that doesn't require too much thought or emotional investment. And it holds the individual accountable. This is an example of a system.

A TIME FOR REFLECTION: ASSESSING NEW EXPERIENCES

Every time we take a step forward, we want to give ourselves the opportunity to pause for a moment and take stock of the experience. There is no right or wrong. Speaking of narratives, even in alternative sexuality communities, folks can get bogged down in rigid, unnecessary rules.

There is no right way to have a relationship, and there is no right way to have sex. The only thing that matters is how everyone involved feels about it. So once you've broken new ground and tried new things, it's very important to go back and reflect on how it feels and what it means for you.

In the psychoanalytic literature, one of the most common phrases you will find is the term "corrective emotional experience." This is a very important concept that I mentioned earlier, and I would now like to take a deeper look at it, since it so accurately describes a slice of the journey we are undertaking. A corrective emotional experience simply means any new experience that provides us with a brand-new way of understanding it, usually through experiencing different emotions that require us to challenge old assumptions.

The corrective emotional experience requires three distinct steps: (1) the experience itself, (2) understanding one's subjective reaction to the experience, and (3) processing the connection between one's subjectivity and the experience, in other words, making meaning of the experience.

It's often not enough to wait passively for an experience to happen, so we must go forward with active intentionality to plan a course of action. This is what we've covered earlier in this chapter. We addressed the second part, understanding one's subjectivity, in the sections on mindfulness and awareness. So now we are left with the final stage, meaning making. It is this final aspect of the corrective emotional experience that is most transformative and cements the emotional learnings of the entire process.

Remember that in the previous section, we described the process of anchoring. Anchoring is one of the key ingredients in the process of meaning making. In other words, the act of understanding the significance of a corrective emotional experience anchors the experience for further work. Let's go back to Nick in chapter 7 as an example. In his case, the act of revisiting his old memory is the action, the experience of observing himself in a different emotional state while still retaining the memory is the awareness part, and then coming to the conclusion that the shame was caused by the other boy, not something that was inherent to him, was the last part of making meaning of his experience.

Now we have an anchor. My goal at this point is to expand on this new level of awareness so that it is reinforced and becomes Nick's default belief system. I do so by often bringing us back to this realization, having him revisit it at times, instructing him to hold onto his expansive, energetic self as he discusses his internalized shame. In other words, this new realization has become the anchor. And we build our work on expanding from that anchor.

THE NEED FOR SELF-COMPASSION

Sometimes trying new things brings up more discomfort. We may experience a renewed sense of guilt or shame. Sometimes these feelings mean that we need to reevaluate what we thought we would get from the experience. Sometimes these feelings are mere artifacts of old schemas that we are outgrowing. At these times, instead of finding ourselves mired in regret and self-criticism, it is very important to be able to connect with a part of ourselves that can extend self-compassion.

The further I go in my work, the more I become certain that self-compassion is one of the key ingredients that we need for our sexual journeys. Indeed, if I were now to be asked what is the most important takeaway that I can provide anyone through psychotherapy, I would answer that it would be the tools to cultivate self-compassion. When it really comes to it, I believe that self-compassion is one of the quintessential hallmarks of mental health.

So what is self-compassion, and how do we cultivate it? First, I think it's important to point out that it's something that's poorly understood. If I ask clients, for example, whether they are able to experience self-compassion, they will invariably get a blank look and state that of course they have self-compassion or something to that effect. And this may be a client who struggles mightily with self-criticism, depression, anxiety, or any other internal conflict that would create distress.

I'll say, let's imagine that there is a distressed child standing on the corner of Fifth Avenue and Forty-Fifth Street (near my office) and this child is in tatters; the child is barefoot, dirty, and crying for help. Now let's imagine that everyone just walked by and ignored this child, that no one comes over to help or soothe the child . . . would we consider these people to be compassionate? Of course not. Now let's take a look at the similar situation where you are feeling distressed, where you are in pain and struggling with painful emotions, and you are unable to come to your own defense and soothe yourself. Would we consider you to be self-compassionate? Probably not.

This is often where I see the looks change from confusion to realization. Because in essence, if we are unable to soothe ourselves, to look out for ourselves when we are feeling sad, depressed, lonely, or anxious, then on some level we either haven't developed or don't know how to access our internal capacity for self-compassion. In these times, we may look for soothing outside of ourselves. In substances, for example. Or in food. Or by distracting ourselves, through shopping, gambling, video games, or a number of other entertainments. Or by delving deeper into work. Or, yes, sometimes even through sex. In essence, much of compulsive behavior is based on seeking external soothing due to the inability to find soothing internally—in other words, due to the inability to have self-compassion. I'm only illustrating here the many ways in which a lack of self-compassion can create internal havoc. And yes, lack of self-compassion can and will derail our journey of sexual exploration.

In my own work, I am constantly expanding my knowledge base and searching for and adopting new techniques that might allow my clients to tap into their own natural reservoirs of healing. As we've seen, I may use somatic or mindfulness exercises or sometimes even visualizations to allow my clients to experientially see what it's like to give themselves a little break during their day, to metaphorically give themselves an internal vacation from the stress, worry, and internal dialogue. When they see that they have the self-agency to create this experience for themselves, that is like a crack in the door that we can expand on, and they can then learn to extend that self-compassion to other areas of their life, including in the service of sexual functioning and pleasure. This is what I would consider tapping into our own innate abilities to heal.

In conclusion, sexuality is often a microcosm of the deeper landscape that resides within. The tip of the iceberg, if you will. And learning the tools to self-soothe, to calm our internal world, is the essence of self-compassion. And it is these same tools that allow us to extend that same reassurance, that same pleasure and calm, that same self-created joy to our sexualities and sexual lives.

BRIEF RECAP

When we find ourselves about to make concrete steps toward our journey, we may find ourselves experiencing an additional jolt of anxiety. To move forward, we must adopt a process-oriented focus and surrender to the moment by making contact with our sexually selfish and ruthless desires. We may feel additionally stuck by rigid narratives that we must learn to challenge. To help us stay on track, we develop systems that preserve our willpower. Afterward, we reflect on our experiences with an eye toward making meaning through a self-compassionate lens.

9

SPREADING YOUR WINGS

Peak Sexual Experiences

We've come quite far in our journey. We have gotten past the initial trepidations and made our initial forays. We've been processing our discoveries and using that information to make meaning of our experiences. From there, we can continue with more of the same, explore further, or course correct and try different things. Now it's time to take it to the next level. I imagine you don't just want good sex. You want great sex.

To accomplish this, I would like to revisit belief systems for a moment. That's because great sex is inherently transgressive. It shatters through traditional, self-limiting beliefs and takes us into ecstatic, transcendent states. What scientists sometimes describe as "flow." But what do we need to reach these levels? How do we go about getting there? Let's take a look.

ACHIEVING FLOW

When we take a look at the genesis of any belief system, we have to take into account two key factors: influence and reinforcement. I'll examine both of these in turn. First, no belief system can take hold if an initial seed is not planted, which requires influence. In other words, we believe the things we do because at one point or another, we were influenced by someone or something that had enough effect on us to change or mold our beliefs, in this case about sex and sexuality. As kids we were influenced by our parents, by teachers, by mentors, by peer leaders. As adults our views may be less malleable, but we still have people around us with varying levels of influence. Said differently, we will pay attention to what we learn from those who have influence over us and dismiss or discard what we hear from those who hold no influence. Yeah, influence is important.

But the seeds of belief that are implanted by influence cannot sprout without continued reinforcement. This reinforcement is often done by our own selves through a psychological process called *confirmation bias*. Like influence, confirmation bias involves a selective process whereby we pay attention to certain things and completely ignore others. Through the process of confirmation bias, it is almost like a self-fulfilling prophecy in that we look for evidence that confirms our beliefs (or the seed of the belief) and ignore, compartmentalize, or rationalize away any evidence that disconfirms those beliefs. So let's say someone in a leadership position disseminates his or her belief system to us; that alone is not sufficient to instill belief. We must be able to find ready confirmation in our environment to reinforce that belief or the seed doesn't grow and nothing comes of it. If the president of the United States or the CEO of your company told you that our society has been infiltrated by green aliens, you may look around and find absolutely no confirming evidence and simply dismiss the claim. However, if the local grocer had told you that, you would probably not even be motivated enough to take a look around. Influence and reinforcement, that's what belief systems are all about.

And this now brings us to the subject of "aliveness." I'm taking this term from the skeptic/martial arts trainer Matt Thornton, who applies methods of aliveness both to his martial arts gym and to scientific inquiry.[1] He takes the example of traditional tae kwon do versus Brazilian jujitsu (BJJ). Tae kwon do focuses primarily on kata (or forms) in which the student learns some choreographed movements that are supposedly effective in real altercations. How do we know that these forms are effective? Just believe the teacher. The teacher said (influence) and all the students seem to believe (reinforcement), so I guess it must be true, right? These are how faulty belief systems develop. Please note, I'm not trying to criticize tae kwon do right now, I'm criticizing the methods of learning to fight, specifically choreographed katas.

BJJ, on the other hand, requires active combat ("rolling") on a regular basis as a means of skill development. The teacher will show a technique or two, and then the students spar using real resistance instead of choreographed forms. In this way, they can gauge what does and doesn't work and accurately assess their skill level. The fighting is alive; in other words, it is based on real experience rather than rote repetition or theory. Aliveness is not theory, it is life experience. While belief is authority based, aliveness is *experiential*.

What does this have to do with sexuality? Everything. As a society, we have so many self-limiting negative beliefs about sexuality that exist for no other reason than cultural influence. Sex-negative learning is authority based. How do we know sex is bad? Well, our parents may have told us, and if we got no sex ed in school, we learned implicitly that sex must be bad, and then we hear sex-phobic messaging in the media, and perhaps if we go to a religious institution, we hear the priest or rabbi speak with caution. And how do they all know that sex is bad/dangerous/dirty/fill in the blank? Well, they heard it from their own parents and their teachers and their religious leaders. In this way, belief systems are tautologies—they are circular and self-reinforcing. They have no discernible origin or credible evidence, and indeed they exist solely based on authority.

If we can actually step outside of our (predetermined) beliefs, we allow for the space necessary to form conclusions based on life experience rather than rigid dogma. In other words, we can come to knowledge through the process of our own inherent "aliveness" (the act of living) rather than following "dead patterns" (formulas and theories that work only when the situation is ideal and fall apart under most conditions). These are martial arts terms that I'm using, but I find them to be most applicable in other areas of life that involve the consolidation of new learning, including critical thinking, new skill development, and identity formation—all aspects of healthy sexuality.

And this takes us to the concept of "flow." What is flow? And what does this have to do with aliveness? Psychologist Mihaly Csikszentmihalyi defines flow as the "mental state of operation in which a person performing an activity is fully immersed in a feeling of energized focus, full involvement, and enjoyment in the process of activity." In other words, flow is when an individual is fully engaged in the process of aliveness.[2] The hallmark of flow is "a feeling of spontaneous joy, even rapture." This is the state where all of the negative thoughts and emotions fall away and we are left feeling internal congruence among our thoughts, feelings, and intentions and with a deep sense of connection among our intentions, our actions, and the world around us. The way I look at it, flow is a heightened state of elevated consciousness that allows us to feel a connection to something greater than ourselves. Isn't this what we think about when we talk about amazing sex, intimacy, tantra, and the like? These are all terms interchangeably used to suggest that sex (and other aspects of relationships) can be experienced in flow states.

Now let's ask ourselves: is it possible to achieve flow states in our sexuality without also experiencing aliveness? In other words, if we are caught up in old sexual taboos, sex-phobic mythologies, and other sex-negative dogmas, do we ever allow ourselves the opportunity to actually experience our subjective truths for ourselves? And if so, do we then deprive ourselves of the opportunity to have the kind of connective experience that can come only from open hearts *and* open minds?

IN THE COCOON: THE PROCESS OF NEW IDENTITY FORMATION

In an earlier chapter, I talked about changing the narrative. In this part, I would like to touch on how rigid narratives tie into specific social roles. And one means of achieving peak sexual experiences, as discussed above, is to challenge these social roles.

It is first important to understand what is meant by the term "role." According to the dictionary definition, a role is the "characteristic and expected social behavior of an individual." The key ideas here are that roles are implicitly social in context and are based on agreed-upon (social) expectations. Roles come in many guises. We all have interpersonal roles—such as mother, father, child, brother, sister, and so on. We have work roles—supervisor, apprentice, and so on. And we have many other contextual roles—breadwinner, caretaker, jokester, black sheep, villain, and so on. The more roles we have, the more we can feel boxed in, living up to a multitude of social expectations. Often, we may find ourselves in a multitude of roles—father, mother, brother, sister, son, daughter, husband, wife, breadwinner, boss, entrepreneur, and so on. Every single role foisted upon us (or that we willingly take on) adds another wall to our sense of possibilities and freedom.

Someone, for example, who is a mother and who also has a demanding corporate job and is the breadwinner for the family would probably find it much more difficult to behave with a sense of carefree abandon than someone who was a sixteen-year-old student. These things are obvious. But the one thing that is absolutely essential to keep in mind is that even though we may be boxed in by a great number of roles, our essential psychological needs remain unaltered. If we crave the desire for novelty, wild abandonment, carefreeness, or danger, it doesn't go away because we play a certain set of roles in society. It's still there. And often we simply have to grin and bear it and suppress it away. Or, best case scenario, sublimate it, which basically means to pick up some other hobby or activity that can give us a taste of our cravings.

But at our core, we extend far beyond the limits of what is allowed by the boundaries of our social roles. And all of those elements that fuel our desires—aggression, lust, fear, anxiety, envy, greed—must be smothered and only sometimes come out in our fantasies and dreams or indirectly in passive-aggressive behavior. In this way, we have very limited social outlets for the wide spectrum of our internal desires, and often we must find a way to tolerate "through quiet desperation" the concessions we make to be included in the social pact.

I would argue, however, that there is perhaps one very clear, direct, and transparent way we can obtain access to our internal life in a way that's safe and insulated from social consequences (if handled privately)—our sexualities. Through sex, we can experiment with, test out, and immerse ourselves in the various roles that exist internally but that can never bear the social light of day. Through this kind of sexual role play, we can unleash our aggression, our anxieties, our fears—in short, the darkest recesses of our minds in a way that is contained to that specific sexual episode and in a way that can be discussed, analyzed, and reflected upon.

Through this kind of exploration, an accountant trapped under mountains of payment ledgers can become a ruthless dictator or a benevolent master or a damsel in distress. A homemaker who is harried by taking care of three kids can become a seductress, starlet, or Amazonian queen. The possibilities are endless. In this way, sexual role play allows us access to parts of ourselves that have been previously split off. It allows us the opportunity to much more fully understand ourselves and achieve a sense of integration and wholeness rather than the sense of fragmentation that we may experience from being sectioned off by a host of social roles.

FACING THE SHADOW

Psychoanalyst Carl Jung called these split-off parts the "shadow."[3] To understand how omnipresent the shadow is in our everyday lives, let's take a look at Halloween, a popular holiday, even among adults. My theory is that for many folks, Halloween is the only time of the year that it is socially sanctioned to get in touch with one's "shadow," again, meaning the term used by Jung to refer to the unconscious aspect of oneself that the ego does not identify with. In other words, the shadow is everything about ourselves—our rage, lust, envy, hatred, and greed—that we want to disown. It is the monster within. And it exists in all of us. When we dress up as goblins and monsters on Halloween, we can parade around as Mr. Hyde at least for one day of the year, and the world supports that. The next day, we are back to Dr. Jekyll, and Mr. Hyde gets locked in the closet.

The problem is that the shadow is still always with us—it can never be fully disowned. It will come out every now and then, even if we are not consciously aware of it, and wreak havoc on our psychological and emotional lives. Often the suppression of the shadow creates intense internal conflict in the form of depression, anxiety, and self-defeating behaviors. It often feels unbearable for people to come to terms with their hatred of a parent or their anger at a child. Instead, it all gets pushed down into the unconscious, bubbling to the surface at inopportune times.

One of the most important articles I read (as required reading) in grad school was called "Hate in the Countertransference."[4] Basically it is about the importance of being able to articulate and recognize all of our feelings, including hatred, if we are to be effective as therapists. The same holds true for everyone else. It takes a lot of courage to admit to ourselves that we feel like murdering someone we love and to articulate it to that person. Something like, "You know honey, sometimes I get so angry at the things you do, I almost feel like killing you." That's honest. And that kind of dialogue (if done appropriately, in a measured way) can be some welcome honesty and transparency in the relationship.

But the important idea I want to convey here is that we all have a shadow. And we all have a strong desire to disown it. To push it to our unconscious and pretend it doesn't exist. But by running away from it, we never give ourselves the chance to face it, address it, and change. We just kick the can down the road until things really hit the fan. By helping my clients to face their shadow, I help them not only to fully understand themselves but also to take steps to not be ruled by the shadow.

I am reminded of the play *Marat/Sade*, which originally premiered in West Berlin in 1964 and eventually won the Tony Award in 1966 for Best Play.[5] It is set in the historical Charenton Asylum during the reign of Napoleon and centers on a play staged within the asylum by the Marquis de Sade and using the asylum inmates as actors. The Marquis de Sade (from whom we have the term "sadism") was held in the asylum after his arrest for the anonymous publication of *Justine* and other pornographic tracts.[6] In real life, the director of the hospital did allow de Sade to stage plays within the asylum, often to a public audience. The particular play-within-a-play performed as *Marat/Sade* focuses on the life and assassination of Jean-Paul Marat, a radical journalist who goaded on the French Revolution and was eventually assassinated by a member of a rival faction.[7] As the play unfolds, the marquis pops in now and then to add his commentary to the proceedings.

The central idea of the play is the juxtaposition and contrast between the philosophies of Marat and de Sade. Marat is a political radical who believes that a utopia can be created through social revolution—that a new government of the people and by the people will lift up the poor and oppressed. De Sade, meanwhile, has no use for this type of social idealism. He believes that any revolution will fail as long as human beings retain their natural condition—their anger, hate, thirst for power and vengeance, envy, bloodlust, and sadism. He refuses to take part in the revolutionary proceedings and instead focuses on the indulgence and exploration of all the aforementioned human vices. In essence, he believes that true freedom comes not from government but from breaking free from social constructs to get at the true heart of the human condition.

This philosophical worldview is fairly bleak and cynical, but at the same time Marat's utopianism can be viewed as overly optimistic and naive. In many ways, this argument mirrors a common source of conflict in the annals of philosophical discourse, echoing previous points of contention between such thinkers as Rousseau (who believed in the innate goodness of the "noble savage") and Hobbes (who believed the nature of man was nasty and brutish).[8]

In the end, Marat is assassinated, the revolutionaries all turn on one another, and Napoleon rises from the ashes to seize power. Nothing has changed: one monarch (Napoleon) has replaced another (Louis XVI), the poor and oppressed are still poor and oppressed, and the only thing that has happened is that power has changed hands. Indeed, for all his idealism, Marat's life and death are all for naught. Of course, as the director and playwright, de Sade shows himself to be correct. But we can't dismiss the ways in which history has a way of repeating itself, from the Russian Revolution and communism to the rise of Hitler and the Third Reich. Is utopia ever possible?

This leads me to think of my work as a therapist. Is it possible to create an ideal society that resolves all social problems without each individual working on resolving his or her own internal struggles? Is a society comprising people in conflict, turmoil, and pain able to create a mass structure that can collectively fix all these challenges from the outside? I would like to believe, but I seem to doubt it. And what of this internal exploration that de Sade appears to be alluding to? Is it possible to know oneself better through sexual self-exploration and understanding?

In my mind, tapping into our "shadow" is an integral part of self-knowledge and self-development. It is not only expansive but also transgressive. And transformative. Indeed, great sex is closely aligned with personal growth. And transgression and transformation can come together in only one package—through our sexuality.

AN OPEN MIND IS THE EROTIC MIND

In his seminal sexological work, *The Erotic Mind*, Jack Morin identifies four key cornerstones of eroticism:[9]

- Longing and anticipation
- Violating prohibitions
- Searching for power
- Overcoming ambivalence

Several of these directly address the themes we've covered in this book, and so in many ways, this is a chapter where many of the ideas we've discussed come together in terms of producing a sexual synergy, where the final whole is greater than the sum of its parts.

Let's start with the final one: overcoming ambivalence. As we've seen, ambivalence is a common obstacle in early stages of change. It can immobilize us from actions that would help us achieve true sexual authenticity, but at the same time, the process of overcoming that same ambivalence can propel us to the heights of peak eroticism. Indeed, many of our fantasies serve the purpose of combating some type of internal ambivalence. Psychologist Michael Bader, in his book *Arousal*, details numerous cases of individuals who experience fantasies as an antidote to specific life situations, such as the high-achieving career woman who dreams of being dominated in brutal gang bangs or the young man who fantasizes about scenes of unlimited power as a means of allaying guilt.[10]

I would be cautious in that I don't think all fantasies serve that function. Indeed, as I've indicated, plenty of research suggests that much of our sexuality is made up of innate characteristics. However, Bader mostly catalogued transient rather than life-long fantasies, so in that case, they may very well and most likely do consist of a psychological component of undoing ambivalence. As Morin himself indicated, Attraction (innate predisposition) + Obstacles (ambivalence, psychological factors) = Excitement.

We can draw on these ideas in our work here. Instead of avoiding ambivalence, we can harness its energy toward peak experiences. In other words, rather than "living in our fears" by avoiding the source of the ambivalence (shame, guilt, anxiety), we turn our attention *toward* the ambivalence and utilize the messages we glean toward our self-understanding and exploration of our sexuality. So when Olivia made lists of her beliefs, her fears, and her anxiety points, she was allowing herself to get in touch with the very sources of her ambivalence rather than avoid them and brush them aside.

On the clinical side of this book, if you, gentle reader, glean one and only one bit of usable information, it is that you must *lean* into your ambivalence as a means of transforming it into an energetic source for your sexual development.

Indeed, Jack Morin, in his study of 351 people, determined that the following emotional states may often lead to peak sexual experiences:

- Exuberance—joy, celebration
- Satisfaction—contentment, relaxation
- Closeness—love, affection, connection
- Anxiety—fear, vulnerability
- Guilt—remorse, dirtiness, shame
- Anger—hostility, contempt, resentment, revenge

Notice that half of these are positive—exuberance, satisfaction, and closeness—while the other three are negative emotions—anxiety, fear, guilt, and anger. Recall the work of Sylvan Tomkins and Paul Ekman from chapter 7. These are basically the core emotions spelled out in affect theory and confirmed via research. And so it is through base, foundational emotions that we experience our sexuality and, at our finest hour, peak sexuality.

Also remember that it is these negative emotional states that form the foundation of ambivalence. And so it is the work that we've done to uncover and understand, rather than submerge and repress, our emotions that not only helps us to overcome our ambivalence and expand our sexualities but also to have the most mind-blowing peak experiences.

So in the face of anxiety, what are some additional tools that may allow us to lean into our ambivalence rather than run away? One of the surest ways of assuring an open mind is to adopt an air of curiosity. We can do so by starting our thoughts with the following opener—"I wonder . . ." Could be "I wonder what it would feel like to be touched in this spot." Or "I wonder what would happen if I asked for this specific sexual activity." Or "I wonder whether I would like acting on this fantasy in real life."

"I wonder." It all starts with those two magical words.

If we are unable to get into that headspace, that's a sure-fire sign that we are stuck in our ambivalence. That rather than leaning into our anxiety, we have bunkered down in our comfort zone.

One more bullet-pointed list from the master, Jack Morin. Through his qualitative research, he also discovered the following subjective experiences of those individuals who have gone through peak sexual experiences:

• Sensual and orgasmic intensity
• Reduced inhibitions (muscular armoring)
• Validation given and received
• Mutuality and resonance
• Transcendence of personal boundaries

Of these five items, the first four are obvious. Sure, you are going to experience orgasmic intensity, reduced inhibition, increased validation, and a feeling of mutuality during bouts of sexual intensity. But the last one, personal transcendence, deserves some extra attention. What it means is that fundamentally, sexuality isn't only about a genital rub. It's emotional. It's relational. It's energetic. It's about identity. And most importantly, it's about personal transcendence. So what I'm getting at is that this book and the process detailed within is not just so much about sexual growth but really, fundamentally about personal development and, ultimately, self-transcendence.

And often, the best way to reach that level of transcendence is to bring a partner or two (or three) along for the ride.

10

KEEPING THE FLAME RED-HOT

The Importance of Communication, Trust, and Transparency

Kevin and Roxie, a professional couple in their mid-thirties, entered my office and sat down together on the far end of the couch. Their two-year relationship was falling apart. Therapy was their last shot.

When Roxie called me the prior week, she'd said that her relationship with Kevin was on the rocks. He was struggling with erectile dysfunction, and they hadn't had sex in six months. Numerous thoughts raced through her mind, each one more negative and depressing than the one before. Had he lost interest in her? Was she no longer attractive to him? She had such high hopes for this relationship. She thought maybe he was "the One," but all her dreams for having a family were on the verge of being dashed by his inability to perform.

As I usually do when I meet a couple for the first time, I ask for some information about the history of their relationship—how and when they met, what attracted them to each other, and when the sexual difficulties started.

Roxie said they met at a high-tech industry convention and it was love at first sight. At first, the sex was frequent and intense. Kevin seemed like such a confident guy back then. Self-assured and highly sexual. As Roxie came to know Kevin better, she learned that he was less confident than first seemed and actually had suffered with long-standing anxiety issues. He had dropped out of college his first time around due to anxiety but finally finished with a degree in project management.

When couples come in with sexual complaints, the sex often cannot be separated from the rest of the relationship. Back in the 1960s, sex therapists William Masters and Virginia Johnson developed sensate focus techniques, which are basically touch and communication exercises, for couples that were anxious about getting sexual. These exercises are helpful for the newbie couple but don't address deeper underlying issues for long-term couples whose problems started somewhere during the course of the relationship.

Roxie recalled that sometimes Kevin wasn't completely hard during sex even when they first met, but this problem intensified to the point that sex became impossible. I wondered whether Kevin had experienced these sexual difficulties in the past. He said that sometimes he had trouble performing with previous girlfriends, but nothing like this.

I often tell clients in the first session that we are going to talk about some things that may make them uncomfortable. That they can and should tell me everything that I should know to help them. And that whatever they may have to say, I won't be fazed because I've heard it all before. Sounds good. But it never quite works like this.

Once I get a short history of the relationship, I start to get a sense of where the couple is right now. How are they communicating? Do they still feel as positively about each other now as when they first met? Are their lives interconnected, or are they drifting apart? In Kevin and Roxie's case, they seemed as close as ever. They sat close together, holding hands, taking turns talking and making great eye contact with each other while listening. Seemed like this couple was made for each other. So why couldn't they have sex?

I asked Kevin point-blank, "So, what are you into?"

"What do you mean? Sexually?"

"Yeah, what's the kind of stuff that gets you hard?"

"Uh . . . I don't know."

This is a typical conversation with a client first starting out in sex therapy. Often, because there is so much shame about sex, it is very difficult in the beginning stages of treatment to get a good sense of what the problem really is. It becomes a process of elimination, like being a detective. Usually sex problems are only the tip of the iceberg and represent bigger issues in the relationship.

Inevitably, it turns out that someone has felt let down, angry, or resentful, and the sex has become the collateral damage. Or, more often the case, one partner simply feels that he or she isn't getting his or her needs met and shuts down. And so my job is to find out what each partner in the relationship wants out of sex. Not what one partner thinks the other partner or I want to hear, but what he or she truly wants. Maybe he or she doesn't know. But then it's my job to help the person figure it out.

Asking directly about sexual interests rarely gets a direct answer, but it often provides other important information, such as the degree of shame that the client experiences. In Kevin's case, the shame was intense. Although he made great eye contact with Roxie, he couldn't bear to look directly at me. Kevin looked at the floor and around the room but never could quite bring himself to make eye contact.

I had a hunch at this point that Kevin was hiding something. There was something sexual that he really liked but was too ashamed to even bring up. I took another try, this time less direct.

"What kinds of porn do you watch?"

"Oh, just the usual kind."

"Usual kind? What's that?"

I often like to ask about porn interests because it feels less intrusive to the client. It feels like we're talking about something else, so it seems less direct. We're talking about porn, not about the client's sexual identity. But, of course, knowing what kind of porn the person watches presents a volume of information about that person's sexuality. In this case, Kevin gave a clearly fake and ambiguous answer. As studies have shown, all men have watched porn at one point in their lives, and they sure as heck know what they are looking at.

I was now convinced that not only did Kevin know exactly what he was into, but also it was so embarrassing to him that he would never, ever admit to it. Or at least not in front of Roxie. After some prodding, Kevin went on to explain that he was into leggy blondes with large breasts who liked to give blow jobs. Little did he know that this is the standard answer when someone isn't revealing the truth.

In these situations, the only way to find out what's really going on is to separate the partners. It's amazing the information that comes out once each partner is alone. I scheduled a time to meet Kevin individually the following week.

When Kevin next came in, he seemed like a changed man. He ambled into the office with a big grin and plopped down on the couch as if ready to unburden himself of years of pent-up frustration. Sensing that Kevin welcomed the space apart from Roxie and was ready to open up, I simply asked, "So, what are you really into?"

Without further prompting, Kevin described his sexual fantasies. He was into bondage porn and fantasized about tying Roxie up in bed and making her beg for pleasure. He had it all planned out. He had some rope hidden in one of his drawers and had been practicing tying knots on those nights that Roxie was working late. Square knot. Slipknot. Fisherman's knot. He had studied and mastered all the basics. And he knew exactly what he would do with Roxie. He would tie some simple wrist and ankle restraints, blindfold her, and forcefully penetrate her as she lay prone in bed. Or else he would hog-tie her and make her suck him off in order to please him. He would lie in bed, masturbating to these fantasies, hurrying before Roxie got home. These fantasies were so vivid; they had clearly taken on a large part of his internal world.

I wondered why he wasn't able to share these fantasies with Roxie.

"No way. What would she think of me?" he asked.

"She just might like it. You never know."

Next session was the following week with Roxie. I asked her some similar questions. What turns her on? What would her ideal sex life look like? How could she get her needs met with Kevin? Roxie's responses were amazing. She revealed that she was secretly hoping that Kevin would tie her up, tell her what to do, and take charge in the bedroom. She wanted to be taken, to feel swept away and desired uncontrollably by her partner.

When I next met them as a couple, I told both of them that the other partner had something important to say. In these situations, it's important to set the tone by letting both individuals know that it is a safe space and that I am sure the partner is open to hearing them because I have already vetted what they have to say. Kevin started by talking about what we discussed in his individual session, at which point Roxie shouted, "I would love for you to do that to me!"

"Really?"

"Yes, I've been waiting for you to make a move forever."

I saw Kevin and Roxie for three more sessions after that. Just because they had both realized that they were open to each other's sexual fantasies did not mean that it would all be a smooth ride from then on. Kevin still struggled with internal fears of hurting or disappointing Roxie but, as they both became comfortable articulating their sexual desires, all of Kevin's sexual anxiety and dysfunction disappeared. Last I heard, they are having sex every chance they get.

Couples don't always sync up in this way, though. This was a rare example of a difficult problem being solved so easily. But it illustrates a central point. Kevin felt that he couldn't reveal his true, authentic sexuality to Roxie, so he started losing trust and withdrawing both sexually and emotionally. He believed that he could get his sexual desires met only through private fantasy, and so he preferred to experience his sexuality alone, without having to deal with possible rejection by his partner. But only by incorporating his sexuality into his relationship was he finally able to have the kind of deep and fulfilling relationship that he desired.

TEARING DOWN THE WALL: INCORPORATING YOUR SEXUALITY INTO YOUR RELATIONSHIPS

Clients can often have the wrong idea that sex should come naturally. That it should be spontaneous and easy. That it should just take care of itself. Nothing could be further from the truth.

When couples come in complaining of lack of sex, I always ask first how often they have sex. I've heard everything from several times a week to never. Then I ask what "never" means. Which could also mean several times a week to never. It's all very subjective.

I then ask, if they were to make a list of priorities, where sex would fall on that list. That question often gets a lot of blank looks. People will prioritize everything—career, kids, eating, watching TV, and playing video games—over sex and then wonder why they aren't having enough sex. But I think the reasons behind this discrepancy run deep.

For many people, the act of prioritizing sex brings up buried underlying feelings about sexuality itself. For some it may feel too sexual, as if they are oversexed nymphomaniacs or satyrs or, worse yet, sex addicts if they put too much thought and planning into sex. It may bring up guilty feelings about focusing too much on one's own pleasure. And for others it brings up feelings of sexual inadequacy, that there is something wrong with them if they have to plan something that should come so naturally.

The truth is that sex loses spontaneity for most very early in the relationship. It has to be prioritized, planned, and sometimes even choreographed to make it feel spontaneous. Those couples waiting to have sex for the right opportunity to feel spontaneous often find themselves waiting a very long time.

A good exercise for couples that I recommend is to actually sit down and write out their list of priorities and then compare. If sex is the third priority for Joe but tenth for Sally, then we have a discussion ahead of us. If sex is ninth for Bob and eighth for Larry, then we have a different situation, where both Bob and Larry are probably not having much sex, don't prioritize it much, but are probably looking for something else in their relationship besides sex, such as more emotional intimacy. Sometimes folks think they want more sex but are actually looking for other forms of closeness.

Let's say Joe and Sally are way off on how they prioritize sex. We have a few options. Probably Joe has a higher sex drive than Sally, which is why she doesn't put a high priority on sex. But that is an oversimplification. Sally might have a lower sex drive because of negative experiences in her past, or because Joe has no idea how to please her and doesn't care to learn, or because she is afraid to reveal what she really wants.

Sorting through priorities often looks quite similar to the case of Kevin and Roxie. I separate both individuals and find out about their interests, attitudes, and fantasies about sex. In Kevin's situation, he lost both his erection and his desire because he felt he couldn't get his needs met with Roxie. Let's take a look at another example.

Craig and Paula had been married for five years. Craig said he loved Paula, but their sex life was dead, and he privately confided that he was afraid that he would start looking elsewhere if things didn't improve. Paula felt that she was always the one initiating sex; she wanted it all the time, but Craig kept refusing her advances. In an individual session, Craig revealed that he was secretly dying to have sex with transsexuals or, as he called them, "chicks with sticks."

He wanted to be dominated and anally penetrated and then forced to suck off the transsexual. He had even gone so far as to ask Paula to engage in a scene where she penetrated him doggy-style while wearing a strap-on, which is actually a popular practice known as "pegging." Although Paula was game, she simply did not have that internal dominance that Craig was seeking. He looked back at her and, instead of pleasure, saw fear and anxiety in her eyes. That was the last night they had sex. At this point, sex with Paula was the last thing on his mind.

This is a perfect example of how sexual priorities get flushed down the drain due to sexual disappointments. Paula could never recreate the dominance that Craig was seeking since it was not her style, and because she didn't know what he was trying to recreate, she found herself in the dark about what this experience meant for him and why it was so unfulfilling.

Because Paula was game for the pegging, I thought she'd be open-minded enough to hear about Craig's interest in transsexuals. It was a risk worth taking because otherwise, the relationship was on a crash-course toward doom.

We worked up gradually toward Craig revealing his sexual fantasies, and unsurprisingly, Paula took it in stride. She even seemed relieved, which is often the case, especially when one of the partners suspects that something is being withheld.

We now had several options open to us. Because Craig's sexual fantasies were on the table, both Paula and Craig could make informed decisions about what to do next. They could engage in some role playing that would closer approximate his interests. They could both watch transsexual porn and get him all worked up about that as foreplay. Or they could actually include a transsexual into their sexual repertoire.

For now, Paula and Craig sometimes watch transsexual porn together and do some role playing with the strap-on. Paula is opening up more about some of her own fantasies, such as being with another woman, and they are both negotiating how to go about allowing each other to experience his or her fantasy with a real person in a structured way that feels safe to both.

All of a sudden, sex is now a top priority for Craig. Paula and Craig report feeling closer and more intimate than ever.

AN OPEN BOOK A DAY KEEPS THE COUPLES THERAPIST AWAY: HOW TRANSPARENCY IN RELATIONSHIPS BUILDS TRUST

The case of Paula and Craig illustrates how sexual authenticity and transparency often set the foundation for enhanced trust and closeness in a relationship. However, often one person does not want to hear what the other has to say. One partner may have absolutely no desire to try pegging, bondage, flogging, or any other such thing. What can couples do when they meet with such resistance?

Psychologist David Schnarch writes about exactly such situations, which he calls the "sexual crucible."[1] He believes that exposing true sexual authenticity forces the couple to make important decisions on how they can improve their relationship. I like the premise, but I see things a bit differently.

Bringing one's sexual authenticity out into the open does not necessarily require some kind of head-on conflict. Being sexually authentic, however, does provide for choice. Just as I recommend couples make a list of their priorities and place sex somewhere on that list, I recommend couples make a list of sexual possibilities that they are open to that their partner would enjoy. Of course, to make such a list requires that both partners be aware of the other person's sexual interests and fantasies.

I compare this to creating a menu. Just as a restaurant provides a menu of possible dinner options that can be ordered, so too each partner creates a menu of sexual possibilities from which to choose. And so both partners can plan out and prioritize to spend defined times throughout the week sampling from the menus. A little pegging Monday night, some cock and ball torture Tuesday, rope bondage Wednesday, a little toe licking on a Thursday, some age play on Friday, a heavy dose of spanking on Saturday, and heck, throw in some "water sports" on Sunday for good measure. Now that's a menu.

Of course, most people aren't going to be into all of that, but the idea is that by creating a menu for each person, the couple has the opportunity to have a real and authentic conversation about their sexuality and learn to communicate, negotiate, and build trust through the act of getting their sexual needs met.

What if your partner isn't into some of the stuff on your menu? You can always modify items on the menu to try to make it more comfortable for the other person. She's not into being gagged and tied up? Maybe she would be open to experiment a bit with a blindfold for now and see what it's like to lose control in the moment. What if he's not into anal penetration? You can start by using small things like fingers and massage his prostate to get him warmed up.

Simple enough? Things get much more complicated.

What if your partner isn't open to any of these things? Let's say your partner is into only missionary sex with eyes closed and the lights out. And that's it. Well, that's when things can get down and dirty. At that point, there are three choices. Both partners can agree to live in misery, knowing that at least one of them will never get his or her sexual needs met. Or both partners agree to break it off and go find someone more sexually suitable.

Or most likely, both partners agree to allow one or both to get their sexual needs met elsewhere. Millions of couples live in this arrangement because they value their relationship enough to want to preserve it but also value their partner's sexuality enough to not want to deprive it. The point is that by being sexually authentic, both individuals have the opportunity to be truly seen, get their needs met within the relationship, or make an informed mutual decision on how to move forward in a way that most benefits both parties.

HONORING EACH OTHER'S DIFFERENCES

I have often thought, and now have come to firmly believe, that couples therapy is one of the most powerful ways to get people unstuck, not only as a couple but also as individuals. The reasons for this are multidimensional but in short have everything to do with the concept of "differentiation." What is differentiation? To my knowledge, this is a concept first introduced by family therapist Murray Bowen to describe the level of individuality present within a family system.[2] The more differentiated a family system, the more the people in that family can advocate for themselves and treat one another like separate individuals who have their own wishes and desires rather than as objects that need to be controlled and molded in order for the family system to survive.

I don't work with entire family systems (children, grandparents, extended relatives, etc.), but the same certainly holds true in couples systems. When a couple is poorly differentiated, neither partner can tolerate signs of individuality or advances toward personal autonomy in the other person. Instead, the couple remains stuck in symbiosis, a system marked by unhealthy merger (these couples are the ones who may often be labeled as codependent), and may use a variety of methods to try to keep this balance intact. These methods may include various forms of manipulation (guilt-tripping, coercion, passive-aggressiveness) to manage the threat that is experienced by the other partner pushing toward more differentiation.

I want to emphasize that by differentiation, I don't mean that the partner who is trying to differentiate is going out and doing things on his or her own, which is called practicing; instead, the partner may try to initiate conversations or otherwise call attention to desired changes in the relationship. These discussions, while a necessary phase in any relationship, are intolerable to the undifferentiated partner and often cause tension, conflict, or even more clingy behavior, which pushes the differentiating partner even further away.

So how do I handle these kinds of couples' difficulties stemming from issues of differentiation? First, it is important to understand that research shows that couples that are well differentiated actually do much better than poorly differentiated couples. Couples therapists Ellyn Bader and Pete Pearson, out in the Bay area, compare this process to the individual stages of childhood development outlined by psychoanalyst Margaret Mahler.[3] In this model, the child first experiences symbiosis with the parent, then slowly starts to comprehend its difference from the parent (differentiation), then willfully attempts to assert its independence (practicing), and then finally comes full circle to embracing its relationship with the parent (rapprochement).[4] According to Mahler, all of these stages are necessary for proper childhood development. Similarly, Bader and Pearson argue that differentiation is a necessary step in the development of any romantic relationship.

In short, I don't try to reel in the differentiating partner. Instead, I see my role as a facilitator in helping both partners to differentiate in healthy ways that will allow them to function positively both as individuals and as a couple. As I often tell couples, when you get together, you create three distinct entities—the two individuals, and now the third entity, the couple. If either of these entities disappears, if either of you loses your individual identity, you will undermine the potential future success of the relationship. Differentiation.

How does this play into my work with couples and sexuality? Actually, quite a bit. Often issues in differentiation come out most distinctly in areas revolving around sexuality. For example, what if one partner is looking to explore some long-held fantasies? The very act of articulating his needs or her needs to the partner is an act of differentiation. What if someone is looking to open up the relationship? That discussion is a discussion of differentiation. Now I'm not saying that the other partner should just simply acquiesce and go with whatever is being presented. That passivity would be a very undifferentiated approach, the opposite of what we are aiming at. On the other hand, rage, defensiveness, or withdrawal are also unhelpful responses and are clearly undifferentiated forms of communication. Instead, my goal would be to help both partners to really hear and understand the wishes and desires of their lover and work together to come up with a situation that works for both.

I'm not saying it's easy. And sometimes both people are moving in such opposite directions that there really is no clear common ground. As mentioned earlier, sometimes people can agree (we will do these things together), sometimes they agree to disagree (sublimating desires because the relationship is more important), or DADT (don't ask, don't tell) or some derivative, and sometimes they just disagree (going separate ways because our needs and desires are no longer compatible). I always advocate for the reparation of the relationship, and fortunately, most of the time I can help the relationship survive differentiation and come out stronger than ever on the other end. And those few times where it doesn't work out, my task is to help the couple work together as amicably as possible to move forward in their decision.

But—and here's the most important point—if the couple is unable to move toward differentiation and embrace it, then the relationship stands far less chance of succeeding and not only surviving but thriving. The way I see it, differentiation within a couple is like growing pains. We have to go through some pain in order to come out stronger and more resilient on the other side. And those couples who do often find themselves with a relationship that is much deeper, more transparent, and more authentic than they ever may have imagined before they began differentiating.

BUILDING COLLABORATION

What we are really looking to foster here is a simple, yet magical word—collaboration. But what if the couple already has so much resentment and conflict that they are simply unable to collaborate on anything, let alone sex? Collaboration is very difficult for folks to pull off when they feel flooded with anger since they so often go into a fear-driven (fight or flight) response. Let's talk more about how I handle these situations, specifically anger, resentment, and fear, when it comes to the way that couples communicate. I am indebted to the work of Dan Wile and his writings on collaborative couples treatment for much of my thinking here.[5]

Wile breaks down couples' communication patterns into three main categories. The first two are highly toxic and unproductive and generally occur when one or both partners feel threatened and triggered. The first of these two is antagonistic communication. This means exactly what it sounds like. This is where individuals are harsh, critical, angry in tone, loud, and demeaning. It corresponds to the fight response of animals that feel threatened. Next is the withdrawal form of communication. This corresponds to the flight response. Examples include stating that nothing is wrong when it obviously is and then acting out in a passive-aggressive way, leaving the scene of the discussion, refusing to talk, and shutting down. Stuff like that. Whereas antagonism is too aggressive, withdrawal is extremely avoidant.

Antagonistic and withdrawal styles are often found in the same relational dynamic. Antagonistic individuals may find themselves in partnership with withdrawing individuals, and their triggers fit together like a jigsaw puzzle. Classic push-pull dynamics that perhaps some readers have heard or read about. None of this stuff is productive, but I also want to make clear that it is not necessarily pathological or abnormal. Indeed, we are wired to mobilize to fight or flee when we feel unsafe, so the issue here is not with our natural response to defend ourselves but rather with a more systemic issue of lack of (the subjective feeling of) safety within the relational framework. So what we must do is twofold: build more capacity to tolerate emotional triggers and build more of an overall feeling of safety between the partners.

Let's focus on the building of safety. We do this primarily through the third means of communication—confiding. Confiding communication requires the individual to stay present and discuss one's feelings from a first-person point of view. It demands authenticity and the risk of exposing one's vulnerabilities. Easier said than done when bullets are flying, right? Well, we want to start modeling this kind of behavior in the therapy room so that all partners can internalize the experience of hearing each other this way and then having more capacity to take these skills home with them. It takes time. It's not going to happen overnight, but I want to start helping couples to have the lived experience of being able to communicate with each other on a different level, one that may initially feel safer only because it is being conducted in my consulting office.

Wile calls this "finding one's voice" as opposed to the "losing one's voice" that occurs when we are in fight/flight mode. So what may a confiding communication look like? Sometimes I may model it by speaking on behalf of one or both partners. So, for example, for the withdrawing partner who has lost his/her voice and has become too triggered to be able to stay present in communication, I may say to the other person as if I were the partner, "I would like to tell how I feel but I am too afraid that you might get mad and reject me for it." I would like both partners to hear what that sounds like, for the withdrawing partner to feel what it's like to have voice given to one's internal thoughts and for the antagonistic partner to perhaps hear these truths for the first time.

For the antagonistic partner, I might say, "I feel really hurt when you withdraw from me and I don't know how to get my needs met without trying harder by showing you how mad and upset I am." Something like that. Doesn't have to be exact or perfect; just get the sense of it down. I may have both partners practicing in this way, finding ways of reclaiming their voice a little at a time by letting their partner peek into their authentic selves. And in this way we build safety because our minds seek congruence, and when we have lived experiences, our minds form conclusions in order to explain these events. So when we take careful, measured risks of exposing our true selves in this kind of authentic way, and we are not hurt, and we are not rejected, but instead we see that the results are positive, we then start to transform our beliefs and conclude that we must be safe after all since our voice was heard and validated.

I'll end here for now since I think I've made my point. There are three basic ways that couples communicate, and the first two are tied into primordial, animalistic responses to threat. By practicing the third type, confiding communication, we model a safe space in which we can work to mitigate and reverse the damage created by the first two ineffective modes of communicating.

Now, that we've gotten that out of the way, let's put it all together.

Keeping sex red-hot in the relationship requires several important things:

1. Prioritizing sex
2. Planning it into the couple's daily or weekly schedule
3. Sexual authenticity and openness
4. Creating sexual menus
5. Negotiating the sexual menus

One last item is left—putting the menus into action. This is where it can really get fun. When both individuals know what their partner wants, they can incorporate those fantasies both inside the bedroom and out. For example, they can decide to pick one total menu item for that evening, or both can choose one item from their list, or both can choose one item from the other's list. The possibilities are endless. They can earn menu items by doing certain things outside the bedroom, such as completing a house chore or doing something thoughtful for the other person.

For example, finally fixing that old porch gets two menu items for Felix on Saturday night—some hair pulling and spanking—while that thoughtful anniversary card gets Sarah an extra menu item on Monday and Wednesday—some light bondage Monday and a dash of nipple play on Wednesday. Maybe throw in a little rimming as an added bonus.

In this way, couples feel connected and sexually charged throughout the week. They practice important skills like open communication, transparency, and negotiation. They want to do nice things for each other. They feel collaborative and creative. And their relationship feels playful and fun. What's not to like?

Some of my most successful couples learn to practice these techniques. It's not easy at first. There's a lot of negative social conditioning that gets in the way. It feels awkward to have such open discussions about sexuality. It's hard to open up about things that have felt so shameful for so long. But finally doing so is powerfully rewarding. Those who have the courage to open themselves to sexual authenticity reap the reward of having a relationship that is not only sustainable but keeps sustaining itself. Through undoing sexual repression, individuals find that they can use their sexual authenticity to enrich both their lives and their relationships.

NO MAN IS AN ISLAND: FINDING AND BUILDING COMMUNITY

The steps I've outlined above take time. Years of repression, shame, and fear cannot be undone overnight. But as a sex therapist, I am richly rewarded in seeing individuals undo their shackles, embrace their true and authentic sexual identities, and use it to improve their lives right before my eyes. I think it's very helpful for individuals and couples to have a professional guide to help them through the process. But that guide can't be there forever. Once treatment is over, individuals and couples often find themselves on their own, which is why I recommend finding community for most of them.

In this era of the Internet, information is not hard to find. But often people need a simple push and some guidance to cut through the riff-raff and find their way. Finding a community of like-minded individuals helps people consolidate their gains and continue on their journey among peers who can offer continued encouragement and support.

The best place to start is often the Internet, but with a few caveats. Online, one can find just about anyone and anything. There's a lot of information out there, but much of it is wrong. Also, the anonymity of the Internet encourages many folks who are not very serious to adopt various online personas that they never intend to act on or live out. In other words, there are a lot of time wasters, poseurs, and fakers online. That comes with the territory.

As a result, I often suggest that folks get an idea of what's out there online first and then try to move as soon as possible to meeting people in real life. A good introductory resource for kinky people is Fet-life.com. Fetlife boasts over two million people, most of whom stay online and who you'll never meet in real life, but the point is that there is so much variety on the site that you're bound to find some interesting aspects to learn from. Indeed, it's very empowering for someone who thinks that he or she is the only person on the planet who has some kind of obscure fetish to then realize that there are hundreds of others online all talking about the same thing.

Probably the best part about Fetlife is the events announcements. Through this feature, anyone can see what local events are planned for the upcoming week. As I mentioned previously, in most cities there are newbie events called munches, where kinky folks get together at local diners to meet each other in a low-pressure, nonsexual atmosphere. Most cities have kinky organizations that serve that town. For example, New York has the Eulenspiegel Society, DC has Black Rose, and San Francisco has the Society of Janus.

The same is true for the LGBT community. All large cities have centers that provide mental health and community-based activities for lesbian, gay, and transgender folks. The Gay Center, in New York City, for example, is an outstanding resource. It provides advocacy, cultural events, support services, and educational resources and also hosts events and meetings for other groups of people, such as kinky and polyamorous people.

Most of the activity among polyamorous people happens online, since there are really few physical locations for polyamorous events. There are, however, large conferences and gatherings for poly people with names such as OpenCon and PolyCon. All World Acres, a large clothing-optional resort area in Tampa, Florida, has various poly events throughout the year, including the Southern Polyamory Gathering and other events that draw a heavy poly crowd. Loving More is a national organization with several local chapters that put on events.

Burning Man, a large pansexual event held in late August in Nevada, draws a poly crowd and has a Poly Paradise theme camp. The Human Awareness Institute (HAI) holds relationship and intimacy events both in California and in the Northeast and attracts poly folk who may often be looking to try it out for the first time. Local organizations such as Polyamorous NYC in New York City specifically seek to promote the polyamorous lifestyle within the LGBT community. In fact, there is often a lot of overlap between the LGBT, kinky, and polyamory communities.

Swingers can find numerous resources in virtually every big city. There are large numbers of website personals out there to find other like-minded couples, but like anywhere else, there are a lot of unserious people posing online. My best advice for couples starting out is to go to a few in-person swinger parties to determine their limits. At these events, newbie couples can often merely observe or meet other people without getting involved.

Often couples experiment with soft swinging at first, which is a loose term that could mean being sexual with each other while others observe, or even doing some light sexual things with others, such as kissing or maybe even oral sex. Basically, no penetration. For a lot of couples, it's often a big step to be seen naked by others and watched as they have sex. Couples may decide that soft swinging is enough, or they may feel uncomfortable by the exhibitionism and realize that swinging is best for them only as a fantasy. Or they may love it and want to push the envelope further. Same goes for anyone else exploring his or her sexuality.

Often people find that after exploring the social scene for their particular interests, they settle into a specific circle of people whom they interact with on a more private level. I think that is a normal course of development. Most sexual scenes held in a public space attract new and curious people or more experienced folks who are specifically attracted to the exhibitionistic aspect of public play.

I know that entering a scene is not for everybody, but it is especially helpful for those who are in the early stages of coming to terms with their sexual identity and need the positive reinforcement of community and peers.

The kink community has a guiding principle for any activity of its members: safe, sane, and consensual. I use that lens in counseling my clients. As long as the sexual activity is safe, sane, and consensual, everyone will be okay. I help my clients define their limits so that they are clear on what seems safe to them and can also communicate their consensual desires to a prospective partner.

As long as we put our due diligence into it, even making mistakes can be an enriching experience. We learn and grow through experience, even our mistakes. Even if the experience turned out to be less than expected, as long as we stayed true to firm boundaries, the experience can be used positively to help us understand ourselves better.

For this reason, I encourage my clients to stick their toe into a scene and see what comes out of it. They can always process their experience with me. Not everyone who is exploring his or her sexuality has a therapist. I understand that. But every scene has its elders. I encourage individuals who are looking to explore their sexualities to go to as many in-person educational events as possible. Through these workshops and trainings, they can meet possible mentors who can guide them in a similar way that I might as a therapist.

IN CONCLUSION

Over the course of this book, we've covered a lot of ground. We've discussed how our innate sexual selves are hemmed in and oppressed by a culture that needs conformity for its survival. We've covered all the ways in which our culture tries to indoctrinate us with fear of natural sexual expression and taken a look at how that plays out in the stories of the day, ranging from sex addiction to homosexuality, prostitution, and kink. We've also covered specific techniques that I use as a sex therapist and that anyone can use to break free of this needless and unfortunate nonsense and really start living life in an authentic way, true to one's sexual identity. That said, if you come away from this book with only one central idea, I want you to come away with the knowledge that being sexual—knowing oneself sexually and really experiencing it to its full vitality—is one of our main gifts of living and being human. As long as what you are doing is safe and consensual, acting on your sexual interests is as close as it gets to being "one" with the world.

Before you think I'm getting too New Age, let me leave you with this. Years ago, psychologist Abraham Maslow created a pyramid to represent the hierarchy of human needs.[6] At the bottom are basic needs such as food and shelter. At the top is "self-actualization," a term meant to describe the process of reaching one's full potential. Nothing is greater or more powerful than self-actualization. It is the highest level any human can hope to achieve. According to Maslow, less than 1 percent reach this level.[7]

In my clinical experience, being authentically sexual is self-actualization. It is throwing away layers of social shame and stigma to discover one's core identity and then incorporating that identity into daily life.

By discovering our sexualities, we discard old crap that doesn't work for us and replace it with ways of living that make sense. When we are free to be ourselves, then and only then can we truly live freely.

Happy fucking.

POSTSCRIPT

On the afternoon of May 11, 2015, after many months (even years) of infighting on the members Listserv of the American Association of Sex Educators, Counselors, and Therapists (AASECT), I sent out an e-mail to the entire list but directed specifically toward Alexandra Katehakis, founder and clinical director of the Center for Healthy Sex in Los Angeles.

That e-mail launched a series of events that I believe may be the start of a paradigm shift in my field. I have debated with myself long and hard whether or not I should discuss this in this book, and if so, how I should go about doing it. In the end, I decided to place it in the postscript and offer it to my readers in its entirety and unedited, even if all of it might not make total sense without its proper context. Its proper home is probably in the postscript anyway, as my hope is that my message and the resulting events are only the beginning of something new. Something that hasn't been written yet. Perhaps another chapter? Or, even better, perhaps another book?

> Alex,
> Would you be willing to support a position statement by AASECT that included the language that all erotic minorities and non-normative sexual practices are not a symptom of sex addiction? I'm also referring to people who are dystonic and shamed up about their sexuality—so for example a man who comes to a sex addiction therapist and tells the therapist he feels disturbed by his desires to be spanked, that man would be told that he is not a sex addict and would

be referred out to a sex therapist. Would you support that? What about someone who struggles with monogamy, perhaps monogamy is not part of his sexual configuration? (see the recent Sari van Anders article in *Archives of Sexual Behavior*). Would you support some language about this in the statement? For example, if this man has cheated on his spouse and struggles to be monogamous, he would be treated for his infidelity but his desire for multiple partners would not be diagnosed as a sex addiction? Would you also support that?

If we can come to a common agreement on this and then all work together to have AASECT pass a statement, I think a lot of the debate on this list would wane. You can take all of the folks who spend their life savings on prostitutes, who lose their jobs because they can't stop looking at porn at work and who can't even get to work because they spent all night masturbating and call them whatever you want (although I still wouldn't agree that it's an addiction), but I don't think most people would get that worked up over it, just leave everyone else (mentioned above) out of it.

What do you say?

Needless to say, Alex said yes, and together we went forward, building a coalition of interested clinicians that would help us draft an official organizational position statement, standing up against and condemning any kind of ideology or therapeutic treatment aimed at pathologizing, shaming, or changing any form of sexual expression, as long as it was consensual. It took almost six months and numerous drafts. We did made compromises on some of the language, but that's usually how things roll when it comes to making large-scale organizational changes: one step at a time, each step pushing the ball ever so slightly forward until the goal has been accomplished.

In the spirit of future progress, I proudly present to you the efforts of those six months, that moment in time captured within AASECT's official position statement on "Sexual Expression Including Orientation and Identity." And I dreamily look forward to more progress that is yet ahead. Are you with me?

AASECT POSITION STATEMENT NOVEMBER 2015

Sexual Expression Including Orientation and Identity: Treatment and Education Foundations

It is the position of the American Association of Sexuality Educators, Counselors, and Therapists that we oppose any and all therapy models and interventions as well as any educational programs and curricula that seek to pathologize, dictate, or prescribe a person's sexual orientation, identity, and/or consensual, sexual expression, whether or not it is conventional or atypical. Regardless of how such clinical interventions or educational programs are labeled or named, AASECT recommends all helping and educating professionals to utilize best practices and culturally relevant resources for foundation and reference.

Furthermore: AASECT affirms that sexuality is central to the human experience and sexual rights must be honored in order for sexual health and overall well-being to be obtained. Informed by the best empirical research, AASECT recognizes human sexual experiences as diverse and supports the acceptance of sexual diversity while embracing consensual sexual expression within the framework of human rights and social justice.

AASECT accepts the evidence that human sexual experience includes a vast spectrum of sexual expression, orientation, and identities. These sexualities, between consenting adults when agreed upon, with permission, and assenting, are typically not psychopathological behaviors. Indeed, recent peer-reviewed research on these sexual experiences shows no correlation to pathology.

AASECT further asserts that all people seeking treatment and education about consensual sexual behavior, identity, or orientation deserve accurate information. AASECT accepts that the empirical evidence is reasonably complete on reparative and conversion therapies that attempt to change sexual orientation or identity and shows that these techniques are experimental at best and overwhelmingly ineffective, with harmful consequences for clients widely documented.

AASECT takes the position that social justice plays an essential and foundational role in the organization's mission. Individuals have the right to be free as possible from undue constraints (e.g. discrimination, stigmatization, oppression and violence) along with the freedom to consensual sexual expression. Destigmatizing human sexual expression and experiences as well as creating and maintaining safe space for those who have been traditionally marginalized are essential practices for AASECT members who are predominately mental health practitioners and educators. This overarching goal compels AASECT to disavow any therapeutic and educational effort that, even if unwittingly, violates or impinges on AASECT's vision of human rights and social justice.

NOTES

I. THROUGH THE KEYHOLE

1. Joseph Campbell, *Pathways to Bliss: Mythology and Personal Transformation*, ed. David Kudler (Novato, CA: New World Library, 2004), 6–10.

2. Campbell, *Pathways to Bliss*, 6–10.

3. Samantha J. Dawson, Brittany A. Bannerman, and Martin L. Lalumière, "Paraphilic Interests: An Examination of Sex Differences in a Nonclinical Sample," *Sex Abuse* 28, no. 1 (2016): 20–45, first published in *Sexual Abuse: A Journal of Research and Treatment* (2014).

4. John Money, *Lovemaps: Clinical Concepts of Sexual/Erotic Health and Pathology, Paraphilia, and Gender Transposition of Childhood, Adolescence, and Maturity* (London: Ardent Media, 1986), 215.

5. Ogi Ogas and Sai Gaddam, *A Billion Wicked Thoughts: What the World's Largest Experiment Reveals about Human Desire* (New York: Dutton, 2011), 53.

6. James G. Pfaus, Kirsten A. Erickson, and Stella Talianakis, "Somatosensory Conditioning of Sexual Arousal and Copulatory Behavior in the Male Rat: A Model of Fetish Development," *Physiology & Behavior* 122 (2013): 1–7.

7. Simon Baron-Cohen et al., "Why Are Autism Spectrum Conditions More Prevalent in Males?," *PLoS Biol* 9, no. 6 (2011): e1001081, doi:10.1371/journal.pbio.1001081.

8. Richard A. Lippa, "Sex Differences in Personality Traits and Gender-Related Occupational Preferences across 53 Nations: Testing Evolutionary and Social-Environmental Theories," *Archives of Sexual Behavior* 39, no. 3 (2010): 619–36.

9. Richard Krafft-Ebing, *Psychopathia Sexualis* (Stuttgart: Enke, 1907).

10. Michel Foucault, *The History of Sexuality* (London: Allen Lane, 1978).

11. Sigmund Freud, *The Interpretation of Dreams* (New York: Basic, 2010).

12. Mark Goldfeder and Elisabeth Sheff, "Children in Polyamorous Families: A First Empirical Look," *Journal of Law and Social Deviance* 5 (2013): 150.

13. Warwick Hosking, "Australian Gay Men's Satisfaction with Sexual Agreements: The Roles of Relationship Quality, Jealousy, and Monogamy Attitudes," *Archives of Sexual Behavior* 43, no. 4 (2014): 823–32.

14. Amy C. Moors et al., "Attached to Monogamy? Avoidance Predicts Willingness to Engage (but Not Actual Engagement) in Consensual Non-monogamy," *Journal of Social and Personal Relationships* 32, no. 2 (2015): 222–40.

15. Anthony Giddens, *The Transformation of Intimacy: Sexuality, Love and Eroticism in Modern Societies* (Cambridge: Polity, 2013).

16. Knowledge Networks and Insight Policy Research, *Loneliness among Older Adults: A National Survey of Adults 45+* (Washington, DC: American Association of Retired Persons, 2010), http://assets.aarp.org/rgcenter/general/loneliness_2010.pdf.

17. Ethan Kross et al., "Facebook Use Predicts Declines in Subjective Well-Being in Young Adults," *PLoS ONE* 8, no. 8 (2013): e69841, doi:10.1371/journal.pone.0069841.

18. Lamar Clarkson, "Divorce Rates Falling, Report Finds," CNN, accessed Jan. 10, 2016, http://www.cnn.com/2011/LIVING/05/19/divorce.rates.drop/.

19. Christine R. Harris, "Sexual and Romantic Jealousy in Heterosexual and Homosexual Adults," *Psychological Science* 13, no. 1 (2002): 7–12.

20. Amber Marie Hinton-Dampf, "Non-monogamous Individuals Compared to Monogamous Individuals: The Differences in Their Relationships, Specifically Sexual Risk Behaviors and Level of Trust" (PhD diss., University of Missouri, Kansas City, 2011).

21. Donald L. Mosher, "Three Dimensions of Depth of Involvement in Human Sexual Response," *Journal of Sex Research* 16, no. 1 (1980): 1–42.

22. Cindy M. Meston and David M. Buss, "Why Humans Have Sex," *Archives of Sexual Behavior* 36, no. 4 (2007): 477–507.

23. Joan Roughgarden, *The Genial Gene: Deconstructing Darwinian Selfishness* (Berkeley: University of California Press, 2009).

2. THE BIRDS AND THE BEES

1. Alfred Charles Kinsey, Wardell Baxter Pomeroy, and Clyde Eugene Martin, *Sexual Behavior in the Human Male* (Philadelphia, PA: Saunders, 1948).

2. Alfred Charles Kinsey and Institute for Sex Research, *Sexual Behavior in the Human Female* (Philadelphia, PA: Saunders, 1953).

3. Ivanka Savic and Per Lindström, "PET and MRI Show Differences in Cerebral Asymmetry and Functional Connectivity between Homo-and Heterosexual Subjects," *Proceedings of the National Academy of Sciences* 105, no. 27 (2008): 9403–8.

4. Simon LeVay, "A Difference in Hypothalamic Structure between Heterosexual and Homosexual Men," *Science* 253, no. 5023 (1991): 1034–37.

5. Ray Blanchard, "Fraternal Birth Order and the Maternal Immune Hypothesis of Male Homosexuality," *Hormones and Behavior* 40, no. 2 (2001): 105–14.

6. Dean H. Hamer et al., "A Linkage between DNA Markers on the X Chromosome and Male Sexual Orientation." *Science* 261, no. 5119 (1993): 321–27.

7. A. R. Sanders et al., "Genome-wide Scan Demonstrates Significant Linkage for Male Sexual Orientation," *Psychological Medicine* 45, no. 7 (2015): 1379–88.

8. Brian W. Ward et al., *Sexual Orientation and Health among U.S. Adults: National Health Interview Survey, 2013* (Washington, DC: National Center for Health Statistics, 2014), accessed Jan. 10, 2016, http://www.cdc.gov/nchs/data/nhsr/nhsr077.pdf.

9. Neil Buhrich, J. Michael Bailey, and Nicholas G. Martin, "Sexual Orientation, Sexual Identity, and Sex-Dimorphic Behaviors in Male Twins." *Behavior Genetics* 21, no. 1 (1991): 75–96.

10. J. Michael Bailey, Michael P. Dunne, and Nicholas G. Martin, "Genetic and Environmental Influences on Sexual Orientation and Its Correlates in an Australian Twin Sample," *Journal of Personality and Social Psychology* 78, no. 3 (2000): 524.

11. Peter S. Bearman and Hannah Brückner, "Opposite-Sex Twins and Adolescent Same-Sex Attraction," *American Journal of Sociology* 107, no. 5 (2002): 1179–1205.

12. Tuck C. Ngun and Eric Vilain, "The Biological Basis of Human Sexual Orientation: Is There a Role for Epigenetics?," *Advances in Genetics* 86 (2014): 167–84.

13. Sergio E. Baranzini et al. "Genome, Epigenome and RNA Sequences of Monozygotic Twins Discordant for Multiple Sclerosis," *Nature* 464, no. 7293 (2010): 1351–56.

14. Kurt Freund et al., "Heterosexual Aversion in Homosexual Males." *British Journal of Psychiatry* 122, no. 567 (1973): 163–69.

15. Gerulf Rieger, Meredith L. Chivers, and J. Michael Bailey, "Sexual Arousal Patterns of Bisexual Men," *Psychological Science* 16, no. 8 (2005): 579–84.

16. C. David Tollison, Henry E. Adams, and Joseph W. Tollison, "Cognitive and Physiological Indices of Sexual Arousal in Homosexual, Bisexual, and Heterosexual Males," *Journal of Behavioral Assessment* 1, no. 4 (1979): 305–14.

17. Janet Lever, "Sexual Revelations: The 1994 *Advocate* Survey of Sexuality and Relationships: The Men," *Advocate* 661–62 (1994): 16–24.

18. Gerulf Rieger et al., "Male Bisexual Arousal: A Matter of Curiosity?," *Biological Psychology* 94, no. 3 (2013): 479–89.

19. Richard A. Lippa, "Men and Women with Bisexual Identities Show Bisexual Patterns of Sexual Attraction to Male and Female 'Swimsuit Models,'" *Archives of Sexual Behavior* 42, no. 2 (2013): 187–96.

20. Morag A. Yule, Lori A. Brotto, and Boris B. Gorzalka, "Biological Markers of Asexuality: Handedness, Birth Order, and Finger Length Ratios in Self-identified Asexual Men and Women," *Archives of Sexual Behavior* 43, no. 2 (2014): 299–310.

21. Lori A. Brotto and Morag A. Yule, "Physiological and Subjective Sexual Arousal in Self-Identified Asexual Women," *Archives of Sexual Behavior* 40, no. 4 (2011): 699–712.

22. Martin E. P. Seligman, *What You Can Change . . . and What You Can't: The Complete Guide to Successful Self-Improvement* (New York: Vintage, 2009).

23. Martin S. Weinberg, Colin J. Williams, and Cassandra Calhan, "Homosexual Foot Fetishism," *Archives of Sexual Behavior* 23, no. 6 (1994): 611–26.

24. William Granzig, private communication with author, April 14, 2012.

25. Amy Lykins, e-mail message to author, Feb. 3, 2015.

26. David M. Ortmann and Richard A. Sprott, *Sexual Outsiders: Understanding BDSM Sexualities and Communities* (Lanham, MD: Rowman & Littlefield, 2012), 117.

27. Andreas Spengler, "Manifest Sadomasochism of Males: Results of an Empirical Study," *Archives of Sexual Behavior* 6, no. 6 (1977): 441–56.

28. Charles Moser and Eugene E. Levitt, "An Exploratory-Descriptive Study of a Sadomasochistically Oriented Sample," *Journal of Sex Research* 23, no. 3 (1987): 322–37.

29. Gloria Brame, "BDSM/Fetish Demographics Survey Results," accessed Aug. 8, 2009, http://gloriabrame.com/therapy/bdsmsurveyresults.html.

30. Galen Fous, "Personal Erotic Myth Research Survey Report," accessed Feb. 3, 2016, https://secure.obsurvey.com/r.aspx?id=6D21827B-A66B-457B-89E3-D65E7B98765E.

31. John Alan Lee, "The Social Organization of Sexual Risk," *Alternative Lifestyles* 2, no. 1 (1979): 69–100.

32. Moser and Levitt, "Exploratory-Descriptive Study."

33. Juliet Richters et al., "Demographic and Psychosocial Features of Participants in Bondage and Discipline, 'Sadomasochism' or Dominance and Submission (BDSM): Data from a National Survey," *Journal of Sexual Medicine* 5, no. 7 (2008): 1660–68.

34. Christian C. Joyal, Amélie Cossette, and Vanessa Lapierre, "What Exactly Is an Unusual Sexual Fantasy?," *Journal of Sexual Medicine* 12, no. 2 (2015): 328–40.

35. American Psychiatric Association, *Diagnostic and Statistical Manual of Mental Disorders: DSM-5*, 5th ed. (Arlington, VA: American Psychiatric Publishing, 2013).

36. Peter J. Fagan et al., "A Comparison of Five-Factor Personality Dimensions in Males with Sexual Dysfunction and Males with Paraphilia," *Journal of Personality Assessment* 57, no. 3 (1991): 434–48.

37. Andreas A. Wismeijer and Marcel A. van Assen, "Psychological Characteristics of BDSM Practitioners," *Journal of Sexual Medicine* 10, no. 8 (2013): 1943–52.

38. Kerry L. Jang, W. John Livesley, and Philip A. Vemon, "Heritability of the Big Five Personality Dimensions and Their Facets: A Twin Study," *Journal of Personality* 64, no. 3 (1996): 577–92.

39. Thomas J. Bouchard and Matt McGue, "Genetic and Environmental Influences on Human Psychological Differences," *Journal of Neurobiology* 54, no. 1 (2003): 4–45.

40. Stella Chess and Alexander Thomas, "Temperamental Individuality from Childhood to Adolescence," *Journal of the American Academy of Child Psychiatry* 16, no. 2 (1977): 218–26.

41. A. C. Moors, T. D. Conley, and D. F. Selterman, "Personality Correlates of Attitudes and Desire to Engage in Consensual Non-monogamy among Lesbian, Gay, and Bisexual Individuals" (unpublished manuscript, 2014).

42. Jon Henley, "Paedophilia: Bringing Dark Desires to Light," *Guardian*, Jan. 3, 2013.

43. Laura Kane, "Is Pedophilia a Sexual Attraction?," *Star* (Toronto), Dec. 22, 2013, accessed Jan. 10, 2016, http://www.thestar.com/news/insight/2013/12/22/is_pedophilia_a_sexual_orientation.html.

44. Sarah Goode, "How Can We Prevent Child Abuse if We Don't Understand Paedophilia?," *Independent* (UK), Jan. 7, 2013, accessed Jan. 10, 2016, http://www.independent.co.uk/voices/comment/how-can-we-prevent-child-abuse-if-we-dont-understand-paedophilia-8438660.html.

45. Kathryn Becker-Blease, Daniel Friend, and Jennifer J. Freyd, "Child Sex Abuse Perpetrators among Male University Students" (poster presented at the 22nd Annual Meeting of the International Society for Traumatic Stress Studies, Hollywood, CA, Nov. 4–7, 2006).

46. James M. Cantor et al., "Cerebral White Matter Deficiencies in Pedophilic Men," *Journal of Psychiatric Research* 42, no. 3 (2008): 167–83.

47. Michael C. Seto, "Pedophilia," *Annual Review of Clinical Psychology* 5 (2009): 391–407.

48. Jan Hindman and James M. Peters, "Polygraph Testing Leads to Better Understanding Adult and Juvenile Sex Offenders," *Federal Probation* 65, no. 3 (2000): 8.

3. BE LIKE MIKE

1. Christopher Hooton, "A Long List of Sex Acts Just Got Banned in UK Porn," *Independent*, Dec. 2, 2014, accessed Jan. 10, 2016, http://www.independent.co.uk/news/uk/a-long-list-of-sex-acts-just-got-banned-in-uk-porn-9897174.html.

2. "Egypt's Appalling Crackdown on Gays," *New York Times*, Jan. 5, 2015, accessed Jan. 10, 2016, http://www.nytimes.com/2015/01/06/opinion/egypts-appalling-crackdown-on-gays.html.

3. "Russia: Anit-LGBT Law a Tool for Discrimination," Human Rights Watch, June 29, 2014, accessed Jan. 10, 2016, https://www.hrw.org/news/2014/06/29/russia-anti-lgbt-law-tool-discrimination.

4. Janson Wu, "Uganda's 'Kill the Gays' Bill Is Back," Daily Beast, March 1, 2015, accessed Jan. 10, 2016, http://www.thedailybeast.com/articles/2015/03/01/uganda-s-kill-the-gays-bill-is-back.html.

5. "UN: ISIS Orders Female Genital Mutilation in Iraq," Al Arabiya News, July 24, 2014, accessed Jan 10, 2016, http://english.alarabiya.net/en/News/middle-east/2014/07/24/-ISIS-order-female-genital-mutilation-in-Iraq.html.

6. Michael Shermer and Dennis McFarland, *The Science of Good and Evil: Why People Cheat, Gossip, Care, Share, and Follow the Golden Rule* (New York: Macmillan, 2004), 36.

7. Wilfred R. Bion, "Group Dynamics: A Review," *International Journal of Psychoanalysis* 33, no. 2 (1952): 235–47.

8. Jeff Greenberg, Tom Pyszczynski, and Sheldon Solomon, "The Causes and Consequences of a Need for Self-Esteem: A Terror Management Theory," in *Public Self and Private Self*, ed. Roy F. Baumeister, Springer Series in Social Psychology (New York: Springer, 1986), 189–212.

9. Dunbar, Robin. How many friends does one person need?: Dunbar's number and other evolutionary quirks. Faber & Faber, 2010.

10. Christopher Ryan and Cacilda Jethá. *Sex at Dawn: The Prehistoric Origins of Modern Sexuality* (New York: HarperCollins, 2010).

11. Michel Foucault, *The History of Sexuality* (London: Allen Lane, 1978).

12. Noam Chomsky and Edward Herman, *Manufacturing Consent: The Political Economy of the Mass Media* (New York: Pantheon, 1988).

13. Richard Langworth, ed., *Churchill by Himself: The Definitive Collection of Quotations* (New York: PublicAffairs, 2011), 574.

14. Georg Lukács, *History and Class Consciousness: Studies in Marxist Dialectics* (Cambridge, MA: MIT Press, 1971).

15. Sirens Media, "Balloon Fetish," *Strange Sex*, season 1, episode 5, aired August 1, 2010, TLC Network.

16. Sirens Media, "Weight for It and Desperate Measures," *Strange Sex*, season 2, episode 10, aired May 22, 2011, TLC Network.

17. Sirens Media, "Erotic Aroma and From Pleasure to Pain," *Strange Sex*, season 3, episode 4, aired July 22, 2012, TLC Network.

18. Violet Media, "Addicted to Psychics/Addicted to Body Casting," *My Strange Addiction*, season 6, episode 5, aired Jan. 21, 2015, TLC Network.

19. Sarah Hale, Anne-Lise Jacobsen, and Amy Yap Day, "Wax On, Wax Off," *Sex Sent Me to the ER*, season 1, episode 26, aired Feb. 21, 2015, TLC Network.

20. Sarah Hale, Anne-Lise Jacobsen, and Amy Yap Day, "Lock and Key," *Sex Sent Me to the ER*, season 1, episode 37, aired Feb. 7, 2015, TLC Network.

21. Sarah Hale, Anne-Lise Jacobsen, and Amy Yap Day, "Hot Air Affair," *Sex Sent Me to the ER*, season 1, episode 13, aired June 7, 2014, TLC Network.

22. Indigo Films, "Eye of the Beholder," *My Strange Criminal Addiction*, season 1, episode 4, aired Dec. 22, 2014, Investigation Discovery Network.

23. Indigo Films, "A Taste of the Bizarre," *My Strange Criminal Addiction*, season 1, episode 1, aired Dec. 1, 2014, Investigation Discovery Network.

24. Russell B. Adams, *"King C." Gillette: The Man and His Wonderful Shaving Device* (Boston, MA: Little, Brown, 1978).

25. Susannah Walker, *Style and Status: Selling Beauty to African American Women, 1920–1975* (Lexington: University Press of Kentucky, 2007).

26. David J. Sullivan, "The American Negro—An 'Export' Market at Home!" *Printer's Ink* 208, no. 3 (1944): 90.

27. Blaine J. Branchik, "Out in the Market: A History of the Gay Market Segment in the United States," *Journal of Macromarketing* 22, no. 1 (2002): 86–97.

4. LAW AND ORDER

1. *The Code of the Assura, c. 1075 BCE*, Fordham University *Ancient History Sourcebook*, accessed Feb. 5, 2016, http://legacy.fordham.edu/halsall/ancient/1075assyriancode.asp.

2. Kenneth James Dover, *Greek Homosexuality* (Cambridge, MA: Harvard University Press, 1989), 76.

3. Olivia F. Robinson and C. F. Robinson, *The Criminal Law of Ancient Rome* (London: Duckworth, 1995).

4. Jean-Claude Feray, Manfred Herzer, and Glen W. Peppel, "Homosexual Studies and Politics in the 19th Century: Karl Maria Kertbeny," *Journal of Homosexuality* 19, no. 1 (1990): 23–48.

5. Victor Asal, Udi Sommer, and Paul G. Harwood, "Original Sin: A Cross-National Study of the Legality of Homosexual Acts," *Comparative Political Studies* 46, no. 3 (2013): 320–51.

6. Byrne Fone, *Homophobia: A History* (New York: Picador, 2000).

7. Marcello Maestro, "A Pioneer for the Abolition of Capital Punishment: Cesare Beccaria," *Journal of the History of Ideas* 34, no. 3 (1973): 463–68.

8. Louis Crompton, "Homosexuals and the Death Penalty in Colonial America,"*Journal of Homosexuality* 1, no. 3 (1976): 277–93.

9. Crompton, "Homosexuals and the Death Penalty."

10. Caroline M. Wong, "Chemical Castration: Oregon's Innovative Approach to Sex Offender Rehabilitation, or Unconstitutional Punishment?," *Oregon Law Review* 80, no. 1 (2001): 267–301.

11. Shannon Minter, "Sodomy and Public Morality Offenses under US Immigration Law: Penalizing Lesbian and Gay Identity," *Cornell International Law Journal* 26 (1993): 771.

12. Henry F. Fradella, "Legal, Moral, and Social Reasons for Decriminalizing Sodomy," *Journal of Contemporary Criminal Justice* 18, no. 3 (2002): 279–301.

13. Laurence H. Tribe, "*Lawrence v. Texas*: The 'Fundamental Right' That Dare Not Speak Its Name," *Harvard Law Review* 117, no. 6 (2004): 1893–1955.

14. Heidi Meinzer, "Idaho's Throwback to Elizabethan England: Criminalizing a Civil Proceeding," *Family Law Quarterly* 34, no. 1 (2000): 165–75.

15. MCL 750.158, "Crime against Nature or Sodomy; Penalty," accessed Feb. 5, 2016, http://www.legislature.mi.gov/(S(01dyppz2m2h10hgzrhnqertg))/mileg.aspx?page=GetObject&objectname=mcl-750-158.

16. Khalil Al Hajal, "Michigan Gay Marriage Ban Overturned by Supreme Court," Michigan Live, accessed Feb. 5, 2016, http://www.mlive.com/news/detroit/index.ssf/2015/06/michigan_gay_marriage_ban_over_2.html.

17. Susan Wright, "Second National Survey of Violence & Discrimination against Sexual Minorities," National Coalition for Sexual Freedom (2008), accessed Feb. 5, 2016, https://ncsfreedom.org/images/stories/pdfs/BDSM_Survey/2008_bdsm_survey_analysis_final.pdf.

18. Natasha Barsotti, "BDSM Lifestyler Unfit to Drive a Limo: Police," Daily Xtra, accessed Feb. 5, 2016, http://www.dailyxtra.com/vancouver/news-and-ideas/news/bdsm-lifestyler-unfit-drive-limo-police-12812.

19. Chris White, "The Spanner Trials and the Changing Law on Sadomasochism in the UK," *Journal of Homosexuality* 50, no. 2–3 (2006): 167–87.

20. Marianne Giles, *Criminal Law in a Nutshell*, 3rd ed. (Andover, UK: Sweet & Maxwell, 1993); "Case Comment—Manslaughter: Death Caused by Vigorous Sexual Activity to Which Deceased Consented," *Criminal Law Review* (July 1995): 570–72.

21. Marty Klein and Charles Moser, "SM (Sadomasochistic) Interests as an Issue in a Child Custody Proceeding," *Journal of Homosexuality* 50, no. 2–3 (2006): 233–42.

22. "What Is Incident Reporting & Response," National Coalition for Sexual Freedom, accessed Feb. 5, 2016, https://ncsfreedom.org/key-programs/incident-response/incident-response.html.

23. "In Their Own Words," National Coalition for Sexual Freedom, accessed Feb. 5, 2016,https://ncsfreedom.org/images/stories/pdfs/BDSM_Survey/in_their_own_words.pdf.

24. Christine Harcourt and Basil Donovan, "The Many Faces of Sex Work," *Sexually Transmitted Infections* 81, no. 3 (2005): 201–6.

25. Ronald Weitzer, "Prostitution: Facts and Fictions," *Contexts* 6, no. 4 (2007): 28–33.

26. Lisa Duggan and Nan D. Hunter, *Sex Wars: Sexual Dissent and Political Culture*. New York: Routledge, 2006.

27. James D. Griffith et al., "Pornography Actresses: An Assessment of the Damaged Goods Hypothesis," *Journal of Sex Research* 50, no. 7 (2013): 621–32.

28. Weitzer, "Prostitution: Facts and Fictions."

29. Tanice Foltz, "Escort Services: An Emerging Middle-Class Sex-for-Money Scene," *California Sociologist* 2, no. 2 (1979): 105–33.

30. Sarah E. Romans et al., "The Mental and Physical Health of Female Sex Workers: A Comparative Study," *Australian and New Zealand Journal of Psychiatry* 35, no. 1 (2001): 75–80.

31. Weitzer, "Prostitution: Facts and Fictions."

32. Stephanie Church et al., "Violence by Clients towards Female Prostitutes in Different Work Settings: Questionnaire Survey," *British Medical Journal* 322, no. 7285 (2001): 524–25.

33. Ronald Weitzer, "The Mythology of Prostitution: Advocacy Research and Public Policy," *Sexuality Research and Social Policy* 7, no. 1 (2010): 15–29.

34. A. L. Daalder, *Lifting the Ban on Brothels: Prostitution in 2000–2001* (The Hague: Wetenschappelijk Onderzoek-en Documentatiecentrum, 2004).

35. C. Woodward et al., *Selling Sex in Queensland 2003: A Study of Prostitution in Queensland* (Brisbane: Prostitution Licensing Authority, 2004).

36. Prostitution Law Review Committee, "Report of the Prostitution Law Review Committee on the Operation of the Prostitution Reform Act, 2003" (Wellington: New Zealand Ministry of Justice, 2008), accessed Apr. 17, 2016, http://www.justice.govt.nz/policy/commercial-property-and-regulatory/prostitution/prostitution-law-review-committee/publications/plrc-report/documents/report.pdf.

37. "Hiring," Cupid's Escorts, accessed Dec. 30, 2015, http://www.cupidsescorts.ca/hiring-escorts/.

38. Grace Kong, *Sex Slaves: Polk County*, MSNBC, aired July 8, 2014.

39. Michel Foucault, *The History of Sexuality, Volume One: An Introduction* (New York: Vintage, 1980).

5. FEAR AND LOATHING

1. Charles Silverstein, "The Implications of Removing Homosexuality from the DSM as a Mental Disorder," *Archives of Sexual Behavior* 38, no. 2 (2009): 161–63.

2. "Sexual Integrity for Young Men," L.I.F.E Recovery International, accessed Aug. 20, 2012, http://freedomeveryday.org.

3. Joseph Nicolosi, *Reparative Therapy of Male Homosexuality: A New Clinical Approach* (Northvale, NJ: Jason Aronson, 1997).

4. Brian McGinnis, "Not Strictly Speaking: Why State Prohibitions against Practicing Sexual Orientation Change Efforts on Minors Are Constitutional under First Amendment Speech Principles," *Rutgers University Law Review* 67 (2015): 243.

5. Sona Dimidjian and Steven D. Hollon, "How Would We Know if Psychotherapy Were Harmful?," *American Psychologist* 65, no. 1 (2010): 21.

6. George A. Rekers, O. Ivar Lovaas, and Benson Low, "The Behavioral Treatment of a 'Transsexual' Preadolescent Boy," *Journal of Abnormal Child Psychology* 2, no. 2 (1974): 99–116.

7. Scott Bronstein and Jessi Joseph, "Therapy to Change 'Feminine' Boy Created a Troubled Man, Family Says," CNN, June 10, 2011, accessed Jan. 10, 2016, http://www.cnn.com/2011/US/06/07/sissy.boy.experiment/.

8. Jeff Muskus, "George Rekers, Anti-Gay Activist, Caught with Male Escort 'Rentboy,'" Huffington Post, July 5, 2010, accessed Feb. 5, 2016, http://www.huffingtonpost.com/2010/05/05/george-rekers-anti-gay-ac_n_565142.html.

9. "Gay Prostitute Who Outed Ted Haggard Alleges Date with Idaho Sen. Larry Craig," Fox News, Dec. 3, 2007, accessed Feb. 5, 2016, http://www.foxnews.com/story/2007/12/03/gay-prostitute-who-outed-ted-haggard-alleges-date-with-idaho-sen-larry-craig.html.

10. Netta Weinstein et al., "Parental Autonomy Support and Discrepancies between Implicit and Explicit Sexual Identities: Dynamics of Self-Acceptance and Defense," *Journal of Personality and Social Psychology* 102, no. 4 (2012): 815.

11. Vivienne C. Cass, "Homosexuality Identity Formation: A Theoretical Model," *Journal of Homosexuality* 4, no. 3 (1979): 219–35.

12. Morty Finklestein, "Which Sex Addiction Program Do You Belong In?," The Fix, March 25, 2013, accessed Feb. 5, 2016, https://www.thefix.com/content/sexual-addiction-sex-recovery2002?page=all.

13. Joe Kort, e-mail message to author, Nov. 22, 2015.

14. Laura Italiano, "Call Girl: Eliot Spitzer Liked to Choke Me," *New York Post*, Dec. 29, 2013, accessed Feb. 5, 2016, http://nypost.com/2013/12/29/call-girl-tell-all-eliot-spitzer-liked-to-choke-me-was-into-struggle/; Carl Campanile, "Weiner Caught Sending Dirty Messages and Photos a Year after His Sexting Scandal," *New York Post*, July 24, 2013, accessed Feb. 5, 2016, http://nypost.com/2013/07/24/weiner-caught-sending-dirty-messages-and-photos-a-year-after-his-sexting-scandal/.

15. Janice M. Irvine, *Disorders of Desire: Sex and Gender in Modern American Sexology* (Philadelphia, PA: Temple University Press, 1990), 164–166.

16. American Psychiatric Association, *Diagnostic and Statistical Manual of Mental Disorders: DSM-5*, 5th ed. (Arlington, VA: American Psychiatric Publishing, 2013).

17. Martin P. Kafka, "Hypersexual Disorder: A Proposed Diagnosis for DSM-V,"*Archives of Sexual Behavior* 39, no. 2 (2010): 377–400.

18. David J. Ley, *The Myth of Sex Addiction* (Lanham, MD: Rowman & Littlefield, 2012), 53.

19. Ley, *Myth of Sex Addiction*, 53.

20. Joshua N. Hook et al., "Methodological Review of Treatments for Nonparaphilic Hypersexual Behavior," *Journal of Sex & Marital Therapy* 40, no. 4 (2014): 294–308.

21. Robert Weiss, e-mail message to author, Feb. 8, 2015.

22. "About CSAT Certification and Training," International Institute for Trauma and Addiction Professionals, accessed Dec. 12, 2015, http://www.iitap.com/certification/csat-certification-and-training.

23. Patrick Carnes and Sharon O'Hara, "Sexual Addiction Screening Test (SAST)," *Tennessee Nurse* 54, no. 3 (1991): 29.

24. Jonathan Liew, "All Men Watch Porn, Scientists Find," *Telegraph*, Dec. 2, 2009.

25. Benjamin Edelman, "Red Light States: Who Buys Online Adult Entertainment?," *Journal of Economic Perspectives* 23, no. 1 (2009): 209–20.

26. Terri D. Fisher, Zachary T. Moore, and Mary-Jo Pittenger, "Sex on the Brain? An Examination of Frequency of Sexual Cognitions as a Function of Gender, Erotophilia, and Social Desirability," *Journal of Sex Research* 49, no. 1 (2012): 69–77.

27. Anne Campbell, "The Morning after the Night Before," *Human Nature* 19, no. 2 (2008): 157–73.

28. Patrick Carnes, *Out of the Shadows: Understanding Sexual Addiction* (Center City, MN: Hazelden, 2001).

29. American Psychiatric Association. *Diagnostic and Statistical Manual of Mental Disorders: DSM-5*, 5th ed. (Arlington, VA: American Psychiatric Publishing, 2013).

30. Katherine Ramsland, "The Many Sides of Ted Bundy," *Forensic Examiner*, September 2013, 18.

31. Andrea Kuszewski, "Your Brain on Sexual Imagery," Institute for Ethics & Emerging Technologies, Dec. 1, 2010, accessed Feb. 5, 2016, http://ieet.org/index.php/IEET/more/kuszewski2010121.

32. Valerie Voon et al., "Neural Correlates of Sexual Cue Reactivity in Individuals with and without Compulsive Sexual Behaviours," *PloS one* 9, no. 7 (2014): e102419, doi:10.1371/journal.pone.0102419.

33. Vaughn R. Steele et al., "Sexual Desire, Not Hypersexuality, Is Related to Neurophysiological Responses Elicited by Sexual Images," *Socioaffective Neuroscience & Psychology* 3 (2013).

34. Grubbs, Joshua B. et al., "Internet Pornography Use: Perceived Addiction, Psychological Distress, and the Validation of a Brief Measure," *Journal of Sex & Marital Therapy* 41, no. 1 (2015): 83–106.

35. John Money, *The Destroying Angel: Sex, Fitness & Food in the Legacy of Degeneracy Theory, Graham Crackers, Kellogg's Corn Flakes & American Health History* (Amherst, NY: Prometheus, 1985), 164.

36. Nicola Beisel, "Class, Culture, and Campaigns against Vice in Three American Cities, 1872–1892," *American Sociological Review* 55, no. 1 (1990): 44–62.

37. Money, *The Destroying Angel*, 84.

38. Milton Diamond, Eva Jozifkova, and Petr Weiss, "Pornography and Sex Crimes in the Czech Republic," *Archives of Sexual Behavior* 40, no. 5 (2011): 1037–43; Milton Diamond and Ayako Uchiyama, "Pornography, Rape, and Sex Crimes in Japan," *International Journal of Law and Psychiatry* 22, no. 1 (1999): 1–22; Milton Diamond, "The Effects of Pornography: An International Perspective," *Pornography* 101 (1999): 223–60; Berl Kutchinsky, "Pornography and Rape: Theory and Practice? Evidence from Crime Data in Four Countries Where Pornography Is Easily Available," *International Journal of Law and Psychiatry* 14, no. 1 (1991): 47–64; I. Landripet, A. Stulhofer, and M. Diamond, "Assessing the Influence of Pornography on Sexual Violence: A Cross-cultural Perspective" (paper presented at the International Academy for Sex Research, Amsterdam, Netherlands, July 2006), 12–15.

39. Todd D. Kendall, "Pornography, Rape, and the Internet," Institute of Industrial Economics, Sept. 2006, accessed Dec. 12, 2015, http://idei.fr/sites/default/files/medias/doc/conf/sic/papers_2007/kendall.pdf.

6. CH-CH-CHANGES, TURN AND FACE THE STRANGE

1. James O. Prochaska and Carlo C. DiClemente, "Transtheoretical Therapy: Toward a More Integrative Model of Change," *Psychotherapy: Theory, Research & Practice* 19, no. 3 (1982): 276.

2. Vivienne C. Cass, "Homosexuality Identity Formation: A Theoretical Model," *Journal of Homosexuality* 4, no. 3 (1979): 219–35.

3. Margaret L. Keeling and Maria Bermudez, "Externalizing Problems through Art and Writing: Experience of Process and Helpfulness," *Journal of Marital and Family Therapy* 32, no. 4 (2006): 405–19.

4. James W. Pennebaker and Cindy K. Chung, "Expressive Writing, Emotional Upheavals, and Health," in *Foundations of Health Psychology*, ed. Howard S. Friedman and Roxane Cohen Silver (New York: Oxford University Press, 2007), 263–84.

5. Joan E. Broderick, Doerte U. Junghaenel, and Joseph E. Schwartz, "Written Emotional Expression Produces Health Benefits in Fibromyalgia Patients," *Psychosomatic Medicine* 67, no. 2 (2005): 326–34.

7. THE AUTHENTIC SELF

1. Silvan S. Tomkins, "Affect Theory," in *Approaches to Emotion*, ed. Klaus R. Scherer and Paul Ekman (Hillsdale, NJ: Erlbaum, 1984): 163–95.

2. Paul Ekman and Wallace V. Friesen, *Unmasking the Face: A Guide to Recognizing Emotions from Facial Clues* (Cambridge, MA: Malor, 2003).

3. *Oxford Dictionaries Online*, s.v. "schema," accessed Feb. 5, 2016, http://www.oxforddictionaries.com/us/definition/american_english/schema.

4. Richard G. Morris et al., "Memory Reconsolidation: Sensitivity of Spatial Memory to Inhibition of Protein Synthesis in Dorsal Hippocampus during Encoding and Retrieval," *Neuron* 50, no. 3 (2006): 479–89.

5. Daniela Schiller et al., "Preventing the Return of Fear in Humans Using Reconsolidation Update Mechanisms," *Nature* 463, no. 7277 (2010): 49–53.

6. Marie-H. Monfils et al., "Extinction-Reconsolidation Boundaries: Key to Persistent Attenuation of Fear Memories," *Science* 324, no. 5929 (2009): 951–55.

7. Bruce Ecker and Brian Toomey, "Depotentiation of Symptom-Producing Implicit Memory in Coherence Therapy," *Journal of Constructivist Psychology* 21, no. 2 (2008): 87–150.

8. Peter A. Levine, *Waking the Tiger: Healing Trauma; The Innate Capacity to Transform Overwhelming Experiences* (Berkeley, CA: North Atlantic, 1997).

9. "Nature's Lessons in Healing Trauma: An Introduction to Somatic Experiencing," YouTube video, 27:33, posted by Somatic Experiencing Trauma Institute, Oct. 15, 2014, accessed Feb. 13, 2016, https://www.youtube.com/watch?v=nmJDkzDMllc.

10. Bessel A. van der Kolk, "Clinical Implications of Neuroscience Research in PTSD," *Annals of the New York Academy of Sciences* 1071, no. 1 (2006): 277–93.

11. Bessel van der Kolk, "The Body Keeps the Score" (keynote lecture, International IEDTA Conference, Washington DC, June 27, 2014).

12. Richard J. Lederman, "Medical Treatment of Performance Anxiety," *Anxiety* 1 (1999): 2.

13. Roger K. Pitman et al., "Pilot Study of Secondary Prevention of Posttraumatic Stress Disorder with Propranolol," *Biological Psychiatry* 51, no. 2 (2002): 189–92.

14. Guillaume Vaiva et al., "Immediate Treatment with Propranolol Decreases Posttraumatic Stress Disorder Two Months after Trauma," *Biological Psychiatry* 54, no. 9 (2003): 947–49.

15. Alain Brunet et al., "Effect of Post-retrieval Propranolol on Psychophysiologic Responding during Subsequent Script-Driven Traumatic Imagery in Post-traumatic Stress Disorder," *Journal of Psychiatric Research* 42, no. 6 (2008): 503–6.

16. Thawatchai Krisanaprakornkit et al., "Meditation Therapy for Anxiety Disorders," *Cochrane Database of Systematic Reviews* 1 (2006).

17. "Headspace," accessed Feb. 5, 2016, http://www.headspace.com.

18. "Muse," accessed Feb. 5, 2016, http://www.choosemuse.com.

19. Les Fehmi, *The Open-Focus Brain: Harnessing the Power of Attention to Heal Mind and Body* (Boulder, CO: Shambhala, 2007).

8. GET YOUR SEXY ON

1. Daniel J. Siegel, *The Developing Mind: How Relationships and the Brain Interact to Shape Who We Are* (New York: Guilford, 2015).

2. Noam Chomsky, *Reflections on Language* (New York: Pantheon, 1975), 3.

3. Tara L. Kraft and Sarah D. Pressman, "Grin and Bear It: The Influence of Manipulated Facial Expression on the Stress Response," *Psychological Science* 23, no. 11 (2012): 1372–78.

4. Melinda Wenner, "Smile! It Could Make You Happier," *Scientific American Mind* 20, no. 5 (2009): 14–15.

5. Wenner, "Smile! It Could Make You Happier."

6. Lance Dodes and Zachary Dodes, *The Sober Truth: Debunking the Bad Science behind 12-Step Programs and the Rehab Industry* (Boston: Beacon, 2014).

7. Steven C. Hayes, Kirk D. Strosahl, and Kelly G. Wilson, *Acceptance and Commitment Therapy: An Experiential Approach to Behavior Change* (New York: Guilford, 1999).

8. Alexander L. Chapman, Kim L. Gratz, and Milton Z. Brown, "Solving the Puzzle of Deliberate Self-Harm: The Experiential Avoidance Model," *Behaviour Research and Therapy* 44, no. 3 (2006): 371–94.

9. Gene Combs, *Narrative Therapy: The Social Construction of Preferred Realities* (New York: Norton, 1996).

10. Richard C. Schwartz, *Internal Family Systems Therapy* (New York: Guilford, 1997).

11. Roy F. Baumeister and John Tierney, *Willpower: Rediscovering the Greatest Human Strength* (New York: Penguin, 2011).

9. SPREADING YOUR WINGS

1. Matt Thornton, "Why Aliveness?," *Aliveness 101* (blog), July 30, 2005, accessed Feb. 13, 2016, http://aliveness101.blogspot.com/2005/07/why-aliveness.html.

2. Mihaly Csikszentmihalyi, *Flow: The Psychology of Optimal Experience* (New York: Harper Perennial, 1991).

3. Carl Gustav Jung, *The Portable Jung* (New York: Penguin, 1971).

4. Donald W. Winnicott, "Hate in the Countertransference," *International Journal of Psychoanalysis* 30, no. 2 (1949): 69–74.

5. Peter Weiss and Geoffrey Skelton, *The Persecution and Assassination of Jean-Paul Marat as Performed by the Inmates of the Asylum of Charenton under the Direction of the Marquis de Sade* (Woodstock, IL: Dramatic Publishing, 1964).

6. Marquis de Sade, *Three Complete Novels: "Justine," "Philosophy in the Bedroom," "Eugénie de Franval" and Other Writings* (London: Arrow, 1991).

7. Louis Reichenthal Gottschalk, *Jean Paul Marat: A Study in Radicalism* (Chicago, IL: University of Chicago Press, 1967).

8. Jean-Jacques Rousseau, *"Discourse on Political Economy" and "The Social Contract,"* trans. Christopher Betts (New York: Oxford University Press, 1999); Thomas Hobbes, *Leviathan: With Selected Variants from the Latin Edition of 1668*, ed. Edwin Curley (Indianapolis, IN: Hackett, 1994).

9. Jack Morin, *The Erotic Mind: Unlocking the Inner Sources of Passion and Fulfillment* (New York: HarperCollins, 2012).

10. Michael J. Bader, *Arousal: The Secret Logic of Sexual Fantasies* (New York: St. Martin's, 2003).

10. KEEPING THE FLAME RED-HOT

1. David Moris Schnarch, *Constructing the Sexual Crucible: An Integration of Sexual and Marital Therapy* (New York: Norton, 1991).

2. Murray Bowen, "Toward the Differentiation of Self in One's Family of Origin," in *Georgetown Family Symposium*, vol. 1, ed. E. Andres and J. Lorio (Washington, DC: Georgetown Medical Center, 1974).

3. Ellyn Bader and Peter Pearson, *In Quest of the Mythical Mate: A Developmental Approach to Diagnosis and Treatment in Couples Therapy* (New York: Routledge, 2013).

4. Margaret S. Mahler, "Rapprochement Subphase of the Separation-Individuation Process," *Psychoanalytic Quarterly* 41 (1972): 487–506.

5. Daniel B. Wile, *After the Fight: A Night in the Life of a Couple* (New York: Guilford, 1993).

6. Abraham H. Maslow, "A Dynamic Theory of Human Motivation," in *Understanding Human Motivation*, ed. Chalmers A. Stacey and Manfred DeMartino (Cleveland, OH: Howard Allen, 1958), 26–47.

7. Abraham H. Maslow, "Some Basic Propositions of a Growth and Self-Actualization Psychology," in *Perceiving, Behaving, Becoming: A New Focus for Education* (Washington, DC: Association for Supervision and Curriculum Development, 1962), 34–49.

ACKNOWLEDGMENTS

I would like to thank the following, in no particular order: Matthew Carnicelli, my agent, for getting my proposal in shape and believing in my message. Suzanne Staszak-Silva, my editor, for liking my work. Michael Christian, for his encouragement and guidance through the process of writing a proposal and finding an agent. Henriette Klauser, for telling me how much my proposal initially sucked and then helping me get it to not suck. Joe Winn, for being a good friend and mentor. Winston Wilde, for his supervision and mentoring. David Ley, for the work he does and his availability as a resource. Joe Kort, for being a strong ally. Richard Sprott, for the work he does and engaging me with his collaborative efforts. Zhana Vrangalova, for her help in locating some references. William Granzig, for believing in my potential. Michael Crocker, for helping me start my career. Dulcinea Pitagora, for being a sounding board and a source of collaborative inspiration. And most of all LA, who continuously shows me what true love looks like and without whose emotional support I would be nowhere now.

BIBLIOGRAPHY

Adams, J., and M. White. "Why Don't Stage-Based Activity Promotion Interventions Work?" *Health Education Research* 20, no. 2 (2005): 237–43.

Adams, Russell B. *"King C." Gillette: The Man and His Wonderful Shaving Device.* Boston, MA: Little, Brown, 1978.

American Psychiatric Association. *Diagnostic and Statistical Manual of Mental Disorders: DSM-5.* 5th ed. Arlington, VA: American Psychiatric Publishing, 2013.

Asal, Victor, Udi Sommer, and Paul G. Harwood. "Original Sin: A Cross-National Study of the Legality of Homosexual Acts." *Comparative Political Studies* 46, no. 3 (2013): 320–51.

Bader, Ellyn, and Peter Pearson. *In Quest of the Mythical Mate: A Developmental Approach to Diagnosis and Treatment in Couples Therapy.* New York: Routledge, 2013.

Bader, Michael J. *Arousal: The Secret Logic of Sexual Fantasies.* New York: St. Martin's, 2003.

Bailey, J. Michael, Michael P. Dunne, and Nicholas G. Martin. "Genetic and Environmental Influences on Sexual Orientation and Its Correlates in an Australian Twin Sample." *Journal of Personality and Social Psychology* 78, no. 3 (2000): 524.

Baranzini, Sergio E., J. Mudge, J. C. van Velkinburgh, P. Khankhanian, I. Khrebtukova, N. A. Miller, L. Zhang, et al. "Genome, Epigenome and RNA Sequences of Monozygotic Twins Discordant for Multiple Sclerosis." *Nature* 464, no. 7293 (2010): 1351–56.

Baron-Cohen, Simon, Michael V. Lombardo, Bonnie Auyeung, Emma Ashwin, Bhismadev Chakrabarti, and Rebecca Knickmeyer. "Why Are Autism Spectrum Conditions More Prevalent in Males?" *PLOS Biol* 9, no. 6 (2011): e1001081. doi:10.1371/journal.pbio.1001081.

Baumeister, Roy F., and John Tierney. *Willpower: Rediscovering the Greatest Human Strength.* New York: Penguin, 2011.

Bearman, Peter S., and Hannah Brückner. "Opposite-Sex Twins and Adolescent Same-Sex Attraction." *American Journal of Sociology* 107, no. 5 (2002): 1179–1205.

Becker-Blease, Kathryn, Daniel Friend, and Jennifer J. Freyd. "Child Sex Abuse Perpetrators among Male University Students." Poster presented at the 22nd Annual Meeting of the International Society for Traumatic Stress Studies, Hollywood, CA, Nov. 4–7, 2006.

Beisel, Nicola. "Class, Culture, and Campaigns against Vice in Three American Cities, 1872–1892." *American Sociological Review* 55, no. 1 (1990): 44–62.

Bion, Wilfred R. "Group Dynamics: A Review." *International Journal of Psychoanalysis* 33, no. 2 (1952): 235–47.

Blanchard, Ray. "Fraternal Birth Order and the Maternal Immune Hypothesis of Male Homosexuality." *Hormones and Behavior* 40, no. 2 (2001): 105–14.

Bouchard, Thomas J., and Matt McGue. "Genetic and Environmental Influences on Human Psychological Differences." *Journal of Neurobiology* 54, no. 1 (2003): 4–45.

Bowen, Murray. "Toward the Differentiation of Self in One's Family of Origin." In *Georgetown Family Symposium*, vol. 1, edited by E. Andres and J. Lorio. Washington, DC: Georgetown Medical Center, 1974.

Branchik, Blaine J. "Out in the Market: A History of the Gay Market Segment in the United States." *Journal of Macromarketing* 22, no. 1 (2002): 86–97.

Broderick, Joan E., Doerte U. Junghaenel, and Joseph E. Schwartz. "Written Emotional Expression Produces Health Benefits in Fibromyalgia Patients." *Psychosomatic Medicine* 67, no. 2 (2005): 326–34.

Brotto, Lori A., and Morag A. Yule. "Physiological and Subjective Sexual Arousal in Self-Identified Asexual Women." *Archives of Sexual Behavior* 40, no. 4 (2011): 699–712.

Brunet, Alain, S. P. Orr, J. Tremblay, K. Robertson, K. Nader, and R. K. Pitman. "Effect of Post-retrieval Propranolol on Psychophysiologic Responding during Subsequent Script-Driven Traumatic Imagery In Post-traumatic Stress Disorder." *Journal of Psychiatric Research* 42, no. 6 (2008): 503–6.

Buhrich, Neil, J. Michael Bailey, and Nicholas G. Martin. "Sexual Orientation, Sexual Identity, and Sex-Dimorphic Behaviors in Male Twins." *Behavior Genetics* 21, no. 1 (1991): 75–96.

Campbell, Anne. "The Morning after the Night Before." *Human Nature* 19, no. 2 (2008): 157–73.

Campbell, Joseph. *Pathways to Bliss: Mythology and Personal Transformation*. Edited by David Kudler. Novato, CA: New World Library, 2004.

Cantor, James M., Noor Kabani, Bruce K. Christensen, Robert B. Zipursky, Howard E. Barbaree, Robert Dickey, Philip E. Klassen, et al. "Cerebral White Matter Deficiencies in Pedophilic Men." *Journal of Psychiatric Research* 42, no. 3 (2008): 167–83.

Carnes, Patrick. *Out of the Shadows: Understanding Sexual Addiction*. Center City, MN: Hazelden, 2001.

Carnes, Patrick, and Sharon O'Hara. "Sexual Addiction Screening Test (SAST)." *Tennessee Nurse* 54, no. 3 (1991): 29.

Cass, Vivienne C. "Homosexuality Identity Formation: A Theoretical Model." *Journal of Homosexuality* 4, no. 3 (1979): 219–35.

Chapman, Alexander L., Kim L. Gratz, and Milton Z. Brown. "Solving the Puzzle of Deliberate Self-Harm: The Experiential Avoidance Model." *Behaviour Research and Therapy* 44, no. 3 (2006): 371–94.

Chess, Stella, and Alexander Thomas. "Temperamental Individuality from Childhood to Adolescence." *Journal of the American Academy of Child Psychiatry* 16, no. 2 (1977): 218–26.

Chomsky, Noam. *Reflections on Language*. New York: Pantheon, 1975.

Chomsky, Noam, and Edward Herman. *Manufacturing Consent: The Political Economy of the Mass Media*. New York: Pantheon, 1988.

Church, Stephanie, Marion Henderson, Marina Barnard, and Graham Hart. "Violence by Clients towards Female Prostitutes in Different Work Settings: Questionnaire Survey." *British Medical Journal* 322, no. 7285 (2001): 524–25.

Combs, Gene. *Narrative Therapy: The Social Construction of Preferred Realities*. New York: Norton, 1996.

Crompton, Louis. "Homosexuals and the Death Penalty in Colonial America." *Journal of Homosexuality* 1, no. 3 (1976): 277–93.

Csikszentmihalyi, Mihaly. *Flow: The Psychology of Optimal Experience*. New York: Harper Perennial, 1991.

Daalder, A. L. *Lifting the Ban on Brothels: Prostitution in 2000–2001*. The Hague: Wetenschappelijk Onderzoek-en Documentatiecentrum, 2004.

Dawson, Samantha J., Brittany A. Bannerman, and Martin L. Lalumière. "Paraphilic Interests: An Examination of Sex Differences in a Nonclinical Sample." *Sex Abuse* 28, no. 1 (2016): 20–45. First published in *Sexual Abuse: A Journal of Research and Treatment* (2014).

Diamond, Milton. "The Effects of Pornography: An International Perspective." *Pornography 101* (1999): 223–60.

Diamond, Milton, and Ayako Uchiyama. "Pornography, Rape, and Sex Crimes in Japan." *International Journal of Law and Psychiatry* 22, no. 1 (1999): 1–22.

Diamond, Milton, Eva Jozifkova, and Petr Weiss. "Pornography and Sex Crimes in the Czech Republic." *Archives of Sexual Behavior* 40, no. 5 (2011): 1037–43.

Dimidjian, Sona, and Steven D. Hollon. "How Would We Know if Psychotherapy Were Harmful?" *American Psychologist* 65, no. 1 (2010): 21.

Dodes, Lance, and Zachary Dodes. *The Sober Truth: Debunking the Bad Science behind 12-Step Programs and the Rehab Industry*. Boston: Beacon, 2014.

Dover, Kenneth James. *Greek Homosexuality*. Cambridge, MA: Harvard University Press, 1989.

Duggan, Lisa, and Nan D. Hunter. *Sex Wars: Sexual Dissent and Political Culture*. New York: Routledge, 2006.

Dunbar, Robin. *How Many Friends Does One Person Need? Dunbar's Number and Other Evolutionary Quirks*. London: Faber & Faber, 2010.

Ecker, Bruce, and Brian Toomey. "Depotentiation of Symptom-Producing Implicit Memory in Coherence Therapy." *Journal of Constructivist Psychology* 21, no. 2 (2008): 87–150.

Edelman, Benjamin. "Red Light States: Who Buys Online Adult Entertainment?" *Journal of Economic Perspectives* 23, no. 1 (2009): 209–20.

Ekman, Paul, and Wallace V. Friesen. *Unmasking the Face: A Guide to Recognizing Emotions from Facial Clues*. Cambridge, MA: Malor, 2003.

Fagan, Peter J., Thomas N. Wise, C. W. Schmidt Jr., Yula Ponticas, Randall D. Marshall, and Paul Costa Jr. "A Comparison of Five-Factor Personality Dimensions in Males with Sexual Dysfunction and Males with Paraphilia." *Journal of Personality Assessment* 57, no. 3 (1991): 434–48.

Fehmi, Les. *The Open-Focus Brain: Harnessing the Power of Attention to Heal Mind and Body*. Boulder, CO: Shambhala, 2007.

Feray, Jean-Claude, Manfred Herzer, and Glen W. Peppel. "Homosexual Studies and Politics in the 19th Century: Karl Maria Kertbeny." *Journal of Homosexuality* 19, no. 1 (1990): 23–48.

Fisher, Terri D., Zachary T. Moore, and Mary-Jo Pittenger. "Sex on the Brain? An Examination of Frequency of Sexual Cognitions as a Function of Gender, Erotophilia, and Social Desirability." *Journal of Sex Research* 49, no. 1 (2012): 69–77.

Foltz, Tanice. "Escort Services: An Emerging Middle-Class Sex-for-Money Scene." *California Sociologist* 2, no. 2 (1979): 105–33.

Fone, Byrne. *Homophobia: A History*. New York: Picador, 2000.

Foucault, Michel. *The History of Sexuality*. London: Allen Lane, 1978.

———. *The History of Sexuality, Volume One: An Introduction* (New York: Vintage, 1980).

Fradella, Henry F. "Legal, Moral, and Social Reasons for Decriminalizing Sodomy." *Journal of Contemporary Criminal Justice* 18, no. 3 (2002): 279–301.

Freud, Sigmund. *The Interpretation of Dreams*. New York: Basic, 2010.

Freund, Kurt, R. Langevin, S. Cibiri, and Y. Zajac. "Heterosexual Aversion in Homosexual Males." *British Journal of Psychiatry* 122, no. 567 (1973): 163–69.

Giddens, Anthony. *The Transformation of Intimacy: Sexuality, Love and Eroticism in Modern Societies*. Cambridge: Polity, 2013.

Giles, Marianne. *Criminal Law in a Nutshell*. 3rd ed. Andover, U.K.: Sweet & Maxwell, 1993.

Goldfeder, Mark, and Elisabeth Sheff. "Children in Polyamorous Families: A First Empirical Look." *Journal of Law and Social Deviance* 5 (2013): 150–243.

Gottschalk, Louis Reichenthal. *Jean Paul Marat: A Study in Radicalism*. Chicago, IL: University of Chicago Press, 1967.

Greenberg, Jeff, Tom Pyszczynski, and Sheldon Solomon. "The Causes and Consequences of a Need for Self-Esteem: A Terror Management Theory." In *Public Self and Private Self*, edited by Roy F. Baumeister, 189–212. Springer Series in Social Psychology. New York: Springer, 1986.

Griffith, James D., S. Mitchell, C. L. Hart, L. T. Adams, and L. L. Gu. "Pornography Actresses: An Assessment of the Damaged Goods Hypothesis." *Journal of Sex Research* 50, no. 7 (2013): 621–32.

Grubbs, Joshua B., Fred Volk, Julie J. Exline, and Kenneth I. Pargament. "Internet Pornography Use: Perceived Addiction, Psychological Distress, and the Validation of a Brief Measure." *Journal of Sex & Marital Therapy* 41, no. 1 (2015): 83–106.

Hamer, Dean H., Stella Hu, Victoria L. Magnuson, Nan Hu, and Angela M. L. Pattatucci. "A Linkage between DNA Markers on the X Chromosome and Male Sexual Orientation." *Science* 261, no. 5119 (1993): 321–27.

Harcourt, Christine, and Basil Donovan. "The Many Faces of Sex Work." *Sexually Transmitted Infections* 81, no. 3 (2005): 201–6.

Harris, Christine R. "Sexual and Romantic Jealousy in Heterosexual and Homosexual Adults." *Psychological Science* 13, no. 1 (2002): 7–12.

Hayes, Steven C., Kirk D. Strosahl, and Kelly G. Wilson. *Acceptance and Commitment Therapy: An Experiential Approach to Behavior Change.* New York: Guilford, 1999.

Hindman, Jan, and James M. Peters. "Polygraph Testing Leads to Better Understanding Adult and Juvenile Sex Offenders." *Federal Probation* 65, no. 3 (2000): 8.

Hinton-Dampf, Amber Marie. "Non-Monogamous Individuals Compared to Monogamous Individuals: The Differences in Their Relationships, Specifically Sexual Risk Behaviors and Level of Trust. PhD diss., University of Missouri, Kansas City, 2011.

Hobbes, Thomas. *Leviathan: With Selected Variants from the Latin Edition of 1668.* Edited by Edwin Curley. Indianapolis, IN: Hackett, 1994.

Hook, Joshua N., Rory C. Reid, J. Kim Penberthy, Don E. Davis, and David J. Jennings. "Methodological Review of Treatments for Nonparaphilic Hypersexual Behavior." *Journal of Sex & Marital Therapy* 40, no. 4 (2014): 294–308.

Hosking, Warwick. "Australian Gay Men's Satisfaction with Sexual Agreements: The Roles of Relationship Quality, Jealousy, and Monogamy Attitudes." *Archives of Sexual Behavior* 43, no. 4 (2014): 823–32.

Irvine, Janice M. *Disorders of Desire: Sex and Gender in Modern American Sexology.* Philadelphia, PA: Temple University Press, 1990.

Jang, Kerry L., W. John Livesley, and Philip A. Vemon. "Heritability of the Big Five Personality Dimensions and Their Facets: A Twin Study." *Journal of Personality* 64, no. 3 (1996): 577–92.

Joyal, Christian C., Amélie Cossette, and Vanessa Lapierre. "What Exactly Is an Unusual Sexual Fantasy?" *Journal of Sexual Medicine* 12, no. 2 (2015): 328–40.

Jung, Carl Gustav. *The Portable Jung.* New York: Penguin, 1971.

Kafka, Martin P. "Hypersexual Disorder: A Proposed Diagnosis for DSM-V." *Archives of Sexual Behavior* 39, no. 2 (2010): 377–400.

Keeling, Margaret L., and Maria Bermudez. "Externalizing Problems through Art and Writing: Experience of Process and Helpfulness." *Journal of Marital and Family Therapy* 32, no. 4 (2006): 405–19.

Kendall, Todd D. "Pornography, Rape, and the Internet." Institute of Industrial Economics, Sept. 2006. Accessed Dec. 12, 2015. http://idei.fr/sites/default/files/medias/doc/conf/sic/papers_2007/kendall.pdf.

Kinsey, Alfred Charles, and Institute for Sex Research. *Sexual Behavior in the Human Female.* Philadelphia, PA: Saunders, 1953.

Kinsey, Alfred Charles, Wardell Baxter Pomeroy, and Clyde Eugene Martin. *Sexual Behavior in the Human Male.* Philadelphia: Saunders, 1948.

Klein, Marty, and Charles Moser. "SM (Sadomasochistic) Interests as an Issue in a Child Custody Proceeding." *Journal of Homosexuality* 50, no. 2–3 (2006): 233–42.

Knowledge Networks and Insight Policy Research. *Loneliness among Older Adults: A National Survey of Adults 45+.* Washington, DC: American Association of Retired Persons, 2010. http://assets.aarp.org/rgcenter/general/loneliness_2010.pdf.

Krafft-Ebing, Richard. *Psychopathia Sexualis.* Stuttgart: Enke, 1907.

Kraft, Tara L., and Sarah D. Pressman. "Grin and Bear It: The Influence of Manipulated Facial Expression on the Stress Response." *Psychological Science* 23, no. 11 (2012): 1372–78.

Krisanaprakornkit, Thawatchai, Wimonrat Sriraj, Nawanant Piyavhatkul, and Malinee Laopaiboon. "Meditation Therapy for Anxiety Disorders." *Cochrane Database of Systematic Reviews* 1 (2006).

Kross, Ethan, Philippe Verduyn, Emre Demiralp, Jiyoung Park, David Seungjae Lee, Natalie Lin, Holly Shablack, et al. "Facebook Use Predicts Declines in Subjective Well-Being in Young Adults." *PloS one* 8, no. 8 (2013): e69841. doi:10.1371/journal.pone.0069841.

Kutchinsky, Berl. "Pornography and Rape: Theory and Practice? Evidence from Crime Data in Four Countries Where Pornography Is Easily Available." *International Journal of Law and Psychiatry* 14, no. 1 (1991): 47–64.

Landripet, I., A. Stulhofer, and M. Diamond. "Assessing the Influence of Pornography on Sexual Violence: A Cross-cultural Perspective." Paper presented at the *International Academy for Sex Research*, Amsterdam, Netherlands, July 2006.

Langworth, Richard, ed. *Churchill by Himself: The Definitive Collection of Quotations*. New York: PublicAffairs, 2011.

Lederman, Richard J. "Medical Treatment of Performance Anxiety." *Anxiety* 1 (1999): 2.

Lee, John Alan. "The Social Organization of Sexual Risk." *Alternative Lifestyles* 2, no. 1 (1979): 69–100.

LeVay, Simon. "A Difference in Hypothalamic Structure between Heterosexual and Homosexual Men." *Science* 253, no. 5023 (1991): 1034–37.

Lever, Janet. "Sexual Revelations: The 1994 *Advocate* Survey of Sexuality and Relationships; The Men." *Advocate* 661–662 (1994): 16–24.

Levine, Peter A. *Waking the Tiger: Healing Trauma: The Innate Capacity to Transform Overwhelming Experiences*. Berkeley, CA: North Atlantic, 1997.

Ley, David J. *The Myth of Sex Addiction*. Lanham, MD: Rowman & Littlefield, 2012.

Lippa, Richard A. "Men and Women with Bisexual Identities Show Bisexual Patterns of Sexual Attraction to Male and Female 'Swimsuit Models.'" *Archives of Sexual Behavior* 42, no. 2 (2013): 187–96.

———. "Sex Differences in Personality Traits and Gender-Related Occupational Preferences across 53 Nations: Testing Evolutionary and Social-Environmental Theories." *Archives of Sexual Behavior* 39, no. 3 (2010): 619–36.

Lukács, Georg. *History and Class Consciousness: Studies in Marxist Dialectics*. Cambridge, MA: MIT Press, 1971.

Maestro, Marcello. "A Pioneer for the Abolition of Capital Punishment: Cesare Beccaria." *Journal of the History of Ideas* 34, no. 3 (1973): 463–68.

Mahler, Margaret S. "Rapprochement Subphase of the Separation-Individuation Process." *Psychoanalytic Quarterly* 41 (1972): 487–506.

Maslow, Abraham H. "A Dynamic Theory of Human Motivation." In *Understanding Human Motivation*, edited by Chalmers A. Stacey and Manfred DeMartino, 26–47. Cleveland, OH: Howard Allen, 1958.

———. "Some Basic Propositions of a Growth and Self-Actualization Psychology." In *Perceiving, Behaving, Becoming: A New Focus for Education*, 34–49. Washington, DC: Association for Supervision and Curriculum Development, 1962.

McGinnis, Brian. "Not Strictly Speaking: Why State Prohibitions against Practicing Sexual Orientation Change Efforts on Minors Are Constitutional under First Amendment Speech Principles." *Rutgers University Law Review* 67 (2015): 243.

Meinzer, Heidi. "Idaho's Throwback to Elizabethan England: Criminalizing a Civil Proceeding." *Family Law Quarterly* 34, no. 1 (2000): 165–175.

Meston, Cindy M., and David M. Buss. "Why Humans Have Sex." *Archives of Sexual Behavior* 36, no. 4 (2007): 477–507.

Minter, Shannon. "Sodomy and Public Morality Offenses under US Immigration Law: Penalizing Lesbian and Gay Identity." *Cornell International Law Journal* 26 (1993): 771.

Money, John. *The Destroying Angel: Sex, Fitness & Food in the Legacy of Degeneracy Theory, Graham Crackers, Kellogg's Corn Flakes & American Health History.* Amherst, NY: Prometheus, 1985.

———. *Lovemaps: Clinical Concepts of Sexual/Erotic Health and Pathology, Paraphilia, and Gender Transposition of Childhood, Adolescence, and Maturity.* London: Ardent Media, 1986.

Monfils, Marie-H., Kiriana K. Cowansage, Eric Klann, and Joseph E. LeDoux. "Extinction-Reconsolidation Boundaries: Key to Persistent Attenuation of Fear Memories." *Science* 324, no. 5929 (2009): 951–55.

Moors, Amy C., Terri D. Conley, Robin S. Edelstein, and William J. Chopik. "Attached to Monogamy? Avoidance Predicts Willingness to Engage (but Not Actual Engagement) in Consensual Non-monogamy." *Journal of Social and Personal Relationships* 32, no. 2 (2015): 222–40.

Moors, A. C., T. D. Conley, and D. Selterman. "Personality Correlates of Attitudes and Desire to Engage in Consensual Non-monogamy among Lesbian, Gay, and Bisexual Individuals." Unpublished manuscript, 2014.

Morin, Jack. *The Erotic Mind: Unlocking the Inner Sources of Passion and Fulfillment.* New York: HarperCollins, 2012.

Morris, Richard G., J. Inglis, J. A. Ainge, H. J. Olverman, J. Tulloch, Y. Dudai, and P. A. Kelly. "Memory Reconsolidation: Sensitivity of Spatial Memory to Inhibition of Protein Synthesis in Dorsal Hippocampus during Encoding and Retrieval." *Neuron* 50, no. 3 (2006): 479–89.

Moser, Charles, and Eugene E. Levitt. "An Exploratory-Descriptive Study of a Sadomasochistically Oriented Sample." *Journal of Sex Research* 23, no. 3 (1987): 322–37.

Mosher, Donald L. "Three Dimensions of Depth of Involvement in Human Sexual Response." *Journal of Sex Research* 16, no. 1 (1980): 1–42.

Ngun, Tuck C., and Eric Vilain. "The Biological Basis of Human Sexual Orientation: Is There a Role for Epigenetics?" *Advances in Genetics* 86 (2014): 167–84.

Nicolosi, Joseph. *Reparative Therapy of Male Homosexuality: A New Clinical Approach.* Northvale, NJ: Jason Aronson, 1997.

Ogas, Ogi, and Sai Gaddam. *A Billion Wicked Thoughts: What the World's Largest Experiment Reveals about Human Desire.* New York: Dutton, 2011.

Ortmann, David M., and Richard A. Sprott. *Sexual Outsiders: Understanding BDSM Sexualities and Communities.* Lanham, MD: Rowman & Littlefield, 2012.

Pennebaker, James W., and Cindy K. Chung. "Expressive Writing, Emotional Upheavals, and Health." In *Foundations of Health Psychology,* edited by Howard S. Friedman and Roxane Cohen Silver, 263–84. New York: Oxford University Press, 2007.

Pfaus, James G., Kirsten A. Erickson, and Stella Talianakis. "Somatosensory Conditioning of Sexual Arousal and Copulatory Behavior in the Male Rat: A Model of Fetish Development." *Physiology & Behavior* 122 (2013): 1–7.

Pitman, Roger K., K. M. Sanders, R. M. Zusman, A. R. Healy, F. Cheema, N. B. Lasko, L. Cahill et al. "Pilot Study of Secondary Prevention of Posttraumatic Stress Disorder with Propranolol." *Biological Psychiatry* 51, no. 2 (2002): 189–92.

Prochaska, James O., and Carlo C. DiClemente. "Transtheoretical Therapy: Toward a More Integrative Model of Change." *Psychotherapy : Theory, Research & Practice* 19, no. 3 (1982): 276.

Prostitution Law Committee. "Report of the Prostitution Law Review Committee on the Operation of the Prostitution Reform Act, 2003." Wellington: New Zealand Ministry of Justice, 2008. Accessed Apr. 17, 2016. http://www.justice.govt.nz/policy/commercial-property-and-regulatory/prostitution/prostitution-law-review-committee/publications/plrc-report/documents/report.pdf.

Rekers, George A., O. Ivar Lovaas, and Benson Low. "The Behavioral Treatment of a 'Transsexual' Preadolescent Boy." *Journal of Abnormal Child Psychology* 2, no. 2 (1974): 99–116.

Richters, Juliet, Richard O. de Visser, Chris E. Rissel, Andrew E. Grulich, and Anthony M. A. Smith. "Demographic and Psychosocial Features of Participants in Bondage and Discipline, 'Sadomasochism' or Dominance and Submission (BDSM): Data from a National Survey." *Journal of Sexual Medicine* 5, no. 7 (2008): 1660–68.

Rieger, Gerulf, Allen M. Rosenthal, Brian M. Cash, Joan A. W. Linsenmeier, J. Michael Bailey, and Ritch C. Savin-Williams. "Male Bisexual Arousal: A Matter of Curiosity?" *Biological Psychology* 94, no. 3 (2013): 479–89.

Rieger, Gerulf, Meredith L. Chivers, and J. Michael Bailey. "Sexual Arousal Patterns of Bisexual Men." *Psychological Science* 16, no. 8 (2005): 579–84.

Robinson, Olivia F., and C. F. Robinson. *The Criminal Law of Ancient Rome*. London: Duckworth, 1995.

Romans, Sarah E., Kathleen Potter, Judy Martin, and Peter Herbison. "The Mental and Physical Health of Female Sex Workers: A Comparative Study." *Australian and New Zealand Journal of Psychiatry* 35, no. 1 (2001): 75–80.

Roughgarden, Joan. *The Genial Gene: Deconstructing Darwinian Selfishness*. Berkeley: University of California Press, 2009.

Rousseau, Jean-Jacques. " *Discourse on Political Economy" and "The Social Contract* ." Translated by Christopher Betts. New York: Oxford University Press, 1999.

Ryan, Christopher, and Cacilda Jethá. *Sex at Dawn: The Prehistoric Origins of Modern Sexuality*. New York: HarperCollins, 2010.

Sade, Marquis de. *Three Complete Novels: "Justine," "Philosophy in the Bedroom," "Eugénie de Franval" and Other Writings*. London: Arrow, 1991.

Sanders, A. R., , E. R. Martin, G. W. Beecham, S. Guo, K. Dawood, G. Rieger, J. A. Badner et al. "Genome-wide Scan Demonstrates Significant Linkage for Male Sexual Orientation." *Psychological Medicine* 45, no. 7 (2015): 1379–88.

Savic, Ivanka, and Per Lindström. "PET and MRI Show Differences in Cerebral Asymmetry and Functional Connectivity between Homo- and Heterosexual Subjects." *Proceedings of the National Academy of Sciences* 105, no. 27 (2008): 9403–8.

Schiller, Daniela, Marie-H. Monfils, Candace M. Raio, David C. Johnson, Joseph E. LeDoux, and Elizabeth A. Phelps. "Preventing the Return of Fear in Humans Using Reconsolidation Update Mechanisms." *Nature* 463, no. 7277 (2010): 49–53.

Schnarch, David Moris. *Constructing the Sexual Crucible: An Integration of Sexual and Marital Therapy*. New York: Norton, 1991.

Schwartz, Richard C. *Internal Family Systems Therapy*. New York: Guilford, 1997.

Seligman, Martin E. P. *What You Can Change . . . and What You Can't: The Complete Guide to Successful Self-Improvement*. New York: Vintage, 2009.

Seto, Michael C. "Pedophilia." *Annual Review of Clinical Psychology* 5 (2009): 391–407.

Shermer, Michael, and Dennis McFarland. *The Science of Good and Evil: Why People Cheat, Gossip, Care, Share, and Follow the Golden Rule*. New York: Macmillan, 2004.

Siegel, Daniel J. *The Developing Mind: How Relationships and the Brain Interact to Shape Who We Are*. New York: Guilford, 2015.

Silverstein, Charles. "The Implications of Removing Homosexuality from the DSM as a Mental Disorder." *Archives of Sexual Behavior* 38, no. 2 (2009): 161–63.

Spengler, Andreas. "Manifest Sadomasochism of Males: Results of an Empirical Study." *Archives of Sexual Behavior* 6, no. 6 (1977): 441–56.

Steele, Vaughn R., Cameron Staley, Timothy Fong, and Nicole Prause. "Sexual Desire, Not Hypersexuality, Is Related to Neurophysiological Responses Elicited by Sexual Images." *Socioaffective Neuroscience & Psychology* 3 (2013).

Sullivan, David J. "The American Negro—An 'Export' Market at Home!" *Printer's Ink* 208, no. 3 (1944): 90.

Tollison, C. David, Henry E. Adams, and Joseph W. Tollison. "Cognitive and Physiological Indices of Sexual Arousal in Homosexual, Bisexual, and Heterosexual Males." *Journal of Behavioral Assessment* 1, no. 4 (1979): 305–14.

Tomkins, Silvan S. "Affect Theory." In *Approaches to Emotion*, edited by Klaus R. Scherer and Paul Ekman, 163–95. Hillsdale, NJ: Erlbaum, 1984.

Tribe, Laurence H. "*Lawrence v. Texas*: The 'Fundamental Right' That Dare Not Speak Its Name." *Harvard Law Review* 117, no. 6 (2004): 1893–1955.

Vaiva, Guillaume, F. Ducrocq, K. Jezequel, B. Averland, P. Lestavel, A. Brunet, and C. R. Marmar. "Immediate Treatment with Propranolol Decreases Posttraumatic Stress Disorder Two Months after Trauma." *Biological Psychiatry* 54, no. 9 (2003): 947–49.

Van der Kolk, Bessel. "The Body Keeps the Score." Keynote lecture, International IEDTA Conference, Washington DC, June 27, 2014.

———. "Clinical Implications of Neuroscience Research in PTSD." *Annals of the New York Academy of Sciences* 1071, no. 1 (2006): 277–93.

Voon, Valerie, Thomas B. Mole, Paula Banca, Laura Porter, Laurel Morris, Simon Mitchell, Tatyana R. Lapa et al. "Neural Correlates of Sexual Cue Reactivity in Individuals with and without Compulsive Sexual Behaviours." *PloS one* 9, no. 7 (2014): e102419. doi:10.1371/journal.pone.0102419.

Walker, Susannah. *Style and Status: Selling Beauty to African American Women, 1920–1975.* Lexington: University Press of Kentucky, 2007.

Ward, Brian W, James M. Dahlhamer, Adina M. Galinsky, and Sarah S. Joestl. *Sexual Orientation and Health among U.S. Adults: National Health Interview Survey, 2013.* Washington, DC: National Center for Health Statistics, 2014. Accessed Jan. 10, 2016. http://www.cdc.gov/nchs/data/nhsr/nhsr077.pdf.

Weinberg, Martin S., Colin J. Williams, and Cassandra Calhan. "Homosexual Foot Fetishism." *Archives of Sexual Behavior* 23, no. 6 (1994): 611–26.

Weinstein, Netta, William S. Ryan, Cody R. DeHaan, Andrew K. Przybylski, Nicole Legate, and Richard M. Ryan. "Parental Autonomy Support and Discrepancies between Implicit and Explicit Sexual Identities: Dynamics of Self-Acceptance and Defense." *Journal of Personality and Social Psychology* 102, no. 4 (2012): 815–32.

Weiss, Peter, and Geoffrey Skelton. *The Persecution and Assassination of Jean-Paul Marat as Performed by the Inmates of the Asylum of Charenton under the Direction of the Marquis de Sade.* Woodstock, IL: Dramatic Publishing, 1964.

Weitzer, Ronald. "The Mythology of Prostitution: Advocacy Research and Public Policy." *Sexuality Research and Social Policy* 7, no. 1 (2010): 15–29.

———. "Prostitution: Facts and Fictions." *Contexts* 6, no. 4 (2007): 28–33.

Wenner, Melinda. "Smile! It Could Make You Happier." *Scientific American Mind* 20, no. 5 (2009): 14–15.

White, Chris. "The Spanner Trials and the Changing Law on Sadomasochism in the UK." *Journal of Homosexuality* 50, no. 2–3 (2006): 167–87.

Wile, Daniel B. *After the Fight: A Night in the Life of a Couple.* New York: Guilford, 1993.

Winnicott, Donald W. "Hate in the Countertransference." *International Journal of Psychoanalysis* 30, no. 2 (1949): 69–74.

Wismeijer, Andreas A., and Marcel A. van Assen. "Psychological Characteristics of BDSM Practitioners." *Journal of Sexual Medicine* 10, no. 8 (2013): 1943–52.

Wong, Caroline M. "Chemical Castration: Oregon's Innovative Approach to Sex Offender Rehabilitation, or Unconstitutional Punishment?" *Oregon Law Review 80*, no. 1 (2001): 267–301.

Woodward, C., J. Fischer, J. Najman, and M. P. Dunne. *Selling Sex in Queensland 2003: A Study of Prostitution in Queensland.* Brisbane: Prostitution Licensing Authority, 2004.

Wright, Susan. "Second National Survey of Violence & Discrimination against Sexual Minorities." National Coalition for Sexual Freedom, 2008. Accessed Feb. 5, 2016. https://ncsfreedom.org/images/stories/pdfs/BDSM_Survey/2008_bdsm_survey_analysis_final.pdf.

Yule, Morag A., Lori A. Brotto, and Boris B. Gorzalka. "Biological Markers of Asexuality: Handedness, Birth Order, and Finger Length Ratios in Self-identified Asexual Men and Women." *Archives of Sexual Behavior* 43, no. 2 (2014): 299–310.

INDEX

AASECT, 181, 181–182, 182–184
acceptance, self, 52, 66, 67, 79, 101
Acceptance and Commitment Therapy
    (ACT), 136–137
AIDS, 23, 80
anger, 106, 110, 111, 112, 114, 122, 154,
    155, 158, 172
anxiety, 89, 95–104, 106–108, 112–113,
    115, 116, 119, 120, 128, 132–135,
    142–143, 145, 147, 153, 154, 157–159,
    162, 165, 167; ambivalence, as related
    to, 98, 105, 106, 107, 108, 141, 142,
    157–159; dealing with, 95–98,
    104–105, 112–113, 119, 129–135,
    142–143, 145–146, 157–159; types of,
    105–107
asexuality, 27, 28–29, 41
Association of Sex Educators, Counselors
    and Therapists. See AASECT
attachment, 2, 15, 16

Bader, Ellyn, 170
Bader, Michael, 157
Bailey, Michael, 25
Baron-Cohen, Simon, 13
Baumeister, Roy. See willpower
BDSM, 2, 3, 5, 12, 19, 29, 31–32, 34,
    35–37, 41, 59–62, 143; personality
    traits of participants, 35–37;
    persecution of, 59–28; resources,
    175–176

Bion, Wilfred, 45, 46
bisexuality, 27–28, 29, 41, 80, 81, 122;
    research on, 27–28
Blanchard, Ray, 25
Bowen, Murray. See couples therapy
Brame, Gloria, 31, 32
Bundy, Ted. See sex crimes

Campbell, Joseph, 10–11
Cameron, David, 44, 89
Cantor, James, 39
capitalism, 49–51, 54–55; consumerism,
    and, 50–51, 54–55; criticism of, 50;
    relation of media to, 51–52, 54–55;
    identity formation, and, 54–56
Carnes, Patrick, 85
Cass, Vivienne. See identity, stages of
    change; homosexuality
Censorship, 90
Certified Sex Addiction Therapist
    (CSAT). See sex addiction
Chess, Stella. See temperament
Chomsky, Noam, 50
coherence therapy, 118–119
compassion, 36, 145–147
consensual nonmonogamy, 15–16, 34, 37,
    41
corrective emotional experience, 131, 144
couples therapy, 133, 162–177; confiding
    communication, 172–174; sexual
    menus, 168–169, 174. See also

differentiation
Csikszentmihalyi, Mihaly. *See* flow states

De Sade, Marquis, 14, 155–156; Marat/
    Sade play, 155–156
degeneracy theory, 90
Diagnostic and Statistical Manual (DSM),
    15, 61, 82, 85; criteria for substance
    dependence, 85
differentiation, 169–171
Dunbar, Robin, 47

Ecker, Bruce. *See* coherence therapy
Ekman, Paul, 110, 111, 158
emotions, 25, 36, 68, 86, 87, 91, 105–107,
    109–112, 114–115, 117, 120, 121–123,
    128, 129–132, 142, 144, 145, 158;
    research on, 110–112; types of,
    110–111. *See also* anger, guilt, anxiety,
    shame, fear
epigenetics, 11, 13, 26, 41

fear. *See* anxiety
Fehmi, Les. *See* open focus
feminism, 2, 63
fetishes, 11, 12–14, 24, 27, 29–35, 41,
    52–54, 105, 176; research on, 12,
    29–34; prevalence, 12–13, 29–30,
    31–35; media representations of,
    52–54; origins of, 12–13, 14, 24, 29–31;
    types of, 29–31
Fifty Shades of Grey, 1, 5, 35
Fetlife, 175–176
Foltz, Tanice, 64
Foucault, Michel, 14, 48
flow states, 20, 149, 151–152
Freund, Karl. *See* penile plethysmograph
Freud, Sigmund, 14–15

gender, 4, 12–13, 24, 29–30, 31–32,
    33–34, 38, 39, 40, 109, 176; differences
    in, 12–13, 24. *See also* transgender
genetics. *See* epigenetics
Giddens, Anthony, 17
group formation. *See* assumption groups
Grubbs, Joshua, 89
guilt, 2, 109, 111, 116, 145, 157, 158, 165,
    170

Hamer, Dean, 25
harm reduction, 4
homosexuality, 14–15, 24–29, 40, 41, 44,
    46, 57–59, 70, 76–78, 79, 81;
    discrimination of, 44, 76–78; history of
    attitudes about, 46, 57–59, 76–78;
    history of legislation on, 57–59; history
    of term, 58; homophobia, 55, 78,
    79–80; laws in other countries, 44;
    research on, 24–29; resources, 176;
    same-sex marriage, 1, 5, 6, 16, 55, 57,
    59

identity, 3, 19, 20, 31, 41, 52, 55, 60, 73,
    78, 81, 100–102, 109, 138–140, 151,
    152, 159, 171, 177, 178, 182–184;
    politics of, 55; stages of, 100–102
Internet, 18, 44, 55–56, 83, 89, 175;
    relation to identity, 175; relation to
    loneliness, 18
intimacy, 2, 10, 16–19, 20, 21, 88, 107,
    152, 166; myths surrounding, 16–19;
    types of, 18–20

Jetha, Cecilda, 48
journaling, 105, 137
Jung, Karl. *See* shadow

Karlbeny, Karl Maria. *See* homosexuality,
    history of term
Katehakis, Alexandra, 82, 181
Kinsey, Alfred, 4, 23
Klein, Marty, 61
Krafft-Ebing, Richard von, 12, 14

LaVey, Simon, 25
Lawrence vs Texas. *See* homosexuality,
    history of legislation
LeDoux, Joseph. *See* memory
    reconsolidation
Levine, Peter. *See* somatic experiencing
L.I.F.E. Ministries, 76–77
Lippa, Richard. *See* gender differences
Lovaas, Ivor. *See* reparative therapy
love maps. *See* Money, John

Mahler, Margaret, 170
Makavejev, Dusan, 44
masturbation, 26, 39, 73, 90–91, 164

Maslow, Abraham, 84, 178
media, 1, 2, 6, 18, 29, 32, 34, 43–54, 56,
    68–69, 74–76, 81, 151; *My Strange
    Addiction*, 52; *My Strange Criminal
    Addiction* , 53–54; *Sex Sent Me to the
    ER* , 52, 53; *Sex Slaves*, 68–69; *Strange
    Sex* , 52–53
meditation, 124–126
memory reconsolidation, 115, 117–118
mindfulness, 113, 124–126, 128, 137, 144,
    146
monogamy, 2, 6, 16, 18
Money, John, 4, 12
Morin, Jack, 157–158, 159
Moser, Charles, 31, 32, 61
Mosher, Donald, 19–20

narrative therapy, 138–141, 143, 147, 152
National Coalition of Sexual Freedom
    (NCSF), 37, 59, 61–62; Incident
    Reporting and Response (IRR)
    program, 61; Survey of Discrimination
    and Violence Against Sexual
    Minorities, 61–62; Wright, Susan, 61

Ogas, Ogi, 12
open focus, 126–128
orientation, 5, 11, 16, 24, 25–29, 38,
    40–41, 58, 60, 78–79, 99, 101, 109,
    182–184. *See also* asexuality,;
    bisexuality,; homosexuality
Ortmann, David, 31

partialism,
Pearson, Pete, 170
pedophilia, 33, 38–40, 41, 79; research on,
    38–40
penile plethysmograph (PPG), 26–27, 28,
    39
personality, dimensions of, 35–38, 41, 89
polyamory, 2, 5, 14, 15–16, 18, 29, 37,
    176; personality traits of participants,
    37; research on, 15–16, 37; resources,
    176
pornography, 1, 3, 6, 17, 43–44, 63–64,
    65, 72–73, 79, 81, 83–84, 88–92;
    addiction, 79, 88–92; feminist
    pornography, 63; research on, 64,
    83–84, 89; performers, 1, 65. *See also*
    sex crimes
prostitution. *See* sex work
psychoanalysis, 14–15, 70, 106
PTSD. *See* trauma

reification, 51
Rekers, George. *See* reparative therapy
Reid, Rory, 82
religion, 14, 48, 57, 69, 132–133; relating
    to letting go, 132–134
reparative therapy, 74, 76–79; history of,
    77–78; stance of mental health
    organizations towards, 77, 79
Ryan, Christopher, 48

Schema, 115–119, 128, 129
Schnarch, David. *See* couples therapy
same-sex marriage. *See* homosexuality
Seligman, Martin, 29
Seto, Michael, 39
sex. *See* asexuality, BDSM, bisexuality,
    consensensual nonmonogamy,
    fetishes, homosexuality, monogamy,
    orientation, pedophilia, polyamory,
    pornography, sex addiction, sex
    crimes, sex workers
sex addiction, 1, 6, 23, 63, 70, 71–88, 178,
    181–182; celebrity scandals, 75–76, 82;
    certified sex addiction therapist
    (CSAT), 73, 82–83; controversies
    surrounding, 81–82; industry
    surrounding, 76, 81–82, 84, 86, 87–88;
    media representations of, 74–76, 81;
    Sexual Addiction Screening Test
    (SAST), 83
sex crimes, 91–92
sexual minorities. *See* homosexuality,
    asexuality, gender, BDSM, polyamory,
    fetishes
sex work, 2, 62–69; attitudes of others
    towards, 66–69; legality of, 63–68;
    media representations of, 68–69;
    research on, 62–66; types of, 63–65, 68
shadow, 19, 154, 155, 156
shame, 1, 2, 5, 10, 32, 38, 63, 76, 81, 82,
    83, 103, 106, 107, 109–111, 116, 119,
    122–124, 128, 132, 135, 140, 142–143,
    144–145, 157, 158, 162–163, 175, 178
Sheff, Elisabeth, 15, 31

Shermer, Michael, 45
somatic experiencing, 119–120
Spanner case. *See* BDSM, persecution
Sprott, Richard, 31

temperament, 36, 37, 41
terror management theory, 47
testosterone, 13, 24, 30
Tomkins, Silvan, 110, 112, 158
transgender, 3, 4, 24, 166–167, 176; sex
    workers, 4; pre-op trans women;
    transsexuals, 3, 166–167

transtheoretical stages of change, 98–99,
    102, 108, 129, 142
trauma, 12, 15, 20, 29–30, 35, 41, 73, 77,
    107; childhood, 12, 15, 20, 25, 35, 77;
    propranolol, use of in treatment,
    120–121; research on, 120–121

Weiss, Rob, 82
Weitzer, Ronald. *See* sex work
Wile, Daniel, 172
willpower, 11, 141, 142, 147

ABOUT THE AUTHOR

Michael Aaron, PhD, is a psychotherapist, writer, and speaker, specializing in the field of human sexuality. He is a recognized expert on a variety of sexuality issues, including sexual minorities, alternative/kink/ polyamory lifestyles, sex workers, discordant desire and infidelity in couples, sexual dysfunction and anxiety, gender and orientation confusion, and sexual compulsivity. He has been interviewed in numerous media outlets, online podcasts, and magazines, such as the *New York Times*, the *Wall St Journal*, CNN, Reuters, Huffington Post, *Cosmopolitan*, *Men's Health*, *Women's Health*, *Men's Fitness*, and Vice.com. He is a member of the Advisory Board of *Men's Fitness Magazine* and blogs for *Psychology Today*. He is certified as a Sex Therapist by the American Association of Sex Educators, Counselors and Therapists (AASECT) and is a Diplomate of the American Board of Sexology. His website is http://www.drmichaelaaronnyc.com.